Richard Francis Burton

Zanzibar

City, island and coast, Vol. I

Richard Francis Burton

Zanzibar

City, island and coast, Vol. I

ISBN/EAN: 9783742862891

Manufactured in Europe, USA, Canada, Australia, Japa

Cover: Foto ©Andreas Hilbeck / pixelio.de

Manufactured and distributed by brebook publishing software (www.brebook.com)

Richard Francis Burton

Zanzibar

ANCIENT TOMB AT TONGO-NI.

ZANZIBAR;

CITY, ISLAND, AND COAST.

BY

RICHARD F. BURTON.

IN TWO VOLUMES.
VOL. I.

LONDON:
TINSLEY BROTHERS, 18, CATHERINE ST., STRAND.
1872.
[All Rights reserved.]

JOHN CHILDS AND SON, PRINTERS.

TO

THE MEMORY OF MY OLD AND LAMENTED FRIEND,

John Frederick Steinhaeuser

(F.R.C.S., ETC. ETC., STAFF SURGEON, BOHR AY ARMY).

THIS NARRATIVE OF A JOURNEY,

m WHICH FATE PREVENTED HIS TAKING PART,

IS INSCRIBED

WITH THE DEEPEST FEEDINGS OF AFFECTION AND REGRET.

CONTENTS OE VOL. I.

CHAPTER I.

PAGE

PREPARATORY... 1

CHAPTER II

ARRIVAL AT ZANZIBAR ISLAND   16

CHAPTER III

HOW THE NILE QUESTION STOOD IN THE YEAR   OE GRACE 1856   38

CHAPTER IV.

A STROLL THROUGH ZANZIBAR CITY.. 69

CHAPTER V.

GEOGRAPHICAL AND PHYSIOLOGICAL.. 116
- SECT. I. AFRICA, EAST AND WEST—'ZANZIBAR' EXPLAINED—MENOU-THIAS—POSITION AND FORMATION—THE EAST [AFRICAN CURRENT—NAVIGATION—ASPECT OF THE ISLAND   116
- II. METEOROLOGICAL NOTES—THE DOUBLE SEASONS, Ac.   150
- III. CLIMATE CONTINUED—NOTES ON THE NOSOLOGY OF ZANZIBAR —EFFECTS ON STRANGERS..   .. 176
- IV. NOTEB ON THE FAUNA OF ZANZIBAR..   .. 197
- V. NOTES ON THE FLORA OF ZANZIBAR,.   .. 218
- VI. THE INDUSTRY OF ZANZIBAR..   .. 252

CHAPTEK VI.

VISIT TO THE PRINCE SAYVID MAJID.—THE GOVERNMENT OF ZANZIBAR 266

CHAPTEK VII.

A CHRONICLE OF ZANZIBAR.-THE CAREER OF THE LATE 'IMAM,' SAYVID SAID 276

CHAPTEK VIII.

ETHNOLOGY OF ZANZIBAR.—THE FOREIGN RESIDENTS   312

CHAPTEK IX.

HORSEFLESH AT ZANZIBAR.—THE OUTSKIRTS OF THE CITY, AND THE CLOVE PLANTATIONS... 346

CHAPTEK X.

ETHNOLOGY OF ZANZIBAR.—THE ARABS 308

CHAPTEK XI.

ETHNOLOGY OF ZANZIBAR. -THE WASAWAHILI AND THE SLAVE I RACES...407

CHAPTER Xn.

PREPARATIONS FOR DEPARTURE 469

APPENDIX.

THE UKARA OR UKEREWE LAKE ..   490

PUEEACE.

I FEEL that the reader will expect some allusion to the circumstances which have delayed, till 1871, the publication of a journal ready to appear in *1860*. The following letter will explain the recovery of a long report, forwarded by me in 1857, under an address, very legibly written in ink, upon its cover, to the late Dr Norton Shaw, then Secretary Royal Geographical Society of Great Britain.

'No. 9, of 1865.

'General Department,
Bombay Castle, 28tt *February,* 1865.

·To
    The Under Secretary of State for India,
        London.

* Sir,

	With reference to the packet addressed, as per margin, which was
No. 9, A.	sent to you via Southampton from
The Secretary	the Separate Department, by the
E. Geog. Society,	Overland Mail of the 14th instant,
Whitehall Place,	I have the honour to subjoin for
London.	your information copy of a note on
	the subject from the Hon. W. E. Frere, dated the 5th idem.

PREFACE.

'When searching the strong box belonging to the Bombay Branch of the Royal Asiatic Society yesterday I found the accompanying parcel, directed to the Secretary Royal Geographical Society, with a pencil note upon it, requesting that it might be sent to the Secretary of State, Foreign Office. From the signature in the corner, R. F. B., I conclude that it must be the manuscript he sent to Colonel Rigby at Zanzibar, and which, from some statements of Mr Burton (to which I cannot at present refer, but of which I have a clear recollection), never reached its destination.[1]

'I have not been able to discover when or how the parcel was received, nor how the Bombay Branch of the Royal Asiatic Society was to send it to the Foreign Office, except through Government. I therefore send it to you, and perhaps you would send it to the Under Secretary at the India House, with the above explanation, and request that it be sent to its direction.

I have, &c.,

(Signed) C. Ravenscroft,

Acting Chief Secretary to Government.'

* * * *[1]

It is not a little curious that, as my first report upon the subject of Zanzibar was diverted from its destination,

---

[1] Mr Erere's memory is unusually short... I intrusted the MS. to the Eurasian apothecary of the Zanzibar Consulate, and I suspected (Lake Regions of Central Africa, vol. i. chap. i.) that it had come to an untimely end. The white population at Zanzibar had in those days a great horror of publication, and thus is easily explained how a parcel legibly addressed to the Royal Geographical Society had the honour of passing eight years in the strong box of the 'Bombay Branch of the Royal Asiatic Society.'

so the ' Letts ' containing my excursions to Sa'adani and to Kilwa also came to temporary grief. Annexed by a skipper on the West African coast, appropriated by his widow, and exposed at a London bookseller's stall (labelled outside, 'Burton Original MS. Diary in Africa'), it was accidentally left by the buyer, an English Artillery officer, in the hall of one of H. M.'s Ministers of State. Here being recognized, it was kindly and courteously returned to me. The meteorological observations made by me on the East African seaboard and at other places during the discovery of the Lakes were also, I would remark, mislaid for years, deep hidden in certain pigeonholes at Whitehall Place. May these three accidents be typical of the fate of my East African Expedition, which, so long the victim of uncontrollable circumstance, appears now, after many weary years, likely to emerge from the shadow which overcast it, and to occupy the position which I ever desired to see it conquer.

The two old documents are published with the less compunction as Zanzibar, though increasing in importance and now the head-quarters of an Admiralty Court and of two Mission-Schools, with a printing-press and other civilized appliances, has not of late been worked out. The best authorities are still those who appeared about a quarter of a century ago, always excepting, however, the four magnificent volumes, Baron Carl Clare von der Decken's Reisen in Ost-Afrika, in den Jahren 1859 bis 1861, which I first saw at Jerusalem: there too I had the pleasure of making acquaintance with Dr Otto Kersten, who accompanied the unfortunate traveller during the earlier portion of Ms peregrinations, and who has so ably and efficiently performed Ms part as editor. Had a certain publisher carried out his expressed intention of introducing a resume of this fine work in English dress to the British public, I should have saved myself the trouble of writing these volumes: the Eeisen, however, in the original form are hardly likely to become popular. Moreover, the long interval of a decade has borne fruit: it has given me time to work out the subject, and, better still, to write with calmness and temper upon a theme of the most temper-trying nature, — chap. xii. vol. II. will explain what is meant. Finally, I have sometMng important to say upon the subject . of the so-called Victoria hfyanza Lake.

I had proposed to enrich the Appendix with extracts from Arab and other mediaeval authors, who have treated of Zanzibar, Island and Coast. Such an addition, however, would destroy all proportion between the hook and its subject: I have therefore confined myself to notes on commerce and tariffs of prices in 1857 to 1859, to meteorological observations, and to Capt. Smee's coasting voyage, wMch dates from January, 1811. The latter will supply an excellent birds-eye view of those parts of the Zanzibar mainland wMch were not visited by the East African Expedition.

RICHARD F. BURTON.

London, Oct. 15, 1871.

ZANZIBAR.

PART I.

THE CITY AND THE ISLAND,

'Of a territory within a fortnight's sail of us, we scarcely know more than we do of much of Central Africa, infinitely less than we do of the shores of the Icy Sea.'—
TRANS. BOMBAY GEOG. SOC., vol. xii

'Si fueris sapiens, sapientibus utere factis,
Si ignarus mordax, utere dente tuo.'
Fe. JOAO DE SANT' ANGELO.

ZANZIBAR.

CHAPTER I.

PREPARATIONS POE, DEPAETUEE.

'We were now landed upon the Continent of Africa, the most desolate, desert, and inhospitable country in the world, even Greenland and Nova Zembla itself not excepted.'—Deeoe.

I could not have believed, before Experience taught me, bow sad and solemn is the moment when a man sits down to think over and to write out the tale of what was before the last Decade began. How many thoughts and memories crowd upon the mind! How many ghosts and phantoms start up from the brain—the shreds of hopes destroyed and of aims made futile; of ends accomplished and of prizes won; the failures and the successes alike half forgotten! How many loves and friendships have waxed cold in the presence of new ties ! How many graves have closed over their dead during those short ten years—that epitome of the past !

> 'And. when the lesson strikes the head,
> The weary heart grows cold.'

*   *   *   *   *

The result of a skirmish with the Somal of Berberah (April 19,1855) was, in my case, a visit 'on sick leave ' to England. Arrived there, I lost no time in recovering health, and in volunteering for active Crimean service. The campaign, however, was but too advanced; all 'appointments ' at bead-quarters had been filled up; and new comers, such as I was, could look only to the 'Bashi Buzuks,⁵ or to the 'Turkish Contingent.⁵

My choice was readily made. There was, indeed, no comparison between serving under Major-General *IV.* E. Beatson, an experienced Light-Cavalry man who had seen rough work in the saddle from Spain to Eastern Hindustan; and under an individual, half-civilian, half-reformed Adjutant-General, whose specialty was, and ever had been, foolscap—-literally and metaphorically.

In due time I found myself at the Dardanelles, Chief of Staff in that thoroughly well-abused corps, the Bashi Buzuks. It were ᶜ actum agere⁵ to inflict upon the reader a *rechauffe*, of our troubles,—how the military world declared us to he a hand of banditti, an irreclaimable savagery; how a man, who then called himself TL B. M.'s Consul—but who has long since incurred the just consequences of his misconduct—packed the press, because General Beatson had refused him a lucrative contract; how we awoke one fine morning to find ourselves in a famous state of siege and blockade, with Turkish muskets on the land side, and with British carronades on the water-front; and how finally we, far more sinned against than sinning, were reported hy Mr Consul Calvert to Constantinople as being in a furor of mutiny, intent upon battle and murder and sudden death. These things, and many other too personal for this occasion, will fit better into an autobiography.

The way, however, in which I 'came to grief' (permit me the phrase) deserves present and instant record: it is an admirable comment upon the now universally accepted axiom, 'surtout, pas de zfele,' and upon the Citizen-king's warning words, 'Surtout, ne me faites pas des affaires.'

The Bashi Buzuks, some 3000 sabres, almost all well mounted and better armed, were pertinaciously kept pitched on a bare bill-side, far from tbe scene of action and close to tbe Dardanelles country town, tbat gay and hvely Turkish Coventry, at tbe Hellespont-mouth. In an evil hour I proposed, if my General, who wanted nothing better, would allow me, to proceed in person to Constantinople and to volunteer officially for tbe relief of tbe doomed city, Kars.

Ah, Corydon, Corydon, quae te dementia cepit ?

And I *did* proceed to Stamb'ul; and I *did* volunteer; and a neat hit, indeed, was tbat same public-spmted proceeding !

It would be a lively imagination tbat could conceive tbe scene of storm which resulted from my brazen-faced procedure. The picture has its comic side when looked back upon through tbe mellowing medium of three long lustres. Tbe hopeful eagerness of tbe volunteer; tbe 'proper pride ' in one's corps, tbat bad come forward for an honourable action; tbe fluent proof tbat we could convoy rations enough for tbe gallant and deserted Ottoman garrison, diplomatically left for months to slow death by starvation; and— tbe blank and stunned surprise at tbe hurricane of wrath which burst from tbe high authority to whose ambassadorial ear tbe project was entrusted.

Reported home as a 'brouillon' and turbulent, I again turned lovingly towards Africa—Central and Intertropical—and on April 19, 1856, I resolved to renew my original design of reaching the unknown regions, and of striking the Nile-sources via the Eastern coast. Eor long ages, I knew, explorers had been working, literally, as well as figuratively, against the stream; and, as the ancients had succeeded by a flank march, so the same might be done by us moderns. My Ptolemy told me the tale in very plain and emphatic terms, and although his shore-line shows great inaccuracies, his traditions of the interior, derived from mariners of Tyre and from older writers, appeared far more reliable:—

'He *(soil,* the Tyrian) says that a certain Diogenes, one of those sailing to India, . . . having the Troglyditic region on the right, after 25 days reached the Lakes whence the Nikis flows, and of which the Promontory of the Hhapta is a little more to the south.'[1]

Amongst my scanty literary belongings, on

[1] Georg, lib. i. is. Tbe concluding words are *I>v ion to nv 'Pa7TTii>v aKponjpiov oXcyol vorttonpov.* There is no reason why Bilibaldus Pirkimerus; (Bilibaldi Pirckeymher), Lugd. 1535, should render it, ' quibus *Rhaptum prom onto >lium* paululum est Australius.'

our march to the Tanganyika Lake was a paper (De Azania Africse littore Orientali, Commentatio Physiologica, Bonvise, Pormis Caroli Gengii, mdccclii.) kindly sent to me by the author, Mr George P. de Bunsen. It quoted that same passage which was a frequent solace to me during our 18 months' wanderings, and I still preserve the pamphlet as a memory.

Nor had I forgotten Camoens :—

> 'And there behold the lakes wherein the Nile
> is born, a truth the ancients never knew ;
> see how he bathes, 'gendering the crocodile,
> th' Abassian land, where man to Christ is true:
> behold, how lacking ramparts (novel style!)
> he fights heroic battle with the foe.
> see Meroe, island erst of ancient fame,
> Noba amongst the peoples now its name.' [1]
>
> *Lusiad*, Canto x. 95.

[1] When the Portuguese counselled the Abyssinians to wall their settlements against the Gallas, the former replied like Spartans, 'No; we keep stones to build churches and temples, but we defend our country with our arms and hands ! ' The Coptic 'Nob ' signifies gold (Ritter Erdkunde, Erench translation, 142), the Camoensian 'Noba' is therefore more correct than our modern Nubia, which we find in the monk Burchard (a.d. 1250), '.Ethiopia quse hodie Nubia dicitur.' De Barros (1. iii. xii.) prefers 'a gente dos Nobis.' I have been tempted to add a stanza which is *not* translated from Camoens.

> 95 (a)
> And see the twain from Albion's chalky shore
> go forth th' Egyptian mystic veil to rend :
> the farthest font of Nilus they explore,

This is happier and truer to antiquity than the douhts of José Basilio da Gama :—

> '—the sombre range
> Virginal, ne'er by foot of man profaned,
> Where rise Nile's fountains, if such fountains be.'
> *0 Uruguay*, Canto v.

I consulted my excellent friend tbe late Dr Barth, of Timbuktu, about following tbe footsteps of pilot Diogenes tbe Fortunate. He replied in a kind and encouraging letter, hinting, however, that no prudent man would pledge himself to discover the Nile sources. The Royal Geographical Society benevolently listened once more to my desire of penetrating into the heart of the Dark Continent. An Expeditionary Committee was formed hy Sir Roderick I. Murchison, the late Rear-admiral Beecbey (then President of the Society), Colonel Sykes, Chairman of the Court of Directors of the Hon. East Indian Company, Mr Monckton Milnes (Lord Houghton), Mr Francis Galton, the South African traveller, and Mr John Arrowsmith. I did not hear, strange to say, till many years had passed,

> those mighty waters whence the rivers trend,
> then, 0 dire Chance! O Fortune hard and sore !
> of all their fatal labours yiew the end—
> that lies self-victimed in his natal land,
> this lives afar on friendless foreign strand.'

of the active part which Vice-admiral Sir George Back, the veteran explorer of the Arctic regions, had taken in urging the expedition, and in proposing me as its *head*. Had it been otherwise, this recognition of his kindness would not have come so tardily.

The Committee obtained from Lord Clarendon, then H. M.'s Secretary of State for Foreign Affairs, the sum of £1000, and it was understood that the same amount would be advanced by *the then* ruling Court of *Directors*. Unfortunately it was found wanting. I received, however, on Sept. 13, 1856, formal permission, 'in compliance with the request of the Royal Geographical Society, to be absent from duty as a regimental officer under the patronage of H. B. Majesty's Government, to, be despatched into Equatorial Africa, for a period not exceeding two years, calculated from the date of departure from Bombay, upon the pay and allowances of my rank.' So wrote the Merchant-Sultans.

I was anxious again to take Lieut. John Hanning Speke, because he had suffered with me in purse and person at Berberah, and because he, like the rest of the party, could obtain no redress. Our misfortunes came directly from Aden, indirectly from England. I had proposed to build a fort *at* Berberah, *and* to buy all tbe non-Ottoman ports on tbe western shores of the Red Sea for the trifle of £10,000. In those days of fierce outcry against 'territorial aggrandisement' the Court of Directors looked with horror at such a firebrand proposal, and they were lost in wonder that a subaltern officer should dare to prepare for the Suez Canal, which Lord Palmerston and Mr Robert Stephenson had declared to be impracticable. Therefore the late Dr Buist, editor of the Bombay *Times,* had his orders to write down the 'Somali Expedition.' He was ably assisted by a certain Reverend gentleman, then chaplain at Aden, who had gained for himself the honourable epithet of Shaytan Abyaz, or White Devil, while the apathy of the highest political authority—the Resident at Aden, Brigadier Coghlan—and the active jealousy of his assistant, Captain *Playfair, also* contributed *to* thwart all my views, and to bring about, more or less directly, the bloody disaster which befell us at Berberah, For this we had no redress. The Right Honourable the Oovernor-General of India/the late Lord Dalhousie, of pernicious memory, thought more of using our injuries to cut off the slave-trade than of doing us justice, although justice might easily have been done. After keeping us waiting from April 23, 1855, to June 13, 1857, the spoliator of Oucle was pleased to inform us, laconically and disdaining explanation, that he 'could not accede to the application.'[1]

Nothing could persuade the Court of Directors to dispense with the services of Lieut. Speke, who had, like myself, volunteered for the Crimea, and who, at the end of the War, had resolved to travel for the rest of his leave. I persuaded him to accompany me as far as Bombay, trusting that the just and generous Governor, the late Lord Elphinstone, who had ever warmly supported my projects, and that my lamented friend James Grant Lumsden, then Member of Council, would enable us, despite official opposition at home, to tide over all obstacles.

I have been prolix upon these points, which suggest that the difficulty of reaching the Lunar Mountains, or the 'Invisos Pontes,' were in London, not in Africa; that the main obstacles were

[1] The losses of the Somali expedition (not including those of the Arab and Somali attendants) were as follows :

Lt. Stroyan, I.N. (killed), lost	Co.'s Eupees .	. 1750
Lt. Speke (wounded)	do. .	. 4100
Lt. Burton (do.)	do. .	. 1950
Lt. Herne	do. .	. 500
Shaykh Ahmed	do. .	. 120

Total, Company's Eupees 8420

not savages and malaria, but civilized rivalry and vis inertise; and that the requisites for success were time, means, and freedom from official trammels. Hardly had we reached Cairo (Nov. 6, 1856), and had inspected an expedition fitted out by H. H. the late Abbas Pasha, and admirably organized by the late Marie Joseph Henri Leonie de Lauture, Marquis d'Escayrac (generally known as Comte d'Escayar de Lauture), when an order from the Court of Directors summoned me back to give evidence at some wretched Court-martial pending on Colonel A. Shirley. The document being so worded that it could not be obeyed, we—Eieut. Speke and I—held on our way.

And even when outward bound, I again got into trouble, without being able, as was said of Lord Gough, to get out again. A short stay at Suez, and the voyage down the lied Sea, taught me enough of Anglo-Indian mismanagement and of Arab temper, to foresee some terrible disaster. Again that zeal! Instead of reporting all things couleur de rose, I sent under flying seal, through the lloya,l Geographical Society, with whom I directly corresponded, a long memorandum, showing the true state of affairs, for transmission to the home branch of the Indian Government. This 'meddling in politics ' was 'viewed with displeasure hy Government,' and reminded me of the old saying—

> 'Wha raells wi' what anitber does,
> May e'en gang hame and sboe bis goose.'

The result was a 'wig ' received in the heart of Africa, and—curious coincidence!—accompanying that sheet of foolscap was a newspaper containing news of the Jeddah massacre (June 15, 1858), and of our farcical revenge for the deaths of Messrs Page, Eveillard, and some fourteen souls, nearly the whole Christian colony.[1] It need hardly he mentioned that this catastrophe showed the way to others, especially to the three days 'Tausheh ' of Damascus in 1860.

Fortune had now worked her little worst. We had a pleasant passage to Bombay (Nov. 23, 1856), where affairs assumed a brighter aspect, as we began preparing for the long exploration. Lord Elphinstone, after an especial requisition, allowed Lieut. Speke to accompany me. He also kindly ordered the Hon. East India Company's sloop of war Elphinstone, Captain

---

[1] I could not resist the temptation of printing 'wig' and newspaper paragraph side by side in the Appendix (ii. 428) to my 'Lake Regions of Central Africa.'

Erushard, I.N., to convoy us, knowing liow much importance Orientals attach to appearances—especially to first appearances. My 'father' Erushard gained nothing hy the voyage hut the loss of his pay; therefore is my gratitude to him the greater. Nor must I forget to record the obliging aid of Mr, now Sir Henry L. Anderson, Secretary to the Government of Bombay ; he enabled us to borrow from the public stores a chronometer, surveying instruments, and other necessaries.

Judging that a medical officer would be useful, not only to the members of the expedition, but would also prove valuable in lands where the art of healing is not held destructive, and where Medici are not called 'Caucifici et Sanicidse,' Lord Elphinstone also detached the late Hr J. E. Steinhaeuser, then staff-surgeon, to accompany us. Unfortunately the order came too late. No merchantman happened then to be leaving Aden for Zanzibar, and during the south-west monsoon native craft will not attempt the perilous passage. Nothing daunted, my old and tried friend crossed the Straits to Berberah, with the gallant project of marching down country to join us in the south; nor did he desist till it became evident, from his slow rate of progress, that he could not make Zanzibar in time. Tlie journey through the North-eastern horn of Africa would alone have given a title to Fame. Its danger and difficulty were subsequently proved (October 2,1865) by the wounding of Baron Theodore von Heughlin and by the murder of Baron von der Decken, Dr Link, and others of his party.[1]

The absence of Dr Steinhaeuser lost the East African Expedition more than can be succinctly told. A favourite with 'natives ' wherever he went, a tried traveller, a man of literary tastes and of extensive reading, and better still, a spirit as staunch and determined as ever attempted desperate enterprise,—he would doubtless have materially furthered our views, and in all human probability Lieut. Speke would have escaped deafness and fever-blight, I paralysis and its consequent invalidism. We afterwards wandered together over the United States, and it is my comfort, now that he also is gone, to think that no unkind thought, much less an unfriendly word, ever broke our fair companionship. His

[1] Proceedings Boyal Geographical Society, May 5, 1866. The lamented travellers' notes have now (1869—70) being published under the title of 'Baron Carl Claus von der Decken's Beisen in Ost-Afrika in den Jabren 1859 his 1861. Bearbeitet von Otto Kersten (who accompanied the first expedition). London. Asher.'

memory is doubly dear to me. He was one of the very few who, through evil as well as through good report, disdained to abate an iota of his friendship, and whose regard was never warmer than when all the little world looked its coldest. After long years of service in pestilential Aden, the 'Coal-hole of the East,' he died suddenly of apoplexy at Berne, when crossing Switzerland to revisit his native land. At that time I was wandering about the Brazil, and I well remember dreaming, on what proved to be the date of his death, that a tooth suddenly fell to the ground, followed by a crash of blood. Such a friend, indeed, becomes part of oneself. I still feel a pang as my hand traces these lines.

NOTE.

'The Bashi Bazuks, commanded hy General Beatson, were displaying all the violence and rapacity of their class, little, if at all, restrained hy the presence of their English officers.' Thus writes Mr Jolm "William Kaye in 'Our Indian Heroes ' *(Good Words,* June, 1851), for the greater glorification of a certain General Neill, whose principal act of heroism was *toy* arrest a 'Jack-in-Office Station Master.' Mr Kaye is essentially an official writer, but even official inspiration should 'not be allowed directly to misstate fact.

CHAPTER II.

ARRIVAL AT ZANZIBAR ISLAND.

'There is probably no part of the world where the English Government has so long had a Resident, where there are always some half-a-dozen merchants and planters, of which we know so little as of the capital and part of the kingdom of one of the most faithful of our allies, with whom we have for half a century (since 1804) heen on terms of intimacy.'—Transactions Bombay Geog-. Soc., **1856**.

On December 2, 1856—fourteen long years ago ! —we bade adieu to tbe foul harbour of Bombay the Beautiful, with but a single sigh. The warm-hearted Mr Lumsden saw us on board, wrung our hands with friendly vigour, and hade us go in and win—deserve success if we could not command it. Ho phantom of the future cast a shadow upon our sunny path as we set out, determined either to do or die. I find my journal brimful of enthusiasm. 'Of the gladdest moments in human life, methinks, is the departure upon a distant journey into unknown lands. Shaking off with one mighty effort the fetters of Habit, the leaden weight of Soutine, the cloak of many Cares and the slavery of Home, man feels once more happy. The blood flows with the fast circulation of childhood. Excitement lends unwonted vigour to the mnscles, and the sudden sense of freedom adds a cubit to the mental stature. Afresh dawns the morn of life ; again the bright world is beautiful to the eye, and the glorious face of nature gladdens the soul. A journey, in fact, appeals to Imagination, to Memory, to Hope,—the three sister Graces of our moral being.'[1]

The 181 days spent in sailing 2400 direct miles 'far o'er the red equator ' were short for our occupations. I read all that had been written upon the subject of Zanzibar, from Messer Marco Miglione to the learned Yincent, who always suspected either the existence or the place of the absurd 'Maravi Lake.' We rubbed up our acquaintance with the sextant and the altitude and azimuth ; and we registered barometer and thermometer, so as to have a base for observations ashore. The nearest reference point of known pressure to Zanzibar was then Aden, dis-

---

[1] Somewhat boisterous, "but true. (Note 14 years afterwards.) -

tant above 1000 miles. Under all circumstances the distance was undesirable ; moreover, violent squalls between the Persian Gulf and Cape G-uardafui sometimes depress the mercury half an inch. I shall again refer to this point in Chapter Y.

'Eather Urushard ' was genial, as usual, and under his command every soul was happy. We greatly enjoyed the order, coolness, and cleanliness of a ship of war, after the confusion, the caloric, and the manifold impurities of a Ued Sea passenger-packet. Here were no rattling, heaving throbs, making you tremulous as a jelly in the Caniculi; no coal-smoke, intrusive as on a German Eisen-bahn; no thirst-maddened (cock-) 'roaches ' exploring the entrance to man's stomach; no cabins rank with sulphuretted hydrogen ; no decks whereon pallid and jaundiced passengers shake convulsed shoulders as they rush to and from the bulwarks and the taffrail. Also no 'starboard and larboard exclusiveness '; of flirting abigails tending portly and majestic dames, who look crooked beyond the salvation-pale of their own very small ͨ set '; no peppery civilians rubbing skirts against heedless ͨ griffins'; nor fair lips maltreating the ͨ hapless letter H '; nor officers singing lullabies to their etiolated *enfants terribles,* and lacking but one little dispensation of nature—concerning wbich Humboldt treats—to become tbe best of wet-nurses. Tbe 'Elplrinstone ' belonged not to the category ᶜ Sbippe of Helle,' one of whose squadron I have described in an old voyage to a certain Unhappy Yalley.' We would willingly have prolonged our cruise with the jovial captain, and with the good fellows and gallant gentlemen in the gun-room, over many and many a league of waves.

Of course we had no adventures. We saw neither pirate nor slaver. The tract seemed desert of human life ; in fact, nothing met our eyes but flying-fish at sea, gulls and gannets near shore. The stiff N. East trade never quite failed us, even when crossing the Line, and the Doldrums hardly visited us with a tornado or two— mere off-shore squalls. The good old heart of teak, then aged 33 years, made an average of 150, and an exceptional run of 200 knots, in 24 hours. This was indeed 'gay sailing on the bosom of the Indian Sea.' After 16 days (Dec. 18), before thesolar lamp had been removed, our landfall, a long, low strip at first sky-blue and distance-blurred, had turned purple, and had robed itself in green and gold, with a pomp and a glory of vegetation then new to ns. This was Pemba, one of the three continental islands composing the Zanzibarian archipelago : the Arabs call it Jazirat el Khazra, (Green Island), and no wonder! Verdant and fresh enough must this huge conservatory, this little and even richer Zanzibar, appear to their half-closed ⁴ peepers,' dazed and seared by the steely skies and brazen grounds of Manga[1] (Arabia generally) and Maskat (Muscat), and by the dreadful glare and 'damnable blue ' of the Persian Gulf and the Indian Ocean. We are soon to visit this emerald isle, therefore no more of it at present.

All had hoped to run in that night, but Pate or our evil deeds in the last life otherwise determined. The wind fell with the sun, and during the five minutes of crepuscule we anchored in the sandy bay-strand under Tumbatu Island, S.W. of Point Nunguwi (Owen's Nangowy), the north cape of its big insular brother, Zanzibar. Like the items of this archipelago generally, it is a long cairn-shaped reef of coralline, with its greater length disposed U.S. This well-known norm of great peninsulas has been explained by

[1] Literally rock, rocky ground. Hence the Arabs are called ■Wamanga. Mr Cooley ('Inner Africa Laid Open,' p. 61) blunders pitiably about this word.

a sudden change in the earth's centre of gravity, which caused the waters to rush furiously from the northern hemisphere towards the south pole. As usual, the burning suns, the tepid winds, the sopping dews, and the copious rains clothe the thin soil with an impervious eoat of verdure, overhanging the salt-waters, and boasting a cultivation that would make spring in green Erin look by its side autumn—rusty and yellow-brown.

We landed, and curiously inspected the people of Tumbatu, for we were now beyond Semitico-Abyssinian centres, and we stood in the presence of another and a new race. They are called by the Omani Arabs Makhadim.—helots or serviles—and there is nothing free about them save their morals. Suspicious and fearful, numerous and prolific, poor and ill-favoured, they show all the advantages and the disadvantages of an almost exclusive ichthyophagism. . Skilful in divination, especially by Bao or geomancy, they have retained, despite El Islam, curious practices palpably derived from their wild ancestry of the Blackmoor shore. They repair, for the purpose of 'clear-seeing,' to a kind of Troplionius cave, spend the night in attack of inspiration, and come forth in the morning £ Agelasti, msesti, cogitabundi.' Similarly the Nas-Amun (Nasamone) slept, for insight into futnrity, npon tlieir ancestral graves. The wild highlanders of the East African ghauts have an equally useful den in their grim mountains; and on the West African coast the Krumen consult the 'Great Hebbil,' who lives in a hole amongst the rocks of Grand Cavalla. The traveller who, *pace* my friends of the Anthropological Society, postulates spiritualism or spiritism (as M. Allan Kardec has it), will save himself much mystification, and he will soon find that every race has had, and still has, its own Swedenborg.

The men of Tumbatu at their half-heathen wakes, lay out the corpse, masculine or feminine, and treat it in a way which reminds us of Hamlet's (Act v. 1) 'Where be your gibes now? your gambols, your songs?' A male friend will say to his departed chum—

'O certain person! hut a few days ago I asked thee for cocoa-nut-water and tobacco, which thou deniedest to me—enh? Where is now the use of them?'

'Eellow!' a woman will address the dead, ᶜ dost thou remember making fierce love to me at such and such a time? Much good will thy love do me now that thou art the meat of ugly worms!'

Tlieir abuse is never worse than when lavished by a creditor upon a defunct debtor.

The idea underlying this custom is probably that which suggested the Irish wake—a test if the clay be really inanimate. Nor would I despise, especially during prevalence of plague or yellow fever, in lands where you are interred offhand, any precaution, however barbarous, against the horrors and the shudders of burying alive. Certain Madras Hindoos, after filling *its* mouth with milk and rapping its face with a shankh or conch-shell, grossly insult, as only the 'mild Hindu ' of Bishop Heber can, all its feminine relatives. The practice is also found in the New World. The Aruacas (Arrawaks) of Guiana opened the eyes of the corpse, and switched them with thorns ; smeared the cheeks and lips with lard, and applied alternately sweet and bitter words. This was a curious contrast to the customs of the Brazilian Tupys and the Bolivian Moxos, who, according to Yves d'Evreux and Alcide d'Orbigny, met every morning to bewail their losses, even of their grandfathers and great-grandfathers !

As darkness came on we saw the sands sparkling with lights, here stationary like glow-worms or the corpusant; there flitting about like ignes fatui or fire-flies. Such was the spectacle seen by Columbus and Pedro Gutierrez ('gentleman of the king's bedchamber') on the memorable night when Bahaman Guanahani was discovered. The fishermen burn dry grass and leaves, and the blaze, like the Arabs' 'fire of hunting,' which dazzles the eye of the gazelle, atGacts shoals that are easily speared. Some carried torches in canoes : now the flame floated in crimpled water, which broke up its reflection into a scatter of brilliants ; then it reposed upon mirror-lilce smooths, the brand forming the apex of a red pyramid which seemed to tremble with life, whilst the boat was buried in the darkness of death. And so 'fishy' are these equinoctial seas, that gangs of old women and children may be seen at Pemba, and on the coast, converting their body-clothes into nets, and filling pots, hand over hand, with small fry. I have seen them myself, although a certain critic says, 'No.'

The people of. Tumbatu, like the Greeks, have their good points. They are skilful pilots and stout seamen, diligent in gathering their bread from the waters, and comparatively industrious, considering their enervating, prostrating climate. Their low, jungly ledge wants the sweet element, compelling them to fetch it from Zanzibar—their mainland ; hence travellers have described the islet as uninhabited. The people are mentioned as Moslems hy Yakut (early 13th century), and this island of 'Tambat'.was made a refuge for the inhabitants of Languja or Zanzibar. We inquired in vain about the fort which the Arabs are said to have built there. The skins of Tumbatu are sooty, the effect, according to some, according to others the concomitant, of humid heat. The reader must not charge me with 'trimming' between the rival schools of 'race *versus* climate, the cause of complexion.' Many peoples betray hut a modicum of chromatic and typical change. On the other hand, I have found an approximation of colour as well as of form between the Anglo-American and the Luso-Brazilian; and I have enlarged upon this chromatic heresy, if heresy it he, in- the Highlands of the Brazil (Yol. i. chap. xxxviii.). Einally, when speaking of the permanence of type, it is well to bear in mind that our poor observations hardly extend over 2500 years.

The next morning placed us at the base of our operations, and we were on deck with Aurora. The stout ship 'Elphinstone,' urged hy the cool land breeze, slid down the channel, the sea-river that separates the low-lying and evergreen Zanzibar Island from its reflection, the Mpoa-ni.[1] We were sensibly affected hy the difference between the Sawahil, this part of the East African sea-board which begins at the Juba River, and the grim physiognomy of Somaliland, Region of Eragrant Gums, with its sandy horrors of Berberah, and its granitic grandeurs of Guardafui, which popular apprehension refers to Garde a vons, and which Abyssinian Bruce, according to Ritter (Erdkunde, 2nd Division, § 8),

[1] This is the 'Poane' of '0 Muata Cazemhe ' (p. 323), and there rightly translated, 'Costa de Zanzibar.' Mr Cooley (p. 14, 'The Memoir on the Lake Kegions, &c., reviewed.' London, Stanford, 1864) thus misleads his readers: 'The Cazemhe knew the name of only one place on the coast— Mpoani, near the Querimba Islands.' The word literally means 'on the coast,' or simply 'the. coast.' In the Zangian dialects the terminative '-ni' has two senses. Nowit is a locative, signifying on, in, hy, or near, as, e.g., Nyumba-ni, 'at home' (in the house) ; Mfu'ua-ni, at the place near the Mfu'u tree. Then it is almost pleonastic, as Kisiwa-ni, [1] the island,' and Kisima-ni, 'the well.' Mpoa-ni, a word in general use, is a literal Kisawahili translation of the Arabic Sawakil (plural of Sdhil), 'the shores,' strictly speaking between Mtangata and tbe Eufiji Eiver. Hence, possibly, the Greeks drew their name, [1] AiyiaXor.' The latter is usually identified with the modern Arabic Sayf Tawil, the long strand, not 'bold or declining shore,' as translated by Captain Owen. It extends southwards from the Ea'as el Khayl to Ea'as Awaz (Cape of Change) in the Barr el Khazdin (Ajan or Azania). Of the latter more in Sect. 1, Chapter V.

altered to Gardefan, the Straits of Burial.[1] We were in the depths of the 'dries,' as they are called in West Africa, in the local midwinter, yet this land was gorgeous in its vestment when others would be hybernating in more than semi-nudity.

Truly prepossessing was our first view of tbe then mysterious island of Zanzibar, set off by tbe dome of distant bills, like solidified air, that

---

[1] De Barros by a slip of tbe pen writes (Decades i. 5, 9) Guadrafu. I should explain tbe corrupted 'Guardafui ' not as usual by 'Cabo d'Orfui,' but as a European version of Jurd Hafun,—highland or crest of Hafun. Jurd, in Arabic, means the mountain-top, opposed to the Wusut, shoulders or half-way slopes, and to the Sahl, or low lands. The modern Arabic name of the ancient Aromata Promontarium is Ea'as Asir, the captive headland, a term especially applied to the projection of land, some 2000 feet high, which, viewed from the south, extends farthest seaward to the north-east, as I saw when sailing from Zanzibar to Aden. Hafun, supposed to be the Mosyllum Promontorium of Pliny and the Opone of Ptolemy, the Khakhui of El Idrisi; tbe Jafuni of El Masudi; tbe Carfuna of other Arab geographers, and the Orfui of the moderns, means the surrounded, i.e. by water, because almost an island. Lieutenant Crittenden, I.N. (Aden, April 10, 1848. Transactions of tbe Bombay Geographical Society), describes it as a headland of lime and sandstone nearly square, and 600 to 700 feet high. He remarks that after the Elephas Mons it is the only point on the coast concerning which there can he no mistake. The sites are thus—

Rns Asir (Guardafui) North Easternmost point of Africa N. lat. 11° 50' 0"   Rnper(ll× ; 4"Norris)
Ras Hafun, Easternmost point of Africa   N. lat. ir>° 26' 48" .. (10° 27' 43" ..   )
                                            Difference   • 1°   32"   1° i:v 1G"
Lieutenant Carless, I.N., makes the difference of meridian arc 0° 4' 50"

form tlie swelling line of the Zanzibar coast. Earth, sea, and sky, all seemed Avrappcd in a soft and sensuous repose, in the tranquil life of the Lotus Eaters, in the swoon-like slumbers of the Seven Sleepers, in the dreams of the Castle of Indolence. The sea of purest sapphire, which had not parted with its blue rays to the atmosphere—a frequent appearance near the equator—lay basking, lazy as the tropical man, under a blaze of sunshine which touched every object with a dull burnish of gold. The wave had hardly energy enough to dandle us, or to cream with snowy foam the yellow sandstrip which separated it from the flower-spangled grass, and from the underwood of dark metallic *green*. The breath of the ocean would hardly take the trouble to ruffle the fronds of the palm which sprang, like a living column, graceful and luxuriant, high above its subject growths. The bell-shaped convolvulus (Ipomsea Maritima), supported by its juicy bed of greenery, had opened its pink eyes to the light of day, but was languidly closing them, as though gazing upon the face of heaven were too much of exertion. The island itself seemed over-indolent, and unwilling to rise ; it showed no trace of mountain or crag, but all was voluptuous with gentle swellings, witli the rounded contours of the girl-negress, and the brown-red tintage of its warm skin showed through its gauzy attire of green. And over all bent lovingly a dome of glowing *azure,* reflecting its splendours upon the nether world, whilst every feature was hazy and mellow, as if viewed through 'woven air,' and not through vulgar atmosphere. Most of my countrymen find monotony in these Claude-Lorraine skies, with the pigment and glazing *on.* 1 remember how in Sind they used to bless the storm-cloud, and stand joyously to be drenched in the rain which rarely falls in that leather-coloured land. Zanzibar, however, must be seen on one of her own fine days: like Fernando Po and Pdo de Janeiro, the beauty can look 'ugly ' enough when she pleases.

As we drew nearer and vision became more distinct, we found as many questions for the pilot as did Yasco da Gama of old. Those prim plantations which, from the offing, resembled Italian avenues of oranges, the tea-gardens of China, the vines of romantic Provence, the coffee plantations of the Brazil, or the orange-yards of Paraguay, were the celebrated clove-grounds, and the largest, streaking the central uplands, were crown property. We distinctly felt a heavy spicy perfume, as if passing before the shop of an Egyptian 'attar,' and the sensorium was not the less pleasantly affected, after a hard diet of briny N.E. Trade. Various legends of hair-oil rubbed upon the bulwarks have made many a tricked traveller a shallow infidel in the matter of smelling the land. But we[1] soon learned that off Zanzibar, as off 'Mozamhic,' the fragrant vegetation makes old Ocean smile, pleased with the grateful smell, as of yore. The night breeze from the island is cool and heavy with clove perfume, and European residents carefully exclude the land-wind from their sleeping-rooms.

Eor a little while we glided S. hy E. along the shore, where the usual outlines of a city took from it the reproach of being a luxuriant wilderness. The first was £ Bayt el Ea'as, a large pile, capped with a dingy pent-house of cajar (cocoa leaves), and backed hy swelling ground— here hared for cultivation, there sprinkled with dense dark trees, masses of verdure sheltering hut and homestead. Followed at the distance of a mile, the Royal Cascine and Harem of Mto-ni, the Rivulet.[1] Our ancient ally 'Sayyid Said,

---

[1] Yefc we read of the 'great river Matoney,' and of 'travellers crossing the great Eiver Mtony.' Mto, in the language

Imam of Maskat and Sultan of Zanzibar and tbe Sawahil,' bad manifestly not attempted African copies of bis palaces in Arabian Shinaz and Bat'bab, pavilions with side-wings and flanking towers, tbe buildings half castle half chateau, so much affected by tbe feudal lords of Oman. He preferred an Arabo-African modification, here valuable for 'sommer-frisch.'

Tbe demesne of Mto-ni has a quaint manner of Gothic look, pauperish and mouldy, like the schloss of some duodecimo Teutonic Prince, or long-titled, short-pursed, placeless, and pensionless German Serenity in the days now happily gone by, when the long drear night of German do-nothingness, has fled before the glorious daybreak of 1866—1870. We can distinguish upon its long rusty front a projecting balcony of dingy planking, with an extinguisher-shaped roof, dwarfed by the luxuriant trees arear, and by the magnificent vegetation which foils up to its very walls. Mto-ni takes its name from a run-

of Zanzibar, is a river or a rivulet; also a pillow. The Quilimani River signifies simply kilima-ni, (w^ter) from the mountain. The meaning of Quilimansi (th^Obi—Webbe—Nile of Makdishu, "Webbe Shebayli, of late christened the Haines River, and called Quilimancy by De Barros, from a settlement now unknown) is still under dispute. It cannot grammatically be made to mean 'mountain-stream, or a mountain with streams,' as Dr Krapf has it.'

nel which, draining the uplands, supplies the 'Palace,' and trickles through a conduit into the sea. "We shall presently visit it.

Entering the coral reef which defends this great store-house of Eastern Intertropical Africa, I remarked that the lucent amethyst of the waters was streaked and patched with verdigris green; the 'light of the waves ' being caused hy shoals, whose golden sands blended with the blue of heaven. The 'Passes of Zanzibar' reminded me in colouration of the 'Gateways of Jeddah,' and as the coral reefs cut like razors, they must be threaded with equal care. So smooth was the surface within the walls, that each ship, based upon a thread of light, seemed to hover over its own reflected image.

And now we could distinguish the normal straight line of Arab town, extending about a mile and a half in length, facing north, and standing out in bold relief, from the varied tints and the grandeur of forest that lay behind. A Puritanical plainness characterized the scene— cathedrals without the graceful minarets of Jeddah, mosques without the cloisters of Cairo, turrets without the domes and monuments of Syria; and the straight stiff sky-line was unrelieved except by a few straggling palms. In tlie centre, and commanding the anchorage, was a square-curtained artless *fort, conspicuous* withal, and fronted hy a still more contemptible battery. To its right and left the Imam's palace, the various Consulates, and the large parallelogrammic buildings of the great, a tabular line of flat roofs, glaring and dazzling like freshly whitewashed sepulchres, detached themselves from the mass, and did their best to conceal the dingy matted hovels of the inner town. Zanzibar city, to become either picturesque or pleasing, must be viewed, like Stambul, from afar.

We floated past the guard-ship, an old 50-gun frigate of Dutch form and Bombay build, belonging to 'His Highness the Sayyid; ' it was modestly named Shah Allum (Alam), or ᵉ King of the World.' The few dark faces on hoard bawled out information unintelligible to our pilot, and showed no colours, as is customary when a foreign cruiser enters the port. We set this down to the fact of their being blacks— 'careless Ethiopians.' But flags being absent from all the masts, and here, as in West Africa, and in the Brazil, every 'house ' flies its own bunting, we decided that there must be some cause for the omission, and we became anxious accordingly.

But not for such small matter would the H. E. I. C.'s ship-of-war 'Elphinstone ' have the trouble of casting loose and of loading her guns gratis. With the Sayyid's plain blood-red ensign at the main, and with union-jack at the fore, she cast anchor in Eront Bay, and gallantly delivered her fire of 21. Thereupon a gay bunting flew up to every truck ashore and afloat, whilst the brass carronades of the 'Victoria,' another item of the Maskat navy, roared a response of 22, and, curious to say, did not blow off a single gunner's arms. We had arrived on the fortieth or last day of Moslem mourning; and the mourning was for Sayyid Said, our native friend and ally, who had for so many years been calling for volunteers and explorers, and from whom the East African expedition had been taught to expect every manner of aid except the pecuniary.

We lost no time in tumbling into a gig and in visiting the British Consulate, a large solid pile, coloured like a twelfth-cake, and shaped like a claret-chest, which lay on its side, comfortably splashed by the sea. Lieut.-Colonel Atkins Hamerton, of the Indian Army, H.B.M.'s Consul and H.E. I. C.'s agent, to whom I was directed to report arrival, was now our mainstay, but we found him in the poorest state of health. He was aroused from lethargy hy the presence of strangers, and after the usual hospitable orders my letters were produced and read. Those entrusted to me hy Lord Elphinstone, and hy his Eminence the learned and benevolent Cardinal "Wiseman, for whom he had the profoundest respect, pleased him greatly; hut he put aside the missive of the Eoyal Geographical Society, declaring that he had been terribly worried for 'copy ' hy sundry writing and talking members of that distinguished body.

I can even now distinctly see my poor friend sitting before me, a tall, broad-shouldered, and powerful figure, with square features, dark, fixed eyes, hair and beard prematurely snow-white, and a complexion once fair and ruddy, but long ago bleached ghastly pale by ennui and sickness. Such had been the effect of the burning heats of Maskat and 'the Gulf,' and the deadly damp of Zanzibar, Island and Coast. The worst symptom in his case—one which I have rarely found other than fatal—was his unwillingness to quit the place which was slowly killing him. At night he would chat merrily about a remove, about a return to Ireland; he loathed the subject in the morning. To esqape seemed a physical impossibility, when he had only to order a few boxes to be packed, and to board the first home-returning ship. In this state the invalid requires the assistance of a friend, of a man who will order him away, and who will, if he refuses, carry him off by main force.

Our small mountain of luggage was soon housed, and we addressed ourselves seriously to the difficulties of our position. That night's rest was not sweet to us. I became as the man of whom it was written—

> 'So coy a dame is Sleep to him,
> That all the weary courtship of his thoughts
> Can't win her to his bed.'

After the disaster in Somali-land, I was pledged, at all risks and under all circumstances, to succeed; and now St Julian, host and patron of travellers, had begun to show me the rough side of his temper. The Consul was evidently unfit for the least exertion. He had in his 'godowns' dozens of chests and cases which he had not the energy to open. H. H. Sayyid Said had left affairs in a most unsatisfactory state. His eldest son, the now murdered Sayyid Suwayni, heir to Maskat, and famous as an anglophobe, had threatened to attack Zanzibar; a menace which, as will afterwards appear, he attempted to carry out. The cadet Sayyid Majid, installed by his father chief of the African possessions, was engrossed in preparations for defence. Moreover, this amiable young prince having lately recovered from confluent small-pox, an African endemic which had during the last few years decimated the islanders, was ashamed to display a pockmarked face to the 'public,' ourselves included. The mainland of Northern Zanzibar about Lamu was, as usual on such occasions, in a state of anarchy. Every man *seized the opportunity of* slaying his enemy, or of refusing to pay his taxes. An exceptionally severe drought had reduced the southern coast of Zanzibar to a state of famine.

Briefly, the gist of the whole was that I had better return to Bombay. But rather than return to Bombay, I would have gone to Hades on that 20th of December, 1856.

NOTE.

Since these *pages* were penned the *Bombay Gasette* of November 11, 1870, announced the death of H. H. Sayyid Majid, Sultan of Zanzibar, and the succession of his brother—Sayyid Burghush.

CHAPTER III.

HOW THE NILE QUESTION STOOD IN THE TEAR OE GRACE 1856.

'Ain) *ptv t/Se rijs ireptppvTov dovog.*
This is the finial of th' encircling earth.

SOPH. PHIL.

IN this chapter I propose briefly to place before the reader the various shiftings of opinion touching the Nile Sources, and especially to show what had been done for Zanzibar and her coast by the theoretical and practical men of Europe between a.d. 1825 and the time of our landing on the Sawdhil, or East African shores.

The details given to Marinus of Tyre by the Arabian merchants, and their verification by the obscure Diogenes, together with the notices of the African lakes on the lower part of the Upper Nile, brought home about a.d. 60 by Nero's exploring Centurions, were never wholly for-

gotten by Europe, which thus unlearned to derive with Herodotus the Nile from Western Africa.[1] As the pages of Marco Polo show, not to quote the voyage of 'Sinbad the Sailor,' Arabs and Persians still frequented these shores; and the Hindu Banyans, established from time immemorial upon the Zanzibar coast, had diffused throughout India some information touching the wealthy land. , The veteran geographer of Africa, Mr James Macqueen, has commented upon the curious fact that the Padmavan of Lieut. Erancis Wilford (vol. iii. of the old Asiatic Researches, £ Course of the River Cali,' as supposed to be derived from the Puranas) is represented by'the beds of floating water-lilies crossed by Captains Speke and Grant, and upon the resemblance between the Amara, or Lake of the Gods, with the Amara people on the N. E. of the so-called Nyanza Lake. These, however, appear to be mere coincidences, or at best the re-
. suits of tales learned upon the coast by the Hindu trader. Before leaving Bombay I applied

[1] The 'Father of History' evidently held to the theory that the modern. Bahr el G-hazal (explored of late hy Mr Petherieh and by the unfortunate Tinn6 family) was the head reservoir of the White Nile. Nor is it. impossible tbat in .long-past ages the lakes or waters in question were fed by a watershed whose eastern declivities still discharge themselves into the higher basin.

to that eminent Sanskritist the Rev. J. Wilson, D.D., for any notices of East Africa which might occur in the sacred writings of the Hindus. He replied that there were none; and I had long before learned that Col. Wilford himself had acknowledged his pandit to have been an impudent impostor.

At the end of the 15th century came the Portuguese explorers, with Strabo, Pliny, and Ptolemy, in their hands, and followed by a multitude of soldiers, merchants, and missionaries, who invested the intertropical maritime regions of Africa, east and west. The first enthusiasm, however, soon passed away. The Portuguese were supplanted by the Dutch, hy the English, and by the Erench; whilst Ptolemy and the Periplus were ousted by Pigafetta, Dapper, and other false improvers of their doctrines. The Ptolemeian Lakes were marched about and countermarched in every possible way. The 'Mountain of the Moon,' prolonged across Africa under the name Jebel Rumri, really became ' Lunatic Mountains.' The change from good to bad geography is well illustrated by two charts published in 1860, by H. E. the Conde de Lavradio. The first is the fac-simile of a map in the British Museum, by Diogo Homem, in 1558. It makes the Nile spring from, two great reservoirs. But the second, hearing the name of Antonio Sances (1623), already reduces these lakes to one central Caspian, which sends forth the Nile, the Congo, and the Zambeze, and which, greatly shrunken, still deforms our maps under the name of Marave. Similarly, the 'Complete System of Geography,' by Emanuel Bowen (1747), places the Zambre Lake in S. lat. 4°—11°, the 'centre from which proceed all the rivers in this part of Africa,' including the Nile.

How popular the subject continued to he may be guessed from the fact that Daniel Defoe (1661—1731), cast his African reading into a favourite form with him, the 'Adventures of Captain Singleton.' He lands his hero about March, 1701, a little south of Cape Delgado, causes him to cross several seas and rivers, the latter often flowing northwards, and after a year's wandering, brings him out at the Dutch settlements on the Gold Coast.

TJpon the general question of modern Nile literature the curious reader will consult the well-studied writings of M. Vivien de Saint-Martin. The valuable paper 'On the Knowledge the Ancients possessed of the Sources of the Nile,' by*my friend W. S. "W. Vaux (Transactions of the Boyal Society of Literature, vol. viii., New Series), treats of exploration up the river, beginning from the Ionian colony, established in the upper river hy Psammetichus (circa a.c. 600), and extending to the present day. The learned article by Mr John Hogg, 'On some old Maps of Africa, in which certain of the Central and Equatorial Lakes are laid down in nearly their true positions,'[1] (Transactions of the

---

[1] In 1859 I had written (Journal Royal Geographical Society, vol. xxix. 272) 'The Nyanza, as regards name, position, and even existence, has hitherto been unknown to European geographers; but descriptions of this "sea" by native travellers have been unconsciously transferred by our writers to the Tanganyika of TJjiji, and even to the Nyassa of Kilwa.' Mr Hogg proposes to show that such was not the case. But the map by John Senex (1711) throws into one three or at least two waters. Mercator (Kauffman) lays the 'Garava' lakelet almost parallel with the Zaflan (Zambeze) or Kilwa Lake. Walker (1811) and Lizars (1815) fit in the Tanganyika correctly, whilst the Nyassa is wholly incorrect.

Of the five maps one only, that of John Senex, deserves consideration. 'This great lake placed here by report of the negroes,' alludes, I believe, to legends of the Bahari-ngo (the 'great sea,' vulgarly, Baringo), of which many East African travellers have heard. One Kumu wa Kikandi, a native of Hemba, described the water to Dr Krapf as lying five days' journey from Mount Kenia: in the Introduction to his last travels (p. xlviii.), however, the enterprising missionary identifies it with the so-called Nyanza or Ukerewe Lake. I was told of it by the Wakamba at Mombasah in 1857. The Pfere L6on d'Avanchers (Bulletin de la Soci6t6 de G^ographie, vol. xvii. 164) also collected, when traveling on the East African coast, in August, 1858, information concerning Baha-

Royal Society of Literature, vol. viii.), supplies a compendium of old cartography.

I proceed now to the practical part of this chapter, namely, the actual visits of inspection to Zanzibar, and their results. TJntil the end of the last century, our knowledge was derived almost entirely from those 'domini Orientalis Africse,' the Portuguese. The few exceptions were Sir James Lancaster, who opened to the English the Orient seas. He wintered at the island in 1591; Captain Alexander Hamilton (new account of the East Indies, 1688—1723, Hakluyt's Collection, viii. 258); and M. Saulnier de Mondevit, commanding the king's Corvette, La Prevoyance. The latter, who, in 1786, visited the principal points of Zanzibar, published a chart with 'Observations sur la cóte du Zangueibar ' (Nouvelles Annales des Voyages, vol. vi.), and recommended a Erench establishment at 'Mongalo.'

In Eebruary, 1799, Captain Bissel, R.N., commanding H. M.'s ship Orestes, with the Leopard

ringo, as he writes it. Senex finally disconnects it with 'the Nile, and indeed gives it no drainage at all.
> . I cannot but think that Mr Hogg's learning and research have considerably strengthened my position, and that the so-called Nyanza Lake was, curious to say, the least known, and at the same time the nearest, to European geographers.

carrying Admiral Blankett's flag, touched at the island for refreshments when heating up against the *N. E.* monsoon towards the Eed Sea. He briefly hut faithfully described its geography, and he laid down sailing directions which to this day are retained in Horshurgh. Since then many coasting voyages have been made by naval officers and others, who collected from natives, with more or less fidelity, details concerning the inner country. As early as 1811, Captain Smee and Lieutenant Hardy were sent hy the Bombay government to gather information on the eastern seaboard of Africa, and they brought hack sundry novel details (Transactions Bombay Geographical Society, 1844, p. 23, &c.). Between the years 1822-1826 the whole coast line was surveyed by Captain (afterwards Admiral) W. E. Owen, and by his officers, Captains Yidal, Boteler, and others. Their charts and plans of the littoral, despite sundry inaccuracies, such as placing Zanzibar Island five miles west of its proper position, excited general attention, and were justly termed by a modern author miranda tabularum series. During this Herculean labour, which occupied three years, some 300 of the officers and crew fell victims to the climate of the Coast, to the hardships of hoat-work, and to the ferocity of the natives. In 1822 Sir Robert Townsend Fairfax, Governor and Commander-in-Chief of the Mauritius, after a crusade against the slave-trade in the dominions of Radama, King of the Hovas, commissioned Captain (afterwards Admiral) Fairfax Moresby, of H. M.'s ship Menai, to draft a treaty between England and Maskat for limiting the traffic. The mission was successful. The sale of Somalis, a free people, was made piracy; and the Sayyid's vessels were subject to seizure by the Royal, including the Company's, cruizers, if detected carrying negroes 'to the east of a line drawn from Cape Delgado, passing south of Socotra and on to Diu, the west point of the Gulf of Cambay.[1] In 182.2, the Sayyid's assent having been formally accorded, Captain Moresby left the coast.

In January, 1834, Captain Hart, of H. M.'s ship Imogene, visited Zanzibar, and submitted to the Imperial government brief *notes,* appending a list of the Sayyid's squadron then in the harbour, with their age, tonnage, armature, and other particulars. Still geographers declared that Zanzibar was a more mysterious spot to England and India than parts of Central Africa

[1] This 'restrictive treaty' was published in No. 24 of the Bombay Selection (1856), under the head of 'Persian G-ulf.'

and the shores of the Icy Sea.[1] During the same year the energetic Mr W. Bollaert matured the plan of an expedition, to be conducted hy himself, from Zanzibar across the continent. It was laid before the Geographical Society in 1837, but it was *not* carried out, funds being deficient. In 1835 the U. S. frigate Peacock visited the island during a treaty-making tour, and was supplied with all her wants gratis, the port officials declaring that 'H. H. the Sultan of Muscat had forbidden them to take any remuneration.' The surgeon, Dr Huschenberger (Narrative of a Voyage round the World in 1835—1837), left a realistic description of the city in those its best days. He acknowledges the hospitalities of 'Captain Hasan bin Ibrahim, of the Arab Navy,' superintendent of the 'Prince Said Carlid.' The latter was the late Sayyid Khalid, then 16 years old. The book, being written by a 'Dutch-American ' in 1835, is of course bitterly hostile to England. We are told that the keel of the Peacock, passing between Tumbatu Island and Zanzibar, scraped over coral reefs not in Owen's charts—which may be true. Pollowed the American Captains Eisher,

---

[1] **We must not, however, forget that in 'all-enlightened England ' Smollett could complain of the ' people at the other end of the island knowing as little of Scotland as of Japan.'** _

Drinker, Abbott, and Osgood, and Mr Ross Brown, tben a young traveller in a trading-vessel. He also published a readable account of the rising settlement.

When Admiral Sir Charles Malcolm, a name endeared to eastern geographers, was giving energy and impulse to exploration in Western Asia, the late Lieut. W. Christopher, I. N., commanding the H. E. I. C.'s brig-of-war Tigris, was sent to Zanzibar; he made a practical survey of the coast, and he touched at many places now famous—Kilwa (Quiloa), Mombasah, Brava, Marka, Gob-wen (or the Jub River), and Makdishu, or Hanir, by the Portuguese called Magadoxo. He explored the lower waters of a large stream, the Webbe (Rivejr) Ganana, or Shebayli (Leopard), which he injudiciously named the Haines River; and he visited Giredi and other settlements till then unknown. He wrote (May 8, 1843) a highly interesting and comprehensive account of the seaboard, which was published in the Journal of the Geographical Society (vol. xiv. of 1844). His plans, charts, and other valuable memoranda were forwarded to the Bombay Government, and the enterprising traveller died in July, 1848, at the early age of 36, from the effects of a wound received before Multan.

The honour of having made the first systematic attempt to explore and to open up the Zanzibar interior, is due to the establishment popularly known as the 'Mombas Mission;' its energetic members proved that it was possible to penetrate beyond the coast, and their discoveries excited a spirit of inquiry which led to the exploration of the Lake Legions. In 1842 the Lev. Dr J. Lewis Krapf, being refused readmittance to Shoa, received a ᶜ Macedonian call ' to East Africa; in other words, he undertook in 1842, with the approbation of the Church Missionary Society, a coasting voyage to East Africa south of the line. Having visited Zanzibar Island he journeyed northwards (March 1844), and met with a kind reception at Mombasah where he accidentally landed ; finally he established his head-quarters amongst the Wanyika tribe at Labai Mpia near Mombasah, which then became the base of his operations. He was joined (June 1846) by the Lev. J. Lebmann of Gerlingen in Würtemberg, and by Messrs Erhardt and Wagner—the latter a young German mechanic, who died shortly after arrival. In June 2, 1851, came Messrs Conrad Diehlmann and Christian Pfefferle, who soon died. They were followed by three mechanics, Hagemann, Kaiser, and Metzler, who returned home, and by M. Deimler who retired to Bombay. M. Kebmann after visiting Kadiaro (Oct. 14, 1847) made in May 11, 1843 the first of three important journeys into the ' Jagga ' highlands, and discovered, or rather rediscovered, the much vexed Kilima-njaro. The existence of this mountain bearing eternal snows in eastern intertropical Africa is thus alluded to in the Suma de Geographia of Fernandez de Enciso (1530): 'West of this port (Mombasah) stands the Mount Olympus of Ethiopia, which is exceedingly high, and beyond it are the " Mountains of the Moon," in which are the sources of the Nile.' The discovery was confirmed by Dr Krapf, who after visiting (also in 1848) Euga, the capital of Usumbara, made two journeys (in 1849 and 1851) into TJkambani. During the first he confirmed the position of Kilima-njaro, and he sighted another snowy peak, Kenia, Kegnia, or Kirenia.

The assertions of the missionaries were variously received. M. Yaux was thereby enabled to explain a statement in the Metereologica of Aristotle, where the first or main stream of the Nile is supposed to flow out of the mountain called Silver. Dr Beke accepted the meridional snowy range, and here placed his Mountains of the Moon, a hypothesis first advanced in 1846.

The sceptics were headed hy Mr *W. D.* Cooley, who in 185d had published his £ Claudius Ptolemy and the Nile.' He had identified the mountain of Selene (trsX^vv)) with the snowy highland of 'Semenai ' or 'Samien ' in northern Abyssinia, and thus hy adopting a mere verbal resemblance he had obtained a system of truly[c] lunatic mountains.' Some years before (Journal Royal Geographical Society, vol. xv. 184)5) appeared his paper entitled, 'The Geography of N'yassi, or the great lake of Southern Africa investigated,' a complicated misnomer. The article was written in a clear style and a critical tone, showing ample reading but lacking a solid foundation of fact. It began as usual with Pigafetta and de Barros, and it ended with Gamitto and Monteiro; the peroration, headed * Harmony of Authorities,' was a self-gratulation, a song of triumph concerning the greatness of hypothetical discoveries, which were soon proved to be purely fanciful. Not one man in a million has the instincts of a good comparative geographer, and the author was assuredly not that exceptional man. His monograph did good by awaking the scientific mind, but it greatly injured popular geography. It unhappily asserted (p. 15) that 'in every part of eastern Africa to which our inquiries have extended, snow is quite unknown.' And the author having laid down his law bowed before it, and expected Fact as well as the Public to do the same; he even attacked the text of Ptolemy, asserting that the passages treating of the Nile sources and the Lunar Mountains were an interpolation of a comparatively recent date. In June and November 1863 the late Baron von der Decken, accompanied by X>r Kersten, an accomplished astronomical observer, ascended some 1300 feet, saw a clearly defined limit of perpetual snow at about ,17,000 feet, and by a rough triangulation gave the main peak of Kilima-njaro an elevation of 20,065 feet. Still Mr Cooley, with singular want of candour, denied existence to the snow. It was the same with his ᶜ Single Sea,' which under the meaningless and erroneous name ᶜ N'yassi ' again supplanted Ptolemy's Lakes, and this want of acumen offered the last insult to African geography. Thus was revived the day when the Arab and Portuguese geographers made the three ,Niles (of Egypt, Magadoxo, and Nigritia) issue from one vast reservoir, and thus were the school maps of the world disfigured during half .a generation. The lake also was painfully distorted, simply that it mightᶠ run parallel to the line of volcanic action drawn through the Isle de

Bourbon, tbe north of Madagascar, and the Comoro Islands, and to one of the two lines predominating on the coasts of southern Africa wherever there are no alluvial flats.' It abounded, moreover, in minor but significant errors, such as confounding 'Zanganyika,' a town or tribe, with Tanganyika, the name of the Lake. Of late years Mr Cooley has once more shifted his position, and has declared that he did not intend to provide central intertropical Africa between 'Monomotapa ' and Angola with a single lake. The whole of his paper on the ' Geography of N'yassi ' means that if it mean anything. He is not, however, the only Proteus—hard to find and harder to bind—amongst African geographers.

To conclude this notice of the 'Mombas Mission,' Dr Krapf again visited Puga, where he was followed by Mr Erhardt, add finally the two missionaries ran down the coast, touched at Kilwa, and extended their course to Cape Delgado. In August 1855 Dr Krapf, after 18 years' residence in Africa, bade it farewell; he did not revisit it except for a few months in 1867, when he acted dragoman to the Abyssinian Expedition. In January 1856 appeared what has been called the £ Mombas Mission Map ' (Skizze nach J. Erhardt's Original), the result of exploration and of notices collected from the natives. It was accompanied by a 'Memoir of the Chart of East and Central Africa, compiled hy J. Erhardt and J. ftebmann.' This production was ᶜ remarked upon' by Mr Cooley (Jan. 8, 1856), and in turn his remarks were remarked upon hy Herr Petermann. The peculiar feature of the chart was a • monster slug '-like inland Sea extending from the line to S. Lat. 11°,—an impossible Caspian some 840 miles long x 200 to 300 in breadth. I have already explained that this error arose by the fact that the three chief caravan routes from the Zanzibar coast abut upon three several lakes which, in the confusion of African vocabulary—Nvassa being corrupted to N'yassi, and Nyanza also signifying water—were naturally thrown into one. It was, however, to ascertain the existence of this slug-shaped article that the East African Expedition of 1856—59 was sent out.

The most valuable results of Dr Krapf's labours are his works on the Zanzibarian languages, and these deserve the gratitude of every traveller and student of .African philology. , The principal are,

Messrs Krapf s and Isenberg's imperfect outline of the Galla language (London, 1840).

Messrs Krapf and Isenberg, 'Vocabulary of the Galla Language,' London, 184.0.

Tentamen imbecillum Translationis Evangelii Joannis in linguam Gallorum, London, 1841.

Messrs Krapf's, Isenberg's, and Miihleisen-Arnold's Vocabulary of the Somali tongue (1843).

(Three chapters of Genesis translated into the 'Soahilee ' language, with an introduction by AV. AV. Greenhough: printed in the Journal of the American Oriental Society, 1847, had appeared in the mean time.)

Gospel according to St Luke translated into Kinika, 12mo, Bombay, 1848.

Gospel according to St Mark translated into Kikamba, 8vo, Tubingen, 1850.

Outline of the elements of the Ki-suakeli language, 8vo, Tubingen, 1850.

Vocabulary of 6 East-African languages, small folio, Tubingen, 1850.

Mr Erhardt's vocabulary of the Enguduk Iloigob or Masai tongue, 8vo, Ludwigburg, 1857.

Besides these there are (1860) in MSS., 1. the entire ls[T]ew Testament (Kisawahili). 2, A complete Dictionary of Ki-suahili. 3. The Gospel according to St Matthew (Kikamba). 4. Matthew and Genesis in Galla, &c., &c., &c.

Dr Krapf s last work, a relation historique,

appeared in 1860 (Travels, Hesearch.es, and Missionary Labours, &c., &c., with an Appendix hy Mr P. G. Bavenstein, E.B.G.S. London, Trubner and Co.). I venture to suggest that he might reprint with great advantage to African students his various journals, scattered through the numbers of the 'Church Missionary Intelligencer/ We want them, however, printed textually, with explanatory notes embodying subsequent information.

Meanwdnle the difficulties of East African exploration were complicated by a terrible disaster. M. Maizan, an Ensigne de Yaisseau, resolved to explore the inner lake regions vih the Zanzibar coast, and in 1844 his projects were approved of by his government. Affer the rains of 1845 he landed at the little settlement Bagamoyo, and when barely three days from the seaboard, he was brutally murdered at the village of Dege la Mhora, by one P'hazi Mazungera, chief of the Wakamba, a sub-tribe of the Wazaramo. The distinguished hydrographer Captain Guillain was sent in the brig of war Be Decouedie, to obtain satisfaction for this murder, and the following sentence concludes his remarks upon the subject (Chap. 1, pp. 17—20); 'Tout ce que je veux, tout ce que je dois me rappeler de

Maizan, c'est qu'il dtait intelligent, instruit, cour-*ageux,* et qu'il a piri misirablement a la fleur de l'age *(set.* 26) au d^but d'une enterprise ou il aurait pn rencontrer la gloire.' I have also described (Lake Legions of Central Africa, 1. Cbap. 3), from information collected on tbe. spot, the young traveller's untimely end; and it is still my opinion tbat tbe foul murder was caused more or less directly by tbe Christian merchants of Zanzibar. Dr Krapf's account of tbe catastrophe (Travels, p. 421) abounds in errors. Captain Guiilain was also sent on a kind of bagman's tour, a hawker carrying echantillons of Drench cloth and other produce offered to the Arab market. Mayotta having been ceded in 1841 by the Sakalawa chief, Andrian Souli, to the Drench government, which occupied it militarily in 1843, the first idea was to make of it a second and a more civilized Zanzibar. The coasting voyages and afew short inland trips were thought worthy of being published in three bulky volumes (Documents sur l'Histoire, la Gdographie, et la Commerce de l'Afrique Orientale, reeuellis et ridigds par M. Guiilain, &c.; publics par ordre du Gouvemement. Paris, Bertrand). The additions to Captain Owen's survey are unimportant, but the Drench. officer has diligently collected 'documents pour servir,' which will be useful when a history of the coast shall be written. The worst part of the hook is the linguistic; a sailor, however, .passing rapidly through or along a country, can hardly he expected to learn much of the language.

Meanwhile an important theory concerning the Nile Sources was published by my friend, Dr Charles T. Beke. He had surveyed and explored (Nov. 1840—May 1843) the Abyssinian plateau and the lowlands near the Bed Sea, and he had determined the water-parting of the streams which feed the Nile and the Indian Ocean (Journal Boyal Geographical Society, vol. xii). Whilst Bitter (Erdkunde) and other geographers made the WhiteBiver rise between N. lat. 7° and 8° and even 11°j ■whilst Messrs Antoine d'Abbadie and Ayrton were searching for the Coy Eountains in Enaria and Kaffa (N. lat. 7° 49' and E. long. 36° 2' 9"); and whilst Mr James Maccpieen located 'the .sources of the chief branch of the Bahr-el-abiad in about N. lat. 3°' (Preface xxiv. Geographical Survey of Africa, London, Eellowes, 1840), and[£] at no great distance from the equator ' (Ibid. 235), Dr Beke announced at the Swansea meeting of the British Association, that he would carry the Caput Nili to S. lat. 2°—3° and E. long. 34°; moreover that he would place it 'at a comparatively short distance from the sea coast, within the dominions of the Imam of Maskat.' Kightly judging the eastern coast to be the easiest road into central intertropical Africa, Dr Beke, then secretary to the Geographical Society of London, collected a subscripion for exploring the Nile Sources, via Zanzibar, and sent out Dr Friedrich Bialloblotsky to attempt the discovery. This Professor of Hebrew and literary man presented in February 1849 his credentials to H. M. the Sayyid and to Lieut.-Colonel Hamerton. The latter, backed by Dr Krapf, sent back the explorer to Egypt, without allowing him even to set foot upon the East African shore, and he was justified in so doing. The recent murder of M. Maizan had thrown the coast into confusion, the assassin was at large, and the motives which prompted the deed were still actively at work within the Island of Zanzibar. Dr Bialloblotsky could speak no eastern tongue, at least none that was intelligible in S. Africa; he was completely untrained to travel, he collected ' meteoric ' dust during a common storm at Aden—*magno cum risu* of the Adenites ; he did not know the difference between a sextant and a quadrant, and he asked Lieut.-Colonel Hamerton what a young cocoanut was.

Dr Beke, in his character of 'Theoretical Discoverer of the Nile Sources,' has published the following studies.

'On the Nile and its Tributaries,' a statement of his then novel views (Oct. 28, 1846, and printed in the Journal Boyal Geographical Society, vols. xvii., xviii. of 1847-8). 'The Sources of the Nile: being a General Survey of the Basin of that Elver, and of its Head-streams, with the History of Nilotic Discovery ' (London, Madden, 1860). The appendix contains a summary of Dr Bialloblotsky's projected journey.

f On the Mountains forming the eastern side of the Basin of the Nile, and the origin of the designation, "Mountains of the Moon," applied to them.' This paper, being refused by the Koyal Geographical Society, was read (August 30,1861) before the British Association at Manchester.

'Who discovered the Sources of the Nile?' A letter to Sir Eoderick I. Murchison (Madden, Leadenhall-street, 1863).

'On the Lake Kurd of Arabian Geographers and Cartographers! This paper argues that the equatorial Lake Kura-Kawar, drawn by an Arab, and published in Lelewel's " Geographie du Moyen Age," represents the lakes and marshes of N. lat. 9°.

Dr Beke, it appears, doubly deserves tbe title 'Theoretical Discoverer of the Nile Sources.' He has lately transferred tbe Caput from S. lat. 2°—3° to S. lat. 10° 30'—11°, and from E. long. 34° to E. long. 18°—19°, making tbe stream pass through 43° of latitude, and measuring diagonally one-eighth of the circumference of the globe. ('Solution of the Nile Problem,' Athenaeum, Eeb. 5,1870). The Nile is thus identified with the Kasai, or Kassavi, the Casais of P. J. Baptista (the Pombeiro), tbe Casati of Douville, the Casasi of M. Cooley, the Cassabe of M. J. P. Graya, the Kasaby of Mr Macqueen, and the Kasye or Loke of Dr Livingstone. These 'New Sources ' are in the 'primaeval forests of Olo-Yihenda and Djikoe or Eibokoe (the Quiboque of the Hungarian officer Ladislaus Magyar), in the Mossamba Mountains, about 300 miles from the coast of Benguela. Mr Keith Johnston, jun. believes that the Lufira-Luapula river is the lower course of the Kassavi or Kassabi, which is usually made to rise in S. lat. 12°, near the Atlantic seaboard, and after flowing N. E. and N. as far as about S. lat. 8°, to turn eastward instead of continuing to the N. *W.* and W. He makes it, however, the true head of the Congo, not of the Nile.

Amongst minor explorations, I may mention that of Mr Henry C. Arcangelo, who in 1847 ascended the Juba or Govind River. It is, however, doubtful how far his explorations extended. He was followed in 1849 by Captain Short. In November, 1851, a party of three Moors or Zanzibar Arabs landed at 'Bocamoio ' (the Bagamoyo roadstead village where M. Maizan disembarked), travelled with 40 carriers to the Lake 'Tanganna' (Tanganyika), crossed it in a boat which they built, visited the Muata Cazembe, and reached, after six months, the Portuguese Benguela. The late Mr Consul Brand communicated, through the Poreign Office, this remarkable journey, in which Africa had been crossed, with few difficulties, from sea to sea, and it excited the attention of the Royal Geographical Society (Journal, vol. xxiv. of 1854).

. In 1852 Sir Roderick I. Murchison propounded his theory of the basin-shaped structure of the African interior. This was an important advance upon the great plateau of Lacdpede (Mdmoire, etc., dans les Annales du Musde de l'Histoire Nat., vi. 284), and it abolished' the gardens and terraces of Ritter (Erdkunde, le Plateau ou la Haute Afrique). About the same time Col. Sykes recommended that an expedition be sent from Mombasah to explore the 'Arcannm Magnum,' opining that the discovery of Kilima-njaro and Kenia had limited the area of the bead-waters between S. lat. 2°—4° and E. long. (G-.) 32°—36°, almost exactly the southernmost position of the Nyanza Lake. In March, 1855, Lieut.-Colonel Hamerton forwarded concise but correct notices, 'On various points connected with the H.M. Imam of Muskat,' which was published in the Bombay Selections (No. 24). In Dec. 10, 1855, followed Mr James Macqueen's paper on the 'Present state of the Geography of some parts of Africa (read at the Boyal Geographical Society, April 8 and June 10, 1850), with 'Notes on the Geography of Central Africa,' taken from the researches of Livingstone, Monteiro, Graca, and others (Journal Boyal Geographical Society, vol. xxvi. 109). They show great critical ability. The map accompanying the memoir separated the 'Tanganyenka ' from the Nyassa Lake ; moreover, it disposed the greater axes of these several waters as they should be, nearly upon a meridian. Maps still suffered from that incubus the N'yassi or Single Sea, stretching between S. lat. 7°—12°, and distorted by its 'historien geographe' from the N. S. position occupied by the half-dozen lakes which compose it[1] to a N. *W.* and S. E. rhumb. As afterwards appeared, Mr Macqueen had confused the Tanganyika and Nyanza waters by placing the centre of the former in long. (G.) 29°. This, however, was not suspected when my excellent and venerable friend gave me the rough proofs of his paper, which travelled with me into Central Africa. Mr Macqueen has also done good hy editing (Journal Royal Geographical Society, vol. xxx.) the Journeys of Silva Porto with the Arabs from Benguela to Ibo and Mozambique, and by other labours too numerous to be specified.

A pause in East African exploration followed the departure of Dr Krapf. M. Erhardt, whose project of entering via Kilwa was not supported, had joined his brother missionaries in India. M. Rebmann alone remained at Rabai Mpia.

[1] The 'Nyassi' is, in fact, a general reservoir into which are thrown the Lakes Tanganyika, the Nyassa, the Shirwa, and the four smaller waters, the Liemba, the Bangweolo, the Moero of the great river Chamheze, and the Liemba drained by the Lufira-Luapula stream. The latter, lying, between S. lat. 10°—12°, have lately been reported by T)r Livingstone (Map of the Lake Begion of Eastern Africa, showing the Sources of the Nile recently discovered by Dr Livingstone, with notes, &c.y by Keith Johnston, jun. (Johnston); and we have a Sketch Map of Dr Livingstone's recent Explorations—Eine Karten-■skizze, &c. Erom Dr Petermann's Geographische Mittbeilumgen, Part V., for May, 1870 (Gotha, Perthes).

And whilst under H. H. Abbas Pasha a large and complete Egypto-European expedition was, after the old fashion, organized to ascend the stream, 'ad investigandum caput *Nili* ' (Seneca, Nat. Qusest. vi. 8), the new and practicable route from the Zanzibar coast seemed to have been clean forgotten.

During this lull we landed, as the reader has been told in the last chapter, upon the African isle ' Menouthias.'

NOTE.

I may be excused in here alluding to an assertion often repeated by the 'Geographer of N'gassi,' in his Memoir on the ᶜ Lake Regions of East Africa reviewed ' (London, Stanford, 1864). He makes me 'the easy dupe of the most transparent personal hostility, which wore the respectable mask of the Royal Geographical Society,' and he assures me that I left England 'indoctrinated ' as to what lake or lakes I should find in Central Africa, and so forth.

This fretfulness of mortified vanity would not have been noticed by me had it not been so unfair to the Royal Geographical Society. In the preface of my Memoir (pp. 4—8, Journal Royal Geographical Society, vol. xxix.), I was careful to print all the instructions of the Expeditionary Committee, and I only regretted that they were not more detailed. It is absurd to assert of a traveller that he 'visited the lake regions with a confirmed inclination to divide the lake.' What interest can he have in bringing home any but the fullest and most exact details? The petty differences between himself and the Royal Geographical Society, which Mr Cooley assumes all the world to know, were utterly unknown to me when I left England in 1856; and, greatly despising such things, I have never since inquired into the subject. Returning home in 1859, I learned with surprise that the 'Comparative Geographer' still stood upon his 'Single Sea,' and considered any one who dared to make two or three of it his personal enemy. That such should be the mental state of a gentleman who has not, they say, taken leave of his wits, was a phenomenon which justified my wonder; nor could I believe it till the pages of the *Athenaeum* proceeded to give me proof positive. It is melancholy to see a laborious literary man, whose name might stand so high, thus display the caput mortuum of his intellect.

P.S. Another mortuary notice! . My good old friend Mr Macqueen has also passed away at a ripe age, leaving behind him the memory of a laborious and useful life, especially devoted to the cause of Africa and the Africans.

CHAPTER IV.

A STROLL THROUGH ZANZIBAR CITY.

'E dahi se foi a Ilba de Zanzibar, que he aquem de Mombasa vinte leguas e tao pegada a terra firma que as d4os que passarem per entre ellas, hao de ser vistas.'—De Bacbos. 1, vii. 4.

And first of the Port.

Zanzibar harbour is a fine specimen of the true Atoll, barrier or fringing reef, built upon a subsiding foundation, probably of sandstone. The original lagoon, charged with sediment and washings from the uplands, must have burst during some greater flood, and split into narrow water-ways the one continuous coralline rim. The same influences may account for the gaps in the straight-lined reef whose breach gave a name to Brazilian Pernambuco.

The port varies in depth from 9 to 13 fathoms, with overfalls, and the rise of the tide is 13 feet. Here the Hormos Episalos (statio fluctuosa, or open roadstead of the Periplus, chap. 8) has been converted into a basin hy the industry of the lithophyte. These ants of the ocean have built up an arc of

> 'Sea-girt isles,
> That, like to rich and various gems, inlay
> The unadorned bosom of the deep.'

There is a front harbour and a back bay. The latter enables ships landing cargo to avoid the heavy swell of the N.E. monsoon. The two are separated by Idas Changani[1]—Sandy Point. The name, corrupted to Shangany, has attached itself in our charts to the whole city.

These coral-based islet clumps are readily made in these seas. The rough ridges of a 'wash,' where currents meet, are soon heaped with sea-weed, with drift-wood, and with scatters of parasitical testaceae, which decaying form a thin but fruitful soil. Seeds brought by winds, waves, and birds then germinate ; and matter,

---

[1] Changa (large sands), in the plural Michanga, sands (of great extent). Mchanga (sand generally), at Mombasab and on tbe coast which preserve the older dialect, becomes Mtanga, and means a sandy place. The islanders of Zanzibar, for instance, will say Nti (tbe land or earth), the continentals, Nchi: these prefer Ku Changanyika (to meet together), those Ku Tanganyika. Toreigners often confound cliya with jya, and pronounce, for instance, Msijyami for Msichytina—a lass. The Arabs, who cannot articulate the ch, convert it into their familiar sh, e. g. Ku Skimba for Ku Chimba (to dig).

animal as well as vegetable, is ever added till a liumns-bed is formed for thick shrubbery and trees. Unless deposition and vegetation continue to bind the rock, it is liable to be undermined by the sea, when it forms banks dangerous to navigation.

Dr Euschenberger, repeated by a modern traveller, informs us that there are 'four minor reefs, looking like great arks, whose bows and sterns hang bushing over the waters.' As all the plans show, there are five. The northernmost link of the broken chain is Champani (not 'Cliapany'), the Isle des Erancais of Drench charts. It became a God's-acre for Europeans, whose infidel corpses here, as at Maskat, and in ancient Madeira before the days of Captain Cook, had during less latitudinarian times the choice of the dunghill of tire cove, or of a hole in the street. Formerly it was frequented by turtle-fishers and egg-seekers : 'black Mukogo,'[1] however, has been scared away by visions of fever-stricken, yellow-faced ghosts rising ghastly from the scatter of Christian graves. The bit of sandy bush, distinguished from its neighbours by absence of tall trees, is frequented (1857) by naval and commercial Nimrods, with 'shooting irons '

[1] **Manioc, often erroneously written Maliogo.**

and ᶜ smelling dogs,' curs with clipped ears and shorn tails, bought from bumboat men: *m bon chasseurs,* they shoot the Sayyid's little antelopes which troop up expecting food ; and sometimes these sportsmen make targets of certain buif-coloured objects imperfectly seen through the bushes. The mouldering sepulchres in their neglected clearings make the prospect of a last home here peculiarly unsavoury, almost as bad as in Brazilian Santos. Yet there are traditions of Trench picnics visiting it to eat monkey—a proceeding which might have been interrupted *en ville.*

Westward the line of natural breakwaters is prolonged by Kibondiko, Le Ponton, or the Hulk. A mere mass of jungle, it has never been utilized. The eye, however, rests with pleasure upon the sheet of sparkling foam tumbling white over its coralline outliers, backed by dark purple-blue distance, and fronted by tranquil, leek-green shoal water. Connected with its neighbour by a reef practicable at low tides, it is separated from Changu, or Middle Island, by 'Trench channel,' deep enough for men-of-war. The shoals about it supply a small rock-oyster. The crustacea, however, is uncultivated, and amongst Moslems it is *escargot* to the typical John Bull.

The most important is B;iwi or Turtle Island, a low, dry bank, slightly undulated, with a beautifully verdant undergrowth, fringed and tasseled with the tallest cocoas. The Chelonian (K'hasa) of the East coast, eaten in April and May, by no means equals that of Eernando Po or of Ascension ; moreover, here no man is master of the art and mystery of developing callipash and callipee. Turtle, cooked by a 'cook-boy,' suggests the flesh of small green Saurians (Susmdr), which the haughty Persians of Firdausi thus objected to their Semitic neighbours—

> 'Can the Arab's greed thus have grown so great,
> From his camels' milk and his lizards' meat,
> That he casts on Kayyanian crowns his eye ?
> Fie on tbee ! thou swift-rolliDg world, 0 fie ! '

The tortoise-shell, so often mentioned in the Periplus as an export from Menoutbias (cbap. xv.) and Khapta (chap. xvii.), has until lately been neglected. Like Bombay Calabar, and our Isle of Logs in the olden time, the few acres of Turtle Island were used to 'keep antelopes, goats, and other beasts of delight,' while vicious baboons were deported to it from the city. Below it is the celebrated 'Harpshell Bank,' now mercilessly spoiled. Southernmost is Ghumbi Island, alias La Passe, which, mistaken for the

Turtle, has caused many'a wreck. These mishaps are not always accidental. One day Lieut. - Colonel Hamerton saw, through his glass, the master of a frenchman deliberately stow himself and his luggage in the gig, put off, and leave his ship to run her nose upon the nearest reef.

These islands form the well-known 'Passes,' channels intricate with lithodom-reefs and mollusk-beds. They number four, namely, the northern or English Pass, between Champani and Zanzibar; theN. W. or Erench Pass, between Kibondiko and Changu; the great or middle, between Changu and Bdwi; and the western, south of Bawi. The principal entrance Avas buoyed hy the late Sayyid, but these precautions soon disappeared. Within the line of breakwaters is the anchorage, which may be pronounced excellent; ships ride close to shore in 7 to 8 fathoms, and the area between the islets and the island may be set down at 3'8 square miles. It presents an animated scene. Mosquito fleets of 'ngarawa ' or monoxyles cut the wavelets like flying proas, under the nice conduct of the sable fishermen, who take advantage of the calm weather. The northerners from about Brava have retained the broad-brimmed straAV hat, big as an average parasol. Like that of Malabar, Morocco, and West Africa, it was adopted by their Portuguese conquerors. The machua or ͨ little boats ' of the Lusiads, which De Barros calls 'Sambucos,'[1] are still the same, except that a disproportioned sail of merkani (American domestics), based upon a pair of outriggers, now supplies the primitive propeller,

'd'humas folhas de palma bem tecidas.'

The outrigger is rarely neglected. Here and there a giant shark shoots up from the depths, and stares at the fishermen with a cruel, fixed, and colourless eye, that makes his blood run cold. Only the poorest of poor devils will venture into a 'dug-out,' which is driven before the wind or paddled with a broad, curved, spoon-like blade. These Matumbi, or hollowed logs, form a curious national contrast with the launches and lighters that land European merchandise; ponderous and solid squares, their build shows nothing graceful or picturesque.

The N. E. monsoon is now (December) doing its duty well, and bringing various native craft

[1] I bare described (Pilgrimage to El Medinah and M'eccah) the modem Sambuk of tbe Red Sea, and find the word 'Sonbouk' in the Ereneh translation of lbn Batutah. Sir Gardner Wilkinson quotes Athenams, who makes the 'Sambuca ' (a musical instrument) 'resemble a ship with a ladder placed over it.'

from Madagascar, Mozambique, the minor islands of tbe Indian Ocean, Bombay and Guzerat, the Somali coast, the Bed Sea, Maskat, and the Persian Gulf. Numbering 60 to 70, they anchor close in shore—0 Semites and Hamites, wondrously apathetic!—where the least sea would bump them to bits. About half a mile outside the 'country shipping,' ride, in 5 to 6 fathoms, half a dozen square-rigged merchantmen — Americans, Prench, and Hamburgers; England is not represented. What with bad water, and worse liquor, the Briton finds it hard to live at Zanzibar. All are awaiting cargoes of copal and ivory, of hides, and of the cowries which we used to call 'blackamoor's teeth.'

The quaintest and freshest local build is to us the Mtepe, which the Arabs call Muntafiyali.[1] This lineal descendant of the Ploaria Bhapta (Naviculae Consutae,. Periplus, chap. 16), that floated upon these seas 20 centuries ago, is a favourite from Lamu to Bhlwa. The shell has a beam one-third of its length, and swims the tide buoyantly as a sea-bird. This breadth, combined with elasticity, enables it to stand any

[1] It is written Mutaifiyah in the Arab Chronicle of Mombasah History, translated and included in Captain Owen's work (Voyages to Africa, vol. i. 416, Arabia, etc., London, Bentley, 1833).

amount of grounding and bumping, nor is it ever beached for the S. W. monsoon. It is pegged together, not nailed, and mostly, as the old traveller says, 'sewn, like clothes, with twine.' The tapering mast, raking forwards, carries any amount of square matting, by no means air-tight, and the stern is long and projecting, as if amphisbffinic. The swan-throat of the arched prow is the cheniscus of the classical galley-stem. Necklaced with strips of hide and bunches of talismans, it bears a red head; and the latter, as in the ark of Osiris and in the Chinese junk, has the round eyes painted white, ■—possibly, in the beginning holes for hawsers. The 'Mtepe ' carries from 12 to 20 tons, and can go to windward of everything propelled by wind.

The Badim, from Sur, Sohar, and Maskat, has a standing plank-covering, and being able to make 11 knots an hour is preferred by passengers, Arab loafers, and somers, one being allowed per ton in short trips. Descried from afar through the haze, her preposterous sail has caused the Zanzibarites to fly their flags in anticipation of home news; nearer, the long, narrow, quoin-shaped craft, with towering sternpost and powerful rudder, like the caudal fin of some monstrous fish, presents an exceptional physiognomy. The unconth Arab Dan (dow) dates probably from tbe days of tbe Phoenicians, and is found all over the Indian Ocean. She ranges from 50 to 500 tons, and her sharp projecting bow makes her deck nearly a quarter longer than the keel, giving her, Avhen under Aveigh, a peculiar stumbling, shambling, tottering gait. The open poop is a mass of immense outworks, and there is the normal giant steering-tackle, often secured only hy lashings : a single mast is stepped a little ahead of amidships; it rakes forward, as is the rule of primitive craft, and it supports a huge square sail of coarse material. The Kidau (small dow) is similar, hut with open stern-cabins; it is generally sewn together with coir or rope of cocoa fibre, and caulked with the same. The bottom is paid over with a composition of lime and shark's-oil, which, hardening under water, preserves the hull from sea-worms. Thus sheathed, ships which have made two feet of leakage become tight as if newly coppered. Similarly, the Irish fishermen coat their craft with marl and oil. Talc and tallow are employed in different parts of Europe: and the Chinese use a putty of oil and burnt gypsum; according to others, a composition, of lime and resin of the Ton gshu-tree applied over the oakum of bamboo (Astley, **4, 128**).

The ' Grab ' (properly 'Ghurab,' meaning a raven) is an overgrown Pattimar. A model of the latter craft, primitive and Hindu, was submitted to the British public during *the* Great Exhibition. Rigged harque-lilce, it is wondrous ark-like and uncouth. Baghlahs (she-mules) and Ganjas (Ghancheh), from Cutch, are old tubs with low projecting prows and elevated sterns, elaborately carved and painted. Low down in the fore, their lean bows split like giant wedges the opposing waves, which hiss and seethe as they fly past in broad arrow-heads. Dangerous in heavy seas, these coffins are preserved by popular prejudice for the antique and by the difficulty of choosing other models. Add sundry Batelas, with poop-cabinets, closed and roomy, some with masts struck, others ready to weigh anchor —I am not writing, gentle reader, a report on Moslem naval architecture—and you have an idea of the outlandish fleet, interesting withal, which hethrongs the port of Zanzibar.

The much-puffed squadron of the late Sayyid, stationed during his life at Mto-ni, and now being divided amongst the rival heirs, flanks with its *single* and double tiers *of guns these* peaceful traders, of whom, bv-the-by, some are desperate pirates. The number is imposing; but the decks have no awnings against the weather, the masts are struck and stripped to save rigging, the yards lie fore-and-aft upon the booms, the crews consist of half-a-dozen thievish, servile ᶜ sons of water ' (M'ana Map]; rats and cockroaches compose the live stock; the ammunition is nowhere, and though the quarter and main decks are sometimes swept, everything below is foul with garbage and vermin. The exteriors are dingy; the interiors are so thoroughly rotted by fresh water that the ships are always ready to go down at their anchors. The whole thing is a mistake amongst Arabs, who are fitted only for a 'buggalow,' or at best a ᶜ grab.' The late Sayyid once attempted English sailors, who behaved well as long as they did what they pleased, especially in the minor matters of 'baccy and grog; hut when the dark-faced skipper hegan loud speaking and tall threats, they incontinently thrashed him upon his own quarter-deck, and were perforce 'dismissed the service.' Every captain in the 11. E. Maskat, besides impudently falsifying the muster-rolls, will steal the fighting-lanterns, the hammocks, and other articles useful at home; whilst the care-takers sell in the bazar, junk, rope, and line; copper bolts, brass-work, and carpenter's chests hearing the government mark. When a ship is wanted an Arab Nakhoda (here called Nahoza), a Muallim or sailing-master, and a couple of Sukkanis (pilots), are sent on board with a crew composed of a few Arab non-commissioned officers and 'able seamen,' Baloch, Maskatis, and slaves. The commander, who receives some 50 dollars per lunar month, kills time with the cognac bottle; the sailing-master (7 dollars) dozes like a lap-dog in his own arm-chair on the quarter-deck ; and the seamen do nothing, Jack helping Bill. One of these vessels sent to England a few years ago lost, hy want of provisions and had water, 86 out of its crew—100 men; and can we wonder at it ? A single small screw-steamer, carrying a heavy gun, and manned and commanded hy Europeans, would have been more efficient in warfare, and far more useful in peace, than the whole squadron of hulks. It is, however, vain to assure the Arab brain that mere number is not might; and, indeed, so it is when people believe in it.

The high and glassless windows of H. M.'s Consulate enable us to prospect the city. Zanzibar, in round numbers 6° soutb of tbe line, occupies the western edge and about the midway length of the coral reef that forms the island. The latter is separated by a Manche or channel from the continent, a raised strip of blue land, broken by tall and remarkable cones all rejoicing in names still mysterious enough to flutter the traveller's nerves. The inclination of the island from N.N.W. to S.S.E. shelters the harbour from the Indian Ocean, whilst the bulge of the mainland breaks the force of dangerous Hippalus, the S.W. monsoon. The minimum breadth of the Manche is 16 geographical miles; from the Fort to the opposite coast there are 24, and from the bottom of Menai Bay 35. The Periplus gives to the Menouthian Channel about 300 stadia, in round numbers 30 geographical miles : 600 common stadia correspond, within a fraction of the real measurement, with a degree of latitude ($1°=_3$-6_0 of the earth's circumference). Marinus of Tyre and Ptolemy, however, unduly reduced the latter to 500 stadia.

Zanzibar city is built upon a triangular spit, breaking the line of its wide, irregular, and shallow bay. The peninsula is connected with the island by an isthmus some 300 yards wide, and it is backed by swamp and lagoon, bush and forest.

Arc-shaped, with the chord formed by the sea-frontage, and the segment of the circle facing landwards, its greatest length is from N.E. to S.W., and it is disposed beachways, like the seaports of Oman. The front is a mere 'dicky,' a clean show concealing nncleanness. Instead, however, of a neat marine parade and a T-shaped pier, the foreground is a line of sand fearfully impure. Corpses float at times upon the heavy water; the shore is a cess-pool, and the younger blacks of both sexes disport themselves in an absence of costume which would startle even Margate. Round-barrelled bulls, the saints of the Banyans, and therefore called by us 'Brahmani,' push and butt, by way of excitement, the gangs of serviles who carry huge sacks of cowries, and pile high their hides and logwood. Others wash and scrape ivory, which suggested to a young traveller the idea that the precious bone, here so plentiful, is swept up by the sea. At night the front often flares as if on fire. The cause is lime-burning on the shore, in small, round, built-up heaps.

Another evil, arising from want of quay and breakwater, is that the sea at times finds its way into the lower parts of the town. The nuisance increases, as this part of the Island appears to he undergoing depression, not an uncommon process in fictile madrepore formations. Off Changdni Point, where in 1823 stood a hut-clump and a mosque, four fathoms of water now roll. The British Consulate, formerly many yards distant from the surf, must be protected by piles and rubble. Some of the larger houses have sunk four, and have sloped nine feet from terrace to ground, owing to the instability of their soppy foundations. The 'Tree-island ' of our earliest charts has been undermined and carried away bodily by the waves; whilst to the north the sea has encroached upon Mto-ni, where the Sayyid's flagstaff has four times required removal. On the other hand, about 15 years ago, the 'Middle-Shoal ' of the harbour was awash; now it is high and dry.

In 1835 Dr B/uschenberger estimated the census of Zanzibar at 12,000 souls, of whom two-thirds were slaves. In 1814 Dr Krapf proposed 100,000 as the population of the island, the greater number living in the capital. Captain Guiilain, in 18-16, gave 20,000 to 25,000, slaves included. I assumed the number, in 1857, as 25.000, which during the N.E. monsoon, when a large floating population flocks in, may rise to 40.000, and even to 45,000. The Consular report of 1819 asserts it to be 'about 60,000.'

The city is divided into 18 quarters (Mahallat), each having its own name; and when travellers inform us that it is called 'Hamuz,' Moafilab, or Baur, they simply take a part for the whole.[1] The west-end boasts the best houses, chiefly those which wealthy natives let to stranger merchants. The Central, or Port quarter, is the seat of government and of commerce, whilst few foreigners inhabit the eastern extremities, the hottest and the most unhealthy. The streets are, as they should be under such a sky, deep and winding alleys, hardly 20 feet broad, and travellers compare them with the threads of a tangled skein. In the west-end a pavement of Chunam, or tamped lime, is provided with a gutter, which secures dryness and cleanliness—

[1] The quarters, beginning from Cbangani, the most western, are, the Baghani, which contains the English Consulate; the Mnazi-Moya to the south, with a grave-yard, and a bazar where milk and grain are sold; tbe *Fuga adjoining it, the* Zambarani, the Kajifichemi, the Kunazemi, and the Kambo to the southeast ; the G-urayzani, containing the fort; and the Eurdani with the Custom House; the Kipondab, where the French Consulate is ; the Ziwani (Mitha-pani of the Hindus) further to the south; the Suk Muhogo, where manure and fish are sold; the Melindi, or Melindini, occupied by Hindus, and boasting a bazar; and lastly the Mnawi, the Kokoni, and the Eungu extend to the easternmost quarter, the Malagash, where the Lagoon, an inlet of the sea, hounds the city. I did not hear any of the three names mentioned in the text; they are probably now obsolete.

it is the first that I have seen in an African city. As we go eastward all such signs of civilization vanish; the sun and wind are the only engineers, and the frequent green and black puddles, like those of the filthy Ghetto, or Jews' quarter, at Damascus, argue a preponderance of black population. Here, as on the odious sands, the festering impui'ities render strolling a task that requires some resolution, and the streets are unfit for a decent (white) woman to walk through. I may say the same of almost every city where the negro element abounds.

As in the coast settlements of the Red Sea and of Madagascar, the house material is wholly coral rag, a substance at once easily worked and durable—stone and lime in one. The irregularity of the place is excessive, and it is by no means easy to describe its peculiar physiognomy. The public buildings are poor and mean. The mosques which adorn Arab towns with light and airy turrets, breaking the monotony of square white tenements, magnified claret-chests, are here in the simplest Wahhabi form. About 30 of these useful, but by no means ornamental, 'meeting-houses ' are scattered about the city for the use of the ' established church.' They are oblong rooms, with stuccoed walls, and matted floors; the flat roofs are supported by dwarf rows of square piers and *polygonal* columns; whilst Saracenic arches, broad, pointed, and lanceated, and windows low-placed for convenience of expectoration, with inner emarginations in the normal shape of scallops or crescents, divide the interior. Two Shafei mosques, one called after Mohammed Abd el Kadir, the other from Mohammed el Aughan (Afghan), have minarets, dwindled turrets like the steeples of Brazilian villages; another boasts of a diminutive cone, most like an Egyptian pigeon-tower; and a fourth has a dwarf excrescence, suggesting the lantern of a light-house. The Shiahs, who are numerous, meet for prayer in the Kipondah quarter, and the Kojahs have a ruined mosque outside the city.

The best houses are on the Arab plan familiar to travellers in Ebro-land and her colonies. The type has extended to Prance and even to Galway, where we still find it in the oldest buildings. A dark narrow entrance leads from the street, and the centre of the tenements is a hypsethral quadrangle, the Iberian Patio or Quintal. *We* miss, however, the shady trees, the sweet flowers, and bright verdure with which the southern European and the Hispano-American beautify their dwellings. Here the 'Dir ' is a dirty yard, paved or unpaved, usually encumbered with piles of wood or hides, stored for sale, and tenanted by poultry, dogs, donkeys, and lounging slaves. A steep and narrow, dark and dangerous staircase of rough stone, like a companion-ladder, connects it with the first floor, the 'noble-quarter.' There are galleries for the several storeys, and doors opening upon the court admit light into the rooms. Zanzibarian architecture, as among 'Orientals ' generally, is at a low ebb. The masonry shows not a single straight line ; the arches are never similar in form or size; the floors may have a foot of depression between the middle and the corners of the room; whilst no two apartments are on the same level, and they seldom open into each other. Joiner's work and iron-work must both be brought from India.

The 'azoteas'[1] flat roofs, or rather terraces, are supported by mangrove-trunks, locally called 'Zanzibar rafters,' and the walls, of massive thickness, are copiously 'chunam'd.' Here the inmates delight to spread their mats, and at suitable seasons to 'smell the air.' Banda or bandim, pent-roofed huts of plaited palm-leaf (ma-

[1] The Iberian name (in Arabic   El Sat'h) of tbe flat roof-terrace, borrowed from tbe dry lands of W estern Asia.

kuti or cajan) garnish, the roofs of the native town. Europeans do not patronize these lookouts, fires being frequent and the slaves dangerous. Some foreigners have secured the comfort of a cool night hy building upper cabins of planking, and have paid for the enjoyment in rheumatism, ague, and fever.

Koranic sentences on slips of paper, fastened to the entrances, and an inscription cut in the wooden lintel, secure the house from witchcraft, like the crocodile in Egypt; whilst a yard of ship's cable drives away thieves. The higher the tenement, the bigger the gateway, the heavier the padlock, and the huger the iron studs which nail the door of heavy timber, the greater is the owner's dignity. All seems ready for a state of siege. Even the little square holes pierced high up in the walls, and doing duty as ventilators, are closely barred. As heat prevents the use of g'lass in sleeping-rooms, shutters of plain or painted plank supply its place, and persiennes deform the best habitations. The northern European who sleeps for the first time in one of these blockhouses fairly realizes the first sensations of a jail. Of course the object is defence, therefore the form is still common to Egypt and Zanzibar, Syria and Asia Minor.

THE ROOM.

Arabs here, as elsewhere, prefer long narrow rooms (40 feet x 15 to 20), generally much higher than their breadth, open to the sea-breeze, which is the health-giver; and they close the eastern side-walls against the ᶜ fever-wind,' the cool, damp, spicy land-draught. The Sala or reception-hall is mostly on the ground-floor. It contrasts strongly with our English apartments, where the comfortless profusion and confusion of furniture, and where the undue crowding of ornamental ornaments, spoil the proportions and 'put out' the eye. The protracted lines of walls and rows of arched and shallow niches, which take the place of tables and consoles, are unbroken save by a few weapons. Pictures and engravings are almost unknown ; chandeliers and mirrors are confined to the wealthy; and the result, which in England would be bald and barn-like, here suggests the coolness and pleasing simplicity of an Italian villa—in Italy. A bright-tinted carpet, a gorgeous but tasteful Persian rug for the dais, matting on the lower floor, which is of the usual chunam; a divan in old-fashioned houses; and, in the best of the modern style, half a dozen stiff chairs of East Indian blackwood or China-work, compose the upholstery of an Arab 'palazzo.'

In the rooms of the few who can or will atford such trifles, ornaments of porcelain or glassware, and French or Yankee knicknacks fill the niches. Of course the inner apartments are more showily dressed, hnt these we may not explore.

About half way down the front of the city we debouch upon the ' Gurayza ' or fort. The material is the usual coral-rag, cemented with lime of the same formation, rudely burnt, and the style as well as the name (Igreja—Ecclesia) recall to mind the Portuguese of the heroic sixteenth century. It is one of those na'iye, crenelated structures, flanked by polygonal towers, each pierced for one small gun, and connected by the comparatively low curtains, in which our ancestors put their trust. A narrow open space runs round it, and it is faced by a straight-lined detached battery, commanding the landing, and about 12 yards long. The embrasures of this outwork are so close that the first broadside would blow open the thin wall; and the score of guns is so placed that every bullet striking the fort must send a billet or two into the men that serve them. A *'place d'armes,'* about 50 feet wide, divides the two, and represents the naval and military arsenal—two dozen iron carronades lying piled to tlie right of the first entrance, and as much neglected and worm-eaten as though they belonged to our happy colony, Cape Coast Castle. Amongst the guns of different calibre we find a few fine old brass pieces, one of which bears the dint of a heavy blow. They are probably the plunder of Hormuz or of Maskat, where the small matter of a 'piece of ham wrapped up in paper '[1] caused, in the middle of the seventeenth century, a general massacre of the Portuguese.'

The gateway is the usual intricate barbican. Here in olden times, after the prayers of el Asr (3 p.m.) the governor and three judges, patriarchs with long grey beards, unclean white robes, and sabres in hand, held courts of justice, and distributed rough-and-ready law to peaceful Banyans, noisy negroes, and groups of fierce Arabs. The square bastion projecting from the curtain, now contains upper rooms for the Baloch Jemadar (commandant). The ground-floor is a large vestibule, upon whose shady masonry-henches the soldiery and their armed slaves lounge and chat, laugh and squabble, play and chew betel. On the left of the outer gate is a

[1] Chap. 7. Captain Hamilton's 'Hew Account of the East Indies.'

Cajan slied, where native artists are setting up carriages for the guns whose lodging is now the hot ground. The experiment of firing a piece was lately tried; it reared up and fell backwards, smashing its frail woodwork and killing two artillery 'chattels.'

Travellers have observed that a launch could easily dismantle this stronghold. It was once, the legend runs, attacked and taken by a single 'Jack,' for the honour of whose birthplace Europe and America vainly contend. Determined to liberate two brother-tars from the ignoble bilboes, he placed himself at the head of a party consisting of a Newfoundland dog. He fell upon the guard *sabre au poing*, and, left master of the field, he waved his bandanna in vinous triumph from the battlements. Sad to relate, this Caucasian hero succumbed to Hamitic fraud. The discomfited slaves rallied. Holding a long rope, they ran round and round the enemy, till, wound about like a windlass or a silk cocoon, he was compelled to surrender at discretion.

The interior of the fort is jammed with soldiers' huts, and divided into courts by ricketty walls. Here, too, is the only jail in Zanzibar. The stocks (Makantarah), the fetters, the iron collars, and the heavy waist-chains, do not prevent black man from conversationizing, singing comic songs, and gambling with pebbles. The same was the case with our gruel-houses— 'Kanji-Kdianah,' vulgo 'Conjee-Connah ' — in British India. The Sepoys laughed at them and at our beards. The Bombay Presidency jail is known to Arabs as El Bistan (El Bostan, the Garden), because the courts show a few shrubs, and with Ishmaelites a ᶜ Bistan ' has ever an *ctrriere pensee* of Paradise. But the most mutinous white salt that ever floored skipper would 'squirm ' at the idea of a second night in the black-hole of Zanzibar. Such is the Oriental beau-ideal of a prison—a place whose very name should develope the goose-skin, and which the Chinese significantly call 'hell.'

In my day foreigners visited the prison to see its curio, a poor devil cateran who had beaten the death-drum whilst his headman was torturing M. Maizan. An Arab expedition sent into the interior returned with this wretch, declaring him to be the murderer in chief, and for two years he lay chained in front of the Erench Consulate. Since 1847 he was heavily ironed to a gun, under a mat-shed, where he could neither stand up nor lie down. The fellow looked fat and well, but he died before our return from the interior in 1859.

Below the eastern bastion of the ' Gurayza ' is the most characteristic spot in Zanzibar city, the Salt Market, so called from the heaps of dingy saline sand offered for sale by the Maskati Arabs and the Mekranis. Being near the Custom House, it is always thronged, and like the bazars of Cairo and Damascus it gives an exaggerated idea of the population. There are besides this three other ' Suk.' The Suk Muhogo, or Manioc market, to the south of the city, supplies the local staff of life. It is the sweet variety of Jatropha, called in the Brazil Aypim, or Macacheira, and known to us as white cassava : it will not make wood-meal, called xa*r e,%o}(7)v,* farinha, *the* flour. The poisonous Manioc (Jatropha Manihot) must be soaked in water, or rasped, squeezed, and toasted, to expel its deleterious juice, which the Brazilian 'Indians,' and the people of the Antilles, convert by boiling into sugar, vinegar, and cassareep for 'pepper-pot ' — I heard of this ' black cassava ' in inner East Africa. The Suk Muhogo sells, besides the negro's daily bread, cloth and cotton, grain and paddy, vegetables, and other provisions. The shops are the usual holes in the wall, raised a foot above the street, and the owners sit or squat, writing upon a knee by way of desk, with the slow, absorbing reed-pen and the clotted clammy fluid called ink. Behind, and hard by, is the fish-market, which is tolerably supplied between 4 and 6 p.m.—in the morning you buy the remnants of the last day. Purther eastward, in the Melindini quarter, is the Suk Melindi, where the butchers expose their vendibles. As in most hot countries, the best articles are here sold early, at least before 7 a.m. A scarcity of meat is by no means rare at Zanzibar, and sometimes it has lasted four or five months.

In the Purzani quarter, eastward of and close to the salt bazar, stands the Custom House. This is an Arab bourse, where millions of dollars annually change hands under the foulest of sheds, a long, low mat-roof, supported by two dozen rough tree-stems. Prom the sea it is conspicuous as the centre of circulation, the heart from and to which twin streams of blacks are ever ebbing and flo wing, whilst the beach and the waters opposite it are crowded with shore-boats, big and small. Inland, it is backed by sacks and bales, baskets and packages, hillocks of hides, old ship's-tanks, piles of valuable woods, heaps of ivories, and a heterogeneous mass of waifs and strays; there is also a rude lock-up, for -warehousing the more valuable goods. A small adjacent square shows an unfinished and dilapidated row of arches, the fragments of a new Custom House. It was begun 26 or 27 years ago (1857), but Jayaram, the benevolent and superstitious Hindu who farmed the customs it is said for $150,000 per annum, had waxed fat under the matting, and was not sure that he would thrive as much within stone and lime. This is a general idea throughout the nearer East. The people are full of saws and instances concerning the downfall of great men who have exposed themselves to the shafts of misfortune by enlarging their gates or by building for themselves two-storeyed abodes. But the hat it seems has lately got the better of the turban, and there will be a handsome new building, half paid by the Prince and half by his farmer of Customs.

An open space now leads us to the finest building in the city, the palace of the late Sayyid, which we visit in a future chapter. I may remark that it is the workhouse style, though hardly so ignoble as that of H. Hellenic Majesty; but at Zanzibar the windows are far higher up, and the jail-like aspect is far morn pronounced. Beyond it commences the east-end, and here lives my kind friend M. Cochet, Consul de Erance. He came, expecting to find civilization, whist in the evening, ladies' society, and the pianoforte: he had been hoaxed in Paris about Colonel Hamerton's daughters. Pie is thoroughly disgusted. Even the Consular residence is the meanest of its kind. No wonder that M. Le Capitaine Guiilain was 'froisse dans son amour-propre national ' when he entered it.

Ear better, and more open to the breeze, is the house of the hospitable M. Bdrard, agent to Messrs ftabaud Erdres, of Marseille. The one disadvantage of the site is the quantity of Khoprd, or cocoa-nut meat, split and sun-dried. It evolves, especially at night-time, a noxious gas, and the strongest stomachs cannot long resist the oily, nausea-breeding odour which tarnishes silver, and which produces fatal dysentery. The Zanzibar trade, with the exception of cloves, is not generally aromatic. Copal, being washed in an over-kept solution of soda, smells not, as was remarked to the 'Dragon of "Wantley,' like balsam. And ton upon ton of cowries, strewed in the sun, or piled up in huge heaps till the mollusc decays away, can hardly be deemed Sabaean or even commonly wholesome.

To our right, in rear of the fronting 'dicky,' and at both flanks of the city, is the native town, —a filthy labyrinth, a capricious arabesque of disorderly lanes, and alleys, and impasses, here broad, there narrow; now heaped with offal, then choked with ruins. It would be the work of weeks to learn the threading of this planless maze, and what white man would have the heart to learn it ? Curiosity may lead us to it in earliest morning, before the black world returns to life. During the day sun or rain, mud or dust, with the certain effluvia of carrion and negro, make it impossible to flaner through the foul mass of densely crowded dwelling-places where the slaves and the poor ' pig ' together. The pauper classes are contented with mere sheds, and only the mildness of the climate keeps them from starving. The meanest hovels are of palm-matting, blackened by wind or sun, thatched with cajan or grass, and with or without walls of wattle-and-dab. They are hardly less wretched than the west Ireland shanty. Internally the huts are cut up into a ' but ' and a 'ben,' and are furnished with pots, gourds, cocoa rasps, low stools hewn out of a single block, a mortar similarly cut, trays, pots, and troughs for food, foul mats, and kitandahs or cartels of pa<u>lm</u> -fibre rope twisted round a frame of tlie rudest carpenter's work. The better abodes are enlarged boxes of stone, mostly surrounded by deep, projecting eaves, forming a kind of verandah on poles, and shading benches of masonry or tamped earth, where articles are exposed for sale. The windows are loop-holes, and the doors are miracles of rudeness. Lastly, there are the wretched shops, which supply the few wants of the population.

We are now at the mouth of the Lagoon, which, at high tides, almost encircles the city. I am told that of late years the natives have huilt all round this backwater. In 1857 the Eastern or landward side was bush and plantation. As the waters retired they left behind them a rich legacy of fevers and terrible diseases ; especially in the inner town, a dead flat, excluded from the sea breeze, and exposed to the pestiferous breath of the maremma.

Ships anchoring off this inlet soon stock Erench Islet. The whalers and American and Hamburg vessels, that prefer Changani Point and the west end of the city, often escape without a single case of sickness. Similarly at Havannah, crews exposed to breezes from the Mangrove swamps have lost half their numbers by yellow fever; and tlie liistory of our West Indian settlements proves, if proof be required, bow fatal is nigbt exposure.

Zanzibar, city and island, is plentifully supplied with bad drinking water. Below the old sea-beaeh, and near the shore, it is necessary only to scrape a hole in the soft ground. Throughout the interior the wells, though deep, are dry during the hot season, and the people flock to the surface-draining rivulets. West Africans generally will not drink rain-water for fear of dysentery; and so with us—when showers fell in large drops men avoided it, or were careful to consume it soon lest it should putrefy. The purest element is found at Kokotoni, a settlement on the N. W. coast of the island, and in the Bububu, a settlement some five miles north of the city, where Sayyid Suleyman bin Hamid, once governor of Zanzibar, had a small establishment, and where Hasan bin Ibrahim built a large house called Chuweni or Leopard's Place. So at Sao Paulo de Loanda the drinking' water must he brought from the Bengo river. The best near the city is from a spring which rises behind the royal Cascine, Mto-ni. Here the late Sayyid built a stone tank and an aqueduct 2000 yards long, which, passing through his establishment,

THE WELL. 99

came out upon the beach. Casks could then he filled hy the hose, hut soon the masonry channel got out of repair, and sailors will not willingly drink water flowing through a dwelling-house.

The produce of the town greatly varies. Some wells are hard with sulphate and carbonate of lime, whilst others are salt as the sea itself; and often, as in Sind and Cutch, of two near together one supplies potable and the other undrinkable water. A few to the south of the city are tolerably sweet. The pits are numerous, and a square shaft, usually from 12 to 15 feet deep, may be found at every 10 or 50 yards. There are no casings; the edges are flush with the filthy ground about them, and the sites must frequently be changed, as the porosity of the coral rock and the regular seaward slope direct the drainage into them. Similarly, nearer home the bright sparkling element is not unfrequently charged with all the seeds of disease. When rain has not fallen for some time the water becomes thick as that of a horsepond, and when allowed to stand it readily taints. I could hardly bear to look at the women as they filled with cocoa-shells the jars to be carried off upon their heads.

formerly Europeans were not allowed, for

religious reasons, to ship water from the wells near the town. Also, cask-filling was carried on at low tide, to prevent the supply of the Mto-ni being brackish, and the exhalations of the black mud were of course extra-dangerous. It is no wonder that dysentery and fever resulted from the use of such a 'necessary.' The Trench frigate Le Berceau, after watering here, was visited by the local pest, and lost 90 men on her way home. Even in January, the most wholesome month, Lieut. Christopher had 16 deaths amongst his scanty crew. In this case, however, the lancet, so fatal near the Line, and the deadly Zerambo, or toddy-brandy, were partly to blame. As early as 1824 Captain Owen condemned the supply of Zanzibar, as liable to cause dysentery. It has this effect during and after heavy rains, unless allowed to deposit its animal and vegetable matter. Luring the second visit of H. M. S. Andromache, in August, 1824, Commander Nourse and several of his officers spent one night in a country house, after which the former and the greater number of the latter died. The water, as well as the air, doubtless tended to cause the catastrophe. In the dry season the element sometimes produces, according to natives and strangers, obstinate costiveness. Between Zanzibar and tbe Cape, five brigs lost collectively 125 men from fever, dysentery, and inflammation of tbe neck of tbe vesica; whilst others were compelled to start their casks, and to touch at different 'aguadas ' en route. Hence skippers learned to fear and shun Zanzibar. During her 14 months' exploration of the island and the coast the Ducouedic lost 16 men; and to keep up a crew of 122 to 128, no less than 226 hands were transferred to her from the naval division of Bourbon and Madagascar. Each visit to Unguja was followed by an epidemic attack. Eormerly as many as seven whalers lay in harbour at one time; now (1857) they prefer to water and refresh at Nossi-beh, Mayotta, and especially at the Seychelles, a free port, with a comparatively cool and healthy climate, where supplies are cheap and plentiful.

Besides the lagoon and the water nuisances there is yet another. The drainage of the Zanzibar water-front is good, owing to the slope of the site seaward. But at low tides, and after dark, when the sulphuretted hydrogen is not raised from the sands by solar heat, a veil of noxious gas overhangs the shore, whose whole length becomes exceedingly offensive. This is caused by the shironi (latrinee) opening upon the water edge. 'Intermural sepulture ' is also here common, though not after the fashion of West African Yoruba; and the city contains sundry unenclosed plots of ground, in which dwarf lime-plastered walls, four to five feet long, fancifully terminated above, and showing, instead of epitaph, a china saucer or bits of porcelain set in the stone, denote tombs.

Drainage and cleanliness are panaceas for the evils of malaria where tropical suns shine. Drainage of swamps and lagoons can improve S'a Leone, and can take away the stink from South African barracks. Zanzibar city, I contend, owes much of its fatality to want of drainage, and it might readily he drained into comparative healthiness. But the East African Arab holds the possibility of pestilence and the probability of fever to he less real evils than those of cutting a ditch, of digging a drain, or of opening a line for ventilation. The Dollar-hunters from Europe are a mere floating population, ever looking to the deluge in prospect, and of course unwilling to do every man's business, that is— to drain.

Such was Zanzibar city when I first walked through it. Though dating beyond the days of Arab history, and made, by its insular and central situation, the depbt of the richest trade in Eastern Africa, its present buildings are almost all modern. At the beginning of this our nineteenth century it consisted of a fort and a ragged line of huts, where the 'Suk Muhogo ' now stands. Er B/uschcnbcrgcr (1835) satisfied himself that 'the town of Zanzibar and its inhabitants possess as few attractions for a Christian stranger as any place and people in the wide world.' As late as 1812 this chief emporium of a most wealthy coast boasted but five store-houses of the humblest description, and the east end was a palm plantation. Since my departure the city, as the trade returns show, has, despite unfavourable political circumstances, progressed. A Catholic mission, sent by Erance, has established an hospital, and two schools for boys and girls, and the English Central African Mission has followed suit. These establishments must differ strangely from the normal thing—the white-bearded pedagogue, hugging his bones or rocking himself before a large chintz-covered copy of the Koran, placed upon a stand two feet high, so as to be above man's girdle, and, when done with, swathed in cloth and stowed away. A change, too, there must be in the pupils; formerly half a dozen ragged boys, some reciting with nasal monotonous voices sentences to be afterwards understood by instinct, others scraping the primitive writing-hoard with a pointed stick.

We will now return to the centre of attraction, the Salt Bazar, and prospect the people. The staple material is a double line of black youth and negresses sitting on the ground, with legs outstretched like compasses. At each apes of the angle is a little heap of fruit, salt, sugar, sun-dried manioc, greasy fritters, redolent fish, or square 'fids' of shark-flesh,[1] the favourite 'kitchen' with Wasawahili and slaves; it brings from Maskat and the Benadir a gout so high that it takes away the breath. These vendors vary the tedium of inaction by mat-making, plaiting leaves, 'palavers,' and 'pow-wows,' which argue an admirable conformation of the articulating organs and a mighty lax morality. Sellers, indeed, seem here to double the number of buyers, and yet somehow buying and selling goes on.

Motley is the name of the crowd. One officer in the service of His Highness stalks down the

[1] The Arabs here call the shark 'jarjur,' the "Wasawahili p'hapL I do not know why Captain Ghiillain (ii. 391) says, ¹ le requin, nommS par les Arabs *lebah*—' Lebah is the Somali name for a lion.

market followed by a Hieland tail, proudly, as if be were lord of the three Arabias. Negroes who dislike the whip clear out like hawk-frightened pigeons. A yellow man, with short, thin beard, and high, meagre, and impassive features, he is well-dressed and gorgeously armed. Observe that he is 'breek-less ': trowsers are 'un-Arab,' and unpopular as were the servile braccse amongst the Eomans. The legs, which, though spare, are generally muscular and well-turned, appear beneath the upper coat, which falls to the knee. He adheres to the national sandals, thick soles of undyed leather, with coloured and spangled straps over the instep, whilst a narrow thong passes between the big toe and its neighbour. The • foot-gear gives him that peculiar strut which is deemed dignified, and if he has a long walk before him—a very improbable contingency—he must remove his chaussure. I never yet saw a European who could wear the sandal without foot-chafing.

Eight meek by the side of the Arab's fierceness appears the Banyan, the local Jew. These men are Bhattias from Outch in western India ; unarmed burghers, with placid, satisfied countenances, and plump, sleek, rounded forms, suggesting the idea of happy, well-to-do cows. Such is the effect of a diet which embraces only bread, rice, and milt, sweetmeats, vegetables, and clarified butter.[1] Their skins are smoother and their complexions are lighter than the Arabs'; their features are as high though hy no means so thin. They wear the long mustachio, not the heard, and a Chinese pig-tail is allowed to spring from the poll of the carefully shaven head. These top-knots are folded, when the owners are full-dressed, under high turbans of spotted purple or crimson stuff edged with gold. The latter are complicated affairs, somewhat suggesting the *oldest* fashion of a bishop's mitre ; bound round in fine transverse plaits, not twisted like the Arabs', and peaked in the centre above the forehead with a manner of horn. Their snowy cotton coats fit close to the neck, like collarless shirts; shawl-girt under the arms, they are short-waisted as the dresses of our grandmothers; the sleeves are tight and profusely wrinkled, being nearly double the needful length, and the immaculate loin-cloth displays the lower part of the thigh, leaving the leg bare. Their slippers of red leather are sharp-toed, with points turning upwards and backwards, somewhat as in the knightly days of Europe.

Another conspicuous type is the Baloch mercenary from Mekran or Maskat. A comely, brown man, with regular features, be is distinguished from the Arab by tbe silkiness and tbe superior length of bis flowing beard, which is carefully anointed after being made glossy witb henna and indigo. He adheres to his primitive matchlock, a barrel lengthened out to suit the weak powder in use, damascened with gold and silver, and fastened to the frail stock by more metal rings than the old Trench 'Brown Bess ' ever had. The match is about double the thickness of our whipcord, and is wound in many a coil round the stalk or stock. A curved iron, about four inches long, and forked in the upper part to hold the igniter, plays in a groove cut lengthways through the wood and the trigger, a prolongation of the match-bolder, guides the fire into the open priming-pan. When the match is not immediately wanted it is made fast to a batten under the breeching. (A parenthesis. Were I again to travel in wet tropical lands, I should take with me two flint-guns, which could, if necessary, be converted into matchlocks. Of course they would shoot slow, but they would not want caps, and they would prove serviceable when the percussion gun and the breech-loader would not.) This mercenary carries also two powder-gourds, one containing coarse material for loading, the other a finer article, English, if possible, for priming. He is never without flint, steel, and tinder; and disposed about his person are spare cartridges in reed cases. His sabre is of the Persian form; his dagger is straighter and handier than that of the Arab; and altogether his tools, like his demeanour, are those of a disciplined, or rather of a disciplinable, man.

The wildest and most picturesque figures are the half-breeds from the western shores of the Persian Gulf—light brown, meagre Ishmaels and Orsons, who look like bundles of fibre bound up in highly-dried human skin. Their unkempt elf-locks fall in mighty masses over unclean, saffron-stained shirts, which suggest the 'night-gown ' of other days, and these are apparently the only articles of wear. Their straight, heavy swords hang ever ready by a strap passing over the left shoulder; their right hands rest lovingly upon the dagger-hafts, and their small round targes of boiled hippopotamus hide—one of the 'industries ' of Zanzibar—apparently await immediate use. Leaning on their long matchlocks, they stand cross-legged, with the left foot planted to the right of the right, or vice versa, and they prowl about like beasts of prey, as they are, eyeing the peaceful, busy crowd witb a greedy cut-tbroat stare, or witb the suspicious, side-long glance of a cat o' mountain. ,

These barbarian 'Gulf Arabs ' differ singularly from the muscular porters of Hazramaut, in whose Semitic blood there is a palpable African mixture. They bobble along in pans, like the Hammals of Constantinople, carrying huge bales of goods and packs of bides suspended from a pole, ever chaunting tbe same monotonous grunt-song, and kicking out of tbe way tbe bumped cows tbat are munching fruit and vegetables under tbe shadow of their worshippers, tbe Banyans. Add half a dozen pale-skinned 'Khojahs,' tricky-faced men witb evil eyes,treacherous smiles, lit for tbe descendants of tbe 'Assassins,' straight, silky beards, forked after tbe fashion of ancient Rustam, and armed witb Chinese umbrellas'. Complete tbe group by throwing in a European — bow ghastly appears his blanched face, and bow frightful bis tight garb !
—stalking down tbe streets in tbe worst of tempers, and using bis stick upon tbe mangy 'pariah dogs ' and tbe naked shoulders of the ᶜ niggers ' tbat obstruct him. At times tbe Arabs, when their toes or heels are trampled upon, will turn and fiercely finger their daggers; but a fear

wMcli is by no means personal prevents tlieir going further.

Such is the aristocracy of the land. As in all servile societies, every white man (i.e. non-negro) is his white neighbour's equal; whilst the highest black man (i.e. servile) ranks below the lowest pale-face.

Par more novel to us is the slave population, male and female. What first strikes every stranger is the scrupulous politeness and the ceremonious earnestness of greetings when friends meet. The idea of standing in the broiling sun to dialogue as follows is not a little remarkable :

A. Yambo (pronounced Dyambo) or Hali gana ?•—The state !

B. Yambo Sana—My state is very (good).

A. Siyambo (or amongst the Arabized Wasawahlli, Marhaba)—Bight welcome !

B. Hast thou eaten and slept ?

A. I have made my reverential bow !

B. Yambo ?

A. Siyambo Sana !

B. Like unto gold ?

A. Like unto gold!

B. Like unto coral ?

A. Like unto coral!

B. Like unto pearl ?
A. Like unto pearl!
B. The happiness—Kua-heri! (farewell!).
A. In happiness let us meet, if Allah please !
B. Hem!
A. Hem! (drawn out as long as possible).

The fact is they are going about 'Ku amkfa,' to salute their friends, and to waste time by running from house to house. Even freemen generally begin their mornings thus, and idle through the working hours.

The males tie, for only garh, a yard of cotton round the waist, and let it fall to the knees; bead necklaces and similar trash complete the costume. Like all negroes they will wear, if possible, the shock-head of wool, which is not pierceable by power of any sun; and they gradually unclothe down to the feet, which, requiring most defence, are the least defended—'Fashion ' must account for the anomaly. To the initiated eye the tattoo distinguishes the vast confusion of races. The variety of national and tribal marks, the stars, raised lumps and scars, the beauty-slashes and carved patterns, further diversified by the effects of pelagra, psoris, and small-pox, is a Chinese puzzle to the new-comer. Domestic slaves, bearing their burdens on the head, not on the shoulder, are known hy a comparatively civilized aspect. They copy then masters, and strangers remark that the countenance is cheerful and not destitute of intelligence. The Bozals, or freshly-trapped chattels, are far more original and interesting. See those Nyassa-men, with their teeth filed to represent the cat or the crocodile, chaffing some old Shylock, an Arab dealer in human flesh and blood; or those wild Uzegura-men, with patterned skins and lower incisors knocked out, like the Shilluks to the west of the Nile, scowling evilly, and muttering curses at the Nakhuda (skipper) from Stir, the professional kidnapper of their kind.

The 'fairer' half of black world is not less note-worthy. There is the tall and sooty-skinned woman from Uhiao, distinguished by the shape of her upper lip. A thorn-pierced hole is enlarged with stalks of green reed till it can admit a disk of white-painted wood nearly as big as a dollar. The same is the system of the Dors, the tribe dwelling north of the equator and west of the Nile; their lip-plates equal the thick end of a cheroot; and the ' pelele ' of the southern regions is a similar disk of bamboo, ivory, or tin, which causes the upper lip to project some two inches beyond the nose-tip, giving it an anserine proportion. In the elder women the ornament is especially hideous. As a rule, the South American ᶜ Indians [5] pierce for their labrets the lower lip, evidently the more unclean fashion — no wonder that kissing (should I say osculation ?) is unknown. Yet even amongst the Somal, if you attempt to salute a woman—supposing that you have the right—she will draw back in horror from the act of incipient cannibalism. Often the lip-disk is absent, and then through the unsightly gap a pearly tooth is seen to gleam, set off by the outer darkness of 'Spoonbill's' skin. This woman, broad-shouldered and thick-waisted, is almost as stalwart as her Mhias, whose tattoo (chale) is a single line forked at both ends :[1] in others the cuticle and cutis are branded, worked, and raised in an intricate embroidery over all the muscular trunk. An abnormal equality of strength and stature between the sexes prevails amongst many

[1] Uhiao is the Iao of Mr Cooler, who calls the people M'yau (Mhiao) and Miyao (Wahiao). They are the 'Monjou ' of Salt, and the Mujao of the Portuguese. M. Macqueen (On the Geography of Central Africa) says, 'The inhabitants on the west side of the Lake are called Yoah, and are Mohammedans.' They are still pagans. Capt. Guiilain (1, 390) remarks, ¹ Les historiens Portuguais nous paraissent avoir donnd au pays le nom que les indigenes donnent a ses habitants. Moudjaou, on plut&t Moniho et, par contraction, M'iao aignifie nn homme da pays de Iao.' TThiao would he the country; Mhiao and Wabiao (singular and plural), its people.

African tribes, especially tbe agricultural, where women are the workers. The same may be observed in parts of North Britain and of *northern* Europe. The difference in this matter between the Teutonic and the Latin races never struck me so strongly as when seeing German families land at Bio de Janeiro.

The half-caste Zanzibar girl enviously eyes the Arab woman, a heap of unwashed cottons on invisible feet, with the Maskat masque exposing only her unrecognizable eyeballs. The former wears a single loose piece of red silk or chequered cotton. Her frizzly hair is twisted into pigtails ; her eyelids are stained black; her eyebrows are lengthened with paint; her ear-rims are riddled with a dozen holes to admit rings, wooden buttons, or metal studs, whilst the slit lobes, distended by elastic twists of coloured palm-leaf, whose continual expansion prodigiously enlarges the aperture, are fitted with a painted disk, an inch and a half in diameter. The same device was practised (according to the missionary Gumilla) by the Aberne tribe of the Orinoco. If pretty, and therefore wealthy, she wears heavy silver earrings run through the shell of the ear; her thumbs have similar decorations, and massive bangles of white metal adorn, like manacles and fetters, her wrists and ancles. One wing of her nose is bored to admit a stud—even the patches of Europe were not more barbarous. The Zanzibarian slave girl shaves her head smooth, till it shows brown and shiny like a well-polished cocoa-nut; and she drags along her ' hopeful '—she has seldom more than one—a small black imp, wholly innocent of clothing. The thing already carries on its head a water-jar bigger than its own 'pot-belly,' and it screams Na-kuja (I come !) to other, small fry disporting itself more amusingly.

CHAPTER Y.

GEOGRAPHICAL AND PHYSIOLOGICAL.

[1] To my surprise, tlie information concerning Zanzibar and the N. E. coast of Africa scarcely contains meagre phrases destitute of precision.'—(Col. Sykes' Journal, R. G. S., vol. xsiii. 1853.) He forgets that entering from the coast is like jumping from the street into the window.—(R. E. B.)

SECTION 1.

Africa, East and West—"Zanzibar" explained—Menoutbias—Position and Formation—The East African Current—Navigation—Aspect of the Island.

It is an old remark tbat Africa, tbe continent which became an island hy the nnion of the twin seas in the year of grace 1869, despite her exuberant wealth and her wonderful powers of reproduction, is badly made—a trunk without limbs, a monotonous mass of painful symmetry, wanting opposition and contrast, like the uniform dark complexion of her sons and of her fauna—a solid body, like her own cocoa-nut, hard to penetrate from without, and soft within; an 'individual of the earth,' self-isolated hy its savagery from the rest of the world. This is especially true of intertropical Africa.

The western coast was, until the last four centuries, cut off from intercourse with mankind by the storm-lashed waters of the northern approach; and to the present day the unbroken seaboard, so scanty in good harbours, and the dangerous bars and bores which defend the deadly river mouths, render it the least progressive part of the old world.

The more fortunate north-eastern and subtropical shores were enabled by their vast crevasse, the Red and riverless Sea, to communicate with Western Asia, whilst the rich productions, gold and ivory, tortoise-shell and ambergris, the hot sensuous climate—which even now induces the northern sailor to ship in the fatal West African squadron—and the amene scenery of the equatorial regions, invited, during pre-historic ages, merchants, and even immigrants, from rugged Persia and sterile Arabia.

Between the two upper coasts,' eastern and western, there is, as might be expected, great similarity of grim aspect. The northern seaboards offer, for the space of a thousand miles, the same horrid aspect; deceitful roadsteads and dangerous anchorages, forbidding lines of chalky cliff and barren brown sandstone bluff; flat strands and white downs, hazed over by the spray of desert sand; and lowlands backed by maritime sub-ranges, masses of bald hill and naked mountains, streaked with dry wadis and water-courses, that bear scatters of dates and thorns, and which support miserable villages of tents or huts. The fierce and wandering tribes, Berber, Arab, and Arabo-African—an especially 'crooked and perverse generation,'—ate equally dangerous to the land traveller and to the shipwrecked mariner.

As sterile and unlovely for the same cause— the absence of tropical rains—are the southern regions of the great Nineteenth Century Island. Good harbours are even rarer than in the north, and the seas about the Cape of Hope, sweeping up unbroken from the South Pole, are yet more perilous. The highlands fringing the southern and eastern coasts arrest the humid winds, and are capable of sunporting an extensive population ; but the interior and the western coast, being lowlands, are wild and barren. The South African or Kafir family, which has overrun this soil, is still for the most part in the nomade state, and its 'evident destiny' is to disappear before the European colonist.

The central and equatorial land, 34° deep, including and bordering upon the zone of almost constant rain, is distinguished by the ojipressive exuberance of its vegetation and by the consequent insalubrity of its climate. The drainage of the interior, pouring with discoloured efflux to the ocean, in large and often navigable channels, subject to violent freshes, taints the water-lines with deadly malaria. The false coasts of coralline or of alluvial deposits—a modern formation, and still forming—fringed with green-capped islets, and broken by sandy bays and by projecting capes, are exposed tojswells and rollers, to surf and surge, to numbing torrents and chilling tornadoes, whilst muddy backwaters and stagnant islets disclose lagoon-valves or vistas through tangled morass, jungle, and hardly penetrable mangrove-swamp. This maremma, the home of fever, is also the seat of trade, but the tribes which occupy it soon die out.

The true coast has already risen high enough above the waters to maintain its level; and the vegetation—-calabashes, palms, and tamarinds—offers a contrast to the swampy growth below. Inland of the raised seaboard are high and jungly mountains and coast-range or ghaut, in many parts yet unvisited by Europeans. Beyond these sierras begins the basin-shaped plateau of Central Equatorial Africa. The inhabitants are mostly inland tribes, ever gravitating towards the coast. They occupy stockaded and barricaded clumps of pent-houses or circular tents, smothered by thicket and veiled, especially after the heavy annual rains, with the 'smokes,' a dense white vapour, moisture made visible by the earth being cooler than the saturated air.[1]

I have elsewhere remarked (The Lake Legions of Central Intertropical Africa; Abeokuta and the Camaroons Mountains, &c.) the striking geological contrast between the two equatorial coasts, eastern and western. The former, south of the Guardafui granites, offers to one proceeding inland from the ocean a succession of corallines, of sandstone and of calcaires, which appear to be an offset from the section of that great zone forming the Somali country. The western coasts, after quitting the basalts and lavas

[1] Dr Livingstone (Zambezi Expedition, x. 213) confounds these African 'smokes' with the blue hazy atmosphere of the 'Indian summers' in America, often the result of grass-burning and prairie fires. During an August on the Syrian coast and a December in the Brazil, I have seen the African 'smokes' as well developed as at Eernando Po.

of the Camaroons, are composed chiefly of the granites and syenites with their degradations of schiste, gneiss, and sandstone. Similarly, in the great Austro-American continent, one shore, that of the Brazil, is granitic, whilst the other, Chili, mainly consists of the various porphyries.

The negroes and negroids of both these inhospitable coasts, an undeveloped and not to be developed race—in this point agreeing with the fauna and flora around them—are the chief obstacles to exploration, and remarkably resemble each other. The productions of the east and west are similar. The voracious shark swims the seas, turtles bask upon the strands and islets, and the crocodile and hippopotamus haunt the rivers. The forests abound in apes and monkeys, and the open plains support the giraffe, the antelope, and the zebra, hog and wild kine (Bos Caflir and B. Brachyceros), herds of elephants and scatters of rhinoceros. The villagers breed goats and poultry. In the healthier regions they have black cattle and sheep, whilst one tribe has acclimatized the ass. The exceeding fertility of the rain-drenched plains gives an amazing luxuriance to cassava and rice, maize, and holcus, cotton, sugar-cane, and wild indigo, banana, lime and orange, ground-nuts and coffee. The hills and torrent-beds yield gold and copper, antimony, and abundance of iron. On both sides of the continent there are rich deposits of the semi-mineral copal. Coal was found by the Portuguese at Tete and in the Zambeze Valley, as related in Dr Livingstone's Pirst Expedition (Missionary Travels, &c., xxxi. 633-4). His second prolonged the coal-field to beyond the Valley of the Pufuma (Povuma) river (xxi. 440), and it wiP probably be found to extend still further.

Dr Krapf declares (Travels, &c., p. 465) that he discovered coal, 'the use of which is stiP unknown to the Abessinians,' on the banks of the Kuang, a river said to rise in the Dembea Province, near Lake Tsana (Coloe Palus). EinaPy, to judge from the analogy of the South American continent, the valuable mineral wiP yet be struck near the western coast, south of the equator.

Erom time immemorial, on both sides of Africa, the continental Islands, like Aradus and Sidon, Tyre and Alexandria, have been favourite places with stranger settlers. They have proved equally useful as forts, impregnable to the wild aborigines, and as depbts for exports and imports.

Second to none in importance is Zanzibar, and the future promises it a still higher destiny.

And first, of the name, which does not occur in Straho, Pliny, or the Periplus. The log-book attributed to Arrian, of Nicomedia, calls the whole shore, 'Continent of Azania; ' probably an adaptation, like Azan, and even Ajan, of the Arabic, Barr el Khazdin, or the Land of Tanks,[1] the coast between Ita'as Hafun and Ra'as el Khayl. So Pliny (vi. 28 and 3d) speaks of the £Azanian Sea³ as communicating with the £ Arabian Gulf.' Ptolemy, however (I. 17, sec. iv. 7), has the followingimportant passage: immediately following this mart (Opone) is another bay, where Azania begins. At its beginning are the promontory Zingis *(tfyyis,* Zingina promontorium), and the tree-topped Mount Phalangis.' The name may have extended from the promontory to the coast, and from the coast to the island. Hr Krapf speaks of a tribe of the £ Zendj ' near the R/ufiji river, but I could not hear of it. It is easy to show that the Pelusian geographer's Opone is the bay south of Ra'as, or Jurd Hafun. Like Pomponius

[1] Dr Krapf (112, Missionary Travels) tells us 'the Somali coast, from Cape G-uardafui southwards, is designated by the Arabs "Dar Ajam," not "Ajan" or "Azan," as the maps wrongly have it, because no Arabic is spoken in it.' Dar Ajam is, I believe, a modern and incorrect phrase.

Mela, Ptolemy evidently made Ms great point de d dp art the Aromata Pxomontorinm et emporium in Barbarico sinn (Cape Guardafui), and he placed it N. lat. 6° 0' 0", instead of N. lat. 11° 50'. This error threw the whole coast 6° (in ronnd numbers, more exactly 5° 50') too far south, and made the world doubt the accurate position of the Nile lakes. Thus, to his latitude of Opone N. 4° add 5° 50', and we have N. lat. 9° 50', the true parallel of Hafun being N. lat. 10° 26'.

Amongst late authors we find the word Zanzibar creeping into use. The Adulis inscription (4th century) gives £ Zingabene '; and its copier, the Greek monk Cosmas Indicopleustes, who proved the globe flat (6th century), calls the 4 unnavigable' ocean beyond Berheria, the 'Sea of Zenj,' and the lands which it bathes 4 Zingium.' ' It is found in Abu Zayd Hasan, generally known as Hunayn bin Ishak (died A.D. 873); in El Mas'udi, who describes it at some length (died A.D. 957); in El Bayruni (11th century), and in the learned 4 Nubian Geographer,' the Sherif El Idrisi (A.D. 1153). Marco Polo (A.D. 1290), who evidently wrote his 37th chapter from hearsay, makes Zanzibar a land of blacks; and, confounding insula with peninsula (in Arabic both being Jezireh), supplies it with a circumference of 2000 miles, and vast numbers of elephants. The India Minor, India Major, and India Tertia of the mediaeval Latin travellers are the Sind, Hind, and Zinj of the Arabs. Ibn Batuta (A.D. 1330,1331), the first Arab traveller who wrote a realistic description of his voyage, has accurately placed Kilwa, which he calls 'Kulua,' in the 'land of the Zunuj.' Finally, we meet with it in El Nowayri, and in Abulfeda, the 'Prince of Arab Geographers,' who both died in the same year, A.D. 1331.

The word Zanj (^), corrupted to Zinj, whence the plural 'Zunuj,' is evidently the Persian Zang or Zangi a black, altered by the Arabs, who ignore the hard Aryan 'Gaf ' (^_f), the 'G ' in our gulf. In the same tongue bar means land or region—not sea or sea-coast—and the compounded term would signify Nigritia or Blackland. In modern Persian Zangi still means a negro, and D' Herbelot says of the 'Zengbis ' that 'they are properly those called Zingari,[1] and, by some, Egyptians and Bohe-

---

[1] My learned and accomplished friend, Dr E. S. Charnoc.li (The Peoples of Transylvania: London, Trubner, 1870, p. 28), agrees with D'Herbelot, and from Zangi derives the racial gipsy names Czigany, It. Zingari, Yar. Cingani, Zingara, Oingari, Port. Ciganos, Q-. Zigeuner. But the Zangi were and are negroes, Wasawahili, whereas the gypsies never were.

mians.' Scholars have not yet shown why the Arab, so rich in nomenclature, borrowed the purely Persian word from his complement the 'Ajam.' They have forgotten that the Persians, who of late years have been credited with the unconquerable aversion to the sea which belongs to the Gallas and the Kafirs, were once a maritime people. 'The indifference or rather the aversion of Persians to navigation ' (M. Guiilain, i. 34, 35) must not he charged to the ancient 'Purs.' Between A.D. 531—579, when Sayf bin Dhu Yezin, one of the latest Himyarite rulers, wanted aid against the Christian Abyssinians, who had held southern Arabia for 72 years, he applied to Khusrau I., better known as Anushirawan, the 23rd king of the Sassanian dynasty, which began with Ardashir Babegan (A.D. 226), and which ended with Yezdegird III. (A.D. 641), thus lasting 415 years. The 'Just Monarch ' sent his fleet to the Roman Port ' (Aden), and slew Masruk. In his day the Persians engrossed, hy means of Hira, Obollah, and Sohar, the rich tracts of Yemen and Hindostan; while Basrah (Bassorah) was founded hy the Caliph Omar, in order to divert the stream of wealth from the Bed Sea, a diversion which will probably soon be repeated. In A.D. 758 the Persians, together with the Arabs, mastered, pillaged, and burnt Canton. Much later (17th century) Shah Abbas claimed Zanzibar Island and coast as an appanage of the suzerainty of Oman.

East Africa still preserves traditions of two distinct colonizations from Persia. The first is that of the ᵉ Emozaydiys,' or 'Emozeides ' (Amm Zayd), who conquered and colonized the sea-board of East Africa, from Berberah of the Somal to Comoro and Madagascar, both included. A second and later emigration (about A.D. 1000) occupied the south Zanzibarian coast, and ruins built by the 'Shirazian dynasty which still lingers, are shown on various parts of the sea-board. Of these Persian occupations more will be found in the following pages. (Part 1, Chap. 1, and Part 2, Chap. 2.)

Persia has left nothing of her widely extended African conquests but a name. In modern days she has become more and more a non-maritime power. She has wholly retired from the coast; and Time, who in these lands works with a will, presently obliterated almost every trace of the stranger. A few ruins at Aden and Berberah, and the white and black sheep of Ormania (Galla-land) and of Somali land, are almost the only vestiges of Persian presence north of the Equator. On the Zangian mainland wells sunk in the rock, monuments of a form now obsolete; mosques with elaborate minarets and pillars of well-cut coralline ; fortified positions, loopholed enclosures, and ruined cities whose names have almost been forgotten, are the results of the civilization which they brought with them southwards.

The limits assigned by the Arab geographers to the ' Land of the Zinj ' are elastic. While some, as Yakut, make it extend from the mouths of the J ub River (S. lat. 0° 14' 30") to Cape Corrientes (S. lat. 24° T 5") and thus include Sofala; others, with El Idrisi, separate from it the latter district, and unjustly make its southern limit the Rufiji River (S. lat. 7° 38'), thus excluding Kilwa. It should evidently extend to Mozambique Island (S. lat. 15° 2' 2"), where the Wasawahili meet the 'Kafir ' races. The length would thus be, in round numbers, 15°=900 geographical miles, whilst the breadth, which is everywhere insignificant, can hardly be estimated.

The Arabs, who love to mingle etymology with legend and fable, derive the word 'Zanzibar ' from the exclamation of its pleased explorers, 'Zayn za'l barr ![5] (fair is this land!). Similar stories concerning Brazilian Olinda and

Argentine Buenos Aires are well known. 'El Sawahil,' the shores, evidently the plural of Sahil, is still applied to the 600 miles of maritime region whose geographical limits are the Jub River and Oape Delgado (S. lat. 10° *41' 2"*, and whose ethnographic boundaries are the Somal and the 'Kafir ' tribes. Others derive it from El Suhayl, the beautiful Canopus which, surrounded by a halo of Arab myth, ever attracts the eye of the southing mariner. The 'Wasawahili, [1] or slave tribes, are fancifully explained by

[1] foreigners—Arab, Persian, and Indian,—call them Sawakili. They call themselves Msawahili in the singular, and "Wasawahili in the plural, always accenting the penultimate syllable. In the Zangian tongues a prefixed M is evidently an abbreviation of Mti, a tree, e. g. Nazi, a cocoa-nut, Mnazi, a cocoa-nut tree, or of Mtu, a man. Before a vowel it is euphoniously exchanged to Mu, e. g. Muarabu, an Arab. The plural form is Wa, a contraction of Watu, men. 'Wa' also is the sign of the personal, or rather of the rational animate plural opposed to 'Ma,' and must not he confounded with the possessive pronoun 'Wa,' of. Mr Cooley (Memoir of the Lake Regions, &c., Reviewed, Stanford, 1861), asserts that 'Wa mtu,'
'of a man,' becomes by rejection of the singular prefix, 'Watu,' men (des hommes): ' consequently it is an error to call the coast people Wamrima and the mountaineers Wakilima. If so, it is an error made by every Kisawahili-speaking man. There are, however, tribes, for instance the Rabai and the Doruma, that do not prefix the normal 'Wa,' toTorm a plural. A prefixed 'Ki,' possibly contracted from 'kitu,' a thing, denotes the language, e. g. Kisawakili: it also acts diminutive, e. g. Kigito, a little mto, or river; and it appears to have at times an adjectival sense. Opposed to it is 'Ji,' an augmentative form,

'Sawwa hllah,' lie 'played tricks,' ■—rascals all.
The coast races who, like their neighbours the
Somal, have their own African names for places,
call Zanzibar Island by the generic term Kisiwa
—insula. It is thus opposed to Mpoa-ni, the
coast, and to Mrim&, the mainland.¹ The latter,

e. g. Jito, a big mto. U, possibly derived from an obsolete
root which survives in *the Kinyika* 'ITatu ' (a *place*), *denotes*
tbe country, e. g. Uzaramo, TJsagara, and Uzungu—Europe the
land of the Wazungu. Some names arbitrarily refuse this
locative, for instance, Khutu, Karagwah, Sanga, Bondei, and
others: we never hear Ukhutu, and so forth. 'IP is also a
sign of abstract words, e. g. Mzuri, a handsome man; TJzuri,
beauty ; Mtajiri, a merchant; Utajiri, merchandise ; Befu,
long ; Urefu, length. I may here remark that Captain Speke's
analysis of Uzaramo and Usagara into U-za-ramo and U-sa-
gara, the country of llamo and Grara, making them 'obviously
triple words,' is wholly inadmissible. The root of national and
tribal names, whatever it may be, is used only exceptionally
amongst the Zangian races. Upon this point I shall presently
offer a few observations.

¹ Captain Guiilain (vol. iii. p. 107, et passim) is correct
upon the subject of the word 'Mrima.' Mr Cooley (Memoir
on the Lake Eegions, &c., p. 8) informs us that 'Wamrima' (the mainland *people)* signifies 'of the mainland;
for it is a mistake to suppose that Mrima is but a dialectic
variation of Mlima (read, Mlima) hill, in its primary sense,
cultivable ground; it is, in truth, a corruption of the
Arabic word Marfi'im, signifying the land to the west, or
under the setting sun. When the early Portuguese navi-
gators told us that the Querimba Islands were peopled hy
the Morimos, we must understand hy this name the people of
the mainland.'

This is an excellent illustration of how dangerous a thing is
p smattering of philology. The 'Arabic word Mara'im ' is
absolutely unknown to the Arahs of Zanzibar. It is evidently

however, is properly speaking limited to the maritime uplands between Tanga and the Pan-

coined out of the dictionary from 'observavifc occiden-
tem solem.' I would also ask how 'Comazinghi is Arabic?' (Geography, art. 15). Similarly, we find (Journal Royal Geographical Society, xix. 190) the Somali [1] Aber' (error for Habr) derived from the Arabic (Hebrew ?) Bar, and explained by Bern! (sons), when it really signifies mother or old woman.

It may be noted that in the Kisawahili of Zanzibar, Mrima is applied to the coast generally, especially between Mtangata and the Rufiji River, and it is mostly synonymous with the Arabs' 'Bar el Moli,' whereas Mlima means a mountain. Prom the latter comes the diminutive Kilima, a hillock, also synonymous in composition with the French mont. It enters into many East African proper names, e.g. Kilima-njaro, Kilima-ni, &c.

I cannot agree with Messrs Norris and Beke, despite their authority as linguists, in stripping the national and racial names of their inflections, e. g. Sagara for Usagara, Zaramo for TJzaramo. Mr Cooley is equally wwong in stating that tbe 'Sawahily and the Arabs write Nika, Zerainu, and Gogo. The Arabs may, the 'Wasawahili do not, thus blunder. Captain Guillain, I have remarked, is no authority. He confounds (vol. i. p. 231) the land of Wak-wak (the Semitic Gallas) with the South African Wamakua; and, worse still, with the 'Vatouahs.' And (vol.i. p. 281) he writes the well-known 'Abhan' of the Somal,

[1] ITebban.' He also unduly neglects the peculiar initial quiescent consonant M, e. g. (i. p. 456) 'Eoumo ' for 'Mfumo.' The bare root-word, I repeat, is never used by the people, who always qualify it by a prepositive. This, in our language Brit or Brut may be the monosyllable upon which Briton and British are built, but it is evidently barbarous to employ it without suffix. In the Zangian tongues the prefixes are clearly primitive words; nouus, not as the Rev. J. L. Doelme explains them in his Zulu-Ivafir Dictionary (Cape Town, 1857), 'pronouns, in the present state of the language, used as nominal forms compounded with other words.

gani river. Zanzibar city is Unguja (pronounced Ungudya, not Anggonya). Tbe word appeal's in an ancient settlement on the eastern coast of the island, and the place is still called Unguja Mku, Old Unguja. Some still call it Lunguja, apparently an older form. We find 'Lendgouya' in the Commercial Traveller Yakut (early thirteenth century) ; but 'Bandgouia ' (Abd el Rashid bin Salih el Bakui, A.D. 1403) is clearly a corruption.

.Finally, Zanzibar has been identified by paheogeographers with the Ptolemean $Msvou Siag$ or $MevovBea$-lag (iv. 9), and with the Mei/ouOi$_{oig}$ of the Periplus (Geog. Grseci Minores of R. Muller, Paris, 1855), in some copies of which Menoutheslas also occurs. Its rivals, however, for this honour are Pemba, Mafiyah (the Monfia of our maps) and Bukini, the northern and north-western parts of Malagash or Madagascar.[1] Ptolemy, it may be observed, places the two important sites, Menouthias and Prasum (or Prassum) in a separate chapter (iv. 9), whereas his principal list of stations is in Book iv. chapter 7. He lays down the site of Menouthias in S. lat.

---

[1] 'What Booken (Bukini) means I do not know.' Wake on the Madecasses. Journal, Anthrop. Soc. No. 28, xxxi., Dr Krapf (Kisuakeli Grammar, p. 106) uses Bukini as Madagascar generally.

12°, and nearly opposite the Lunar Mountain, and the Lakes whence the Nile arises (S. lat. 12° 30'). The mouth of the Bhapta river and Kbapta, the metropolis of Barbaria, are in S. lat. 7°, the Bhapta promontory is in S. lat. 8° 20' 5", and the Prasum promontory in S. lat. 15°. By applying the correction as before, we have for Menouthias S. lat. 6° (the capital of Zanzibar being in S. lat. 6° 9' 6"); for the Lakes, 6° 30', which would nearly bisect Tanganyika; for Bhapta river and city, S. lat. 1° (or more exactly, S. lat. 1° 10'); the mouth of the Jub river being in S. lat. 0° 14°30'; the Bhapta promontory in S. lat. 2° 30', corresponding with the coast about Patta; and finally, for Prasum S. lat. 9° 10'— Cape Delgado being in S. lat. 10° 41' 12."

The account given of Menouthias in the Periplus (written between A.D. 64, Yincent, and A.D. 210, Letronne[1]) is that of an eyewitness : 'After two nychthemeral days (each of 100 miles) towards the west [here the text is evidently corrupt] comes Menouthias, altogether insulated, distant from the land about 300 stadia (30 geo-

---

[1] Captain Gnillain (vol. i. 121—139, et passim) contends, and with much show of reason, that the Periplus was written after the days of Ptolemy (A.D. 139 and A.D. 161). ' Tant de lacunes dans l'ceuvre du grand g^ographe grec, lie semhlent-elles pas assigner k son travail une place toute naturelle entre les 6crits de Marin de Tyr et le P6riple ?'

graphical miles), low and tree-clad. In it are many kinds of birds and mountain tortoises (land turtle ?). It has no other wild beasts but crocodiles (iguanas), and these do not injure man. There are in it sewn boats and monoxyles (canoes), which they use for salt-pans [here the text is defective] and for catching turtle. In this island they trap them after a peculiar fashion with baskets (the modern wigo) instead of nets, letting them down at the mouth of stony inlets ' (chap. i. 15).

The next chapter informs us : 'From which (island) after two runs (each 50 miles)[1] lies the last emporium of the continent of Azania, called Ta Bhapta, thus named from the before-mentioned sewn-together vessels. In it are much ivory and tortoise-shell. The men, who in this country are of the largest size, live scattered (in

---

[1] The daily run (∩ ..S'*) of native craft varies from 40 to 50- knots per diem, and 50 may be assumed as an average. Captain Guiilain estimates it higher, from 48 to 60. Abulfeda gives the Majra or *Zpojjos wyjdrtpipoc,* 100 Hashemi miles = 170 of our geographical miles, here too high a rate unless aided hy currents. Other Arab authors propose 100,000 paces = 100 Boman or Arab miles = 80 geographical miles. The pilot Theophilus (Ptol. i. 9) rated the day and night run in these seas at 1000 stadia = 100 miles, or two Ptolemeian degrees ; the Pelusian geographer having, I have said, reduced the degree to 500 instead of 600 stadia.

the mountains ?), and each tribe in its own place is subject to tyrants ' ('tyranneaulx ' or petty chiefs).

Here, then, we have Bhapta 33 leagues (100 miles — 1° 40') beyond Menouthias. Captain Guiilain (Prem. Partie, p. 115) would make the former correspond with the debouchure of the Oufidji river (Bufiji or Lufiji), in S. lat. 7° 50'. But the Periplus, unlike Ptolemy, alludes only to a port, not to a river mouth, nor does the coast-line here show any promontory. Others have proposed Point Puna (S. lat. 7° 2' 42"), the south-western portal of the Zanzibar manche, near the modern trading port of Mbuamaji, which in former ages may have been more important. D'Anville, Vincent, and De Froberville boldly prefer Kilwa (in round numbers S. lat. 9°), which is distant 157 geographical miles from the southernmost point of Zanzibar, and I think they are right. It is safer in such matters to suspect an error of figures and of distances than of topography, especially where the geographical features are so rvell marked and cannot be found in other places. Computations of ancient courses and log-books can have little value except when they serve to confirm commonly topographical positions. Kilwa has ever been a central station on tbe Zanzibar coast, and tbe slaves brought from tbe interior are still remarkable for size. Moreover, as Dr Beke well observes (Sources of tbe Nile, p. 69), 'In attempting to fix in tbe map of Africa tbe true position of Ptolemy's lakes and sources of tbe Nile, we must discard all notions of tbeir having been determined *absolutely* by means of astronomical observations, special maps of particular localities, or otherwise, and regard them simply as derived from oral information, *and as laid down relatively to some well-known point or points on tbe coast.*'[1]

Zanzibar, tbe principal link in tbe chain of islets which extends from Makdisbu (Magadoxo), in tbe Barr el Benadir or Haven-land, to Cape Corrientes, is a long narrow reef, witb tbe major axis disposed from N. N. W. to S. S. E., and subtending a deep bight or bend in tbe coast, justly enough called tbe Barbaric Gulf. Tbe length is 48'25 geographical miles from Ea'as Nunguwi, *the* northern (S. lat. 5° 42' 8" Raper), to Ea'as Kizimkaz, tbe southern, extremity (S. lat. 6° 27' 7" Baper). Tbe breadth is 18 miles from tbe Port in E. long. 89° 14' 5" Eaper's correction, to tbe continental coast in E. long. (G.)

[1] See Part II. clap. 11.

39° 32' 5'. French travellers assume a max. length of 83 kilometres, and a max. breadth of 33. The capital (S. lat. 6° 9' 6") corresponds in parallel with the Pernambucan province to the west and with Java and central New Guinea to the east. The corrected longitude (laid down by Captain Smee in 1811 as E. lat. 39° 15') gives a difference of Greenwich time 2^h- $3G^m$- and 56^s-. From Southampton round the Cape the run is usually laid down at 8500 miles, via Suez 6200. The Lesseps Canal has shortened the distance from Marseille by 2000 leagues, and thus has placed Zanzibar within 1600 leagues of the great port — in fact, about the distance of the Gaboon ex-colony.

The formation of the island is madrepore, resting upon a core or base of stratified sandstone grit, disposed in beds varying from *15* to 3 feet thick. ' The surface gently inclines towards the sea, and the lines of fracture run parallel with the shores. Three distinct formations occur to one crossing the breadth.[1] The first is a

[1] **Dr Ruschenberger, I know not on what authority, says that the island is undulated and** *crossed* **hy three principal ridges, whose most elevated points are 500 feet high. My information, derived from hearsay, however, not from actual inspection, assures me that the waves of ground are disposed north and south.**

band of grit-based coralline, which runs meridionally, and is most remarkable on the eastern side. This portion, featureless and thinly inhabited, is protected from the dangerous swell and the fury of the Indian Ocean by a broad reef and scattered rocks of polypidoms. The band thins out to the north and south: in the centre, where it is widest, the breadth may he three to four miles, and the greatest height 400 feet. The coral-rag is mostly white and of many shapes, like fans, plants, and trees: the most usual form is the mushroom, with a broad domed head rising from a narrow stem. The texture is exceedingly reticulated and elastic; solid masses, however, occur where neighbouring rocks meet and bind—hence the labyrinth of caverns, raised by secular upgrowth and preserving the original formation. The ground echoes, as in volcanic countries, hollow and vault-like to the tread; the tunnels are frequently without issue for drainage, and when the rain drips in, the usual calcareous phenomena, stalactites and stalagmites, appear. Many of these caves are found on the coast as well as on the island. The carbonate of lime is very pure, and contains brown or yellow-white crystals.

A stony valley, sunk below the level of both flanks, is said to bisect the island from north to south. Into this basin fall sundry small streams, the Mohayra and others, which are lost through the crevices and caverns, and in the cracks and fissures of the grit. There are other drains, forming, after heavy downfalls, swamps and marshes, whence partly the great insalubrity of the interior. The western part of Zanzibar, with its wealth of evergreen vegetation, appears by far the most fertile. It is a meridional band of red clay and sandy hills, running parallel with the corallines of the eastern coast. Here are the most elevated grounds. I found the royal plantation Sebbe or Izimbane, 400 feet (B.P.) above sea-level, or a little higher than the Bermudas. The least productive parts are those covered with dark clay. Heavy rains deposit arenaceous matter upon the surface, and the black humus disappears. On this side of the island also many streamlets discharge into the sea, bearing at their mouths mangrove beds, whose miasmas cause agues, dysenteries, diarrhoeas, and deadly fevers.

The rule established by Dampier and quoted by Humboldt directs us to expect great depth near a coast formed by high perpendicular mountains. Here, as in the rest of the Zanzibarian archipelago, the maritime line, unlike the west

Atlantic islands Tenerife and Madeira, is composed of gently rolling hills. Yet seven fathoms are often found with<u>in</u> a stone-throw of the land, whilst the encircling ledges are steep-to, marked in the charts 4 and ⑧. Evidently, then, the corallines are perched upon the summits of a submarine range which rises sharp and abrupt from abysmal hollows and depressions. As usual too in such formations, the leeward shore line of the island, where occur the lagoon entrances, is more varied and accidented than the eastern. At Pemba this feature will be even more remarkable.

The windward coast, in common with many parts of the continental seaboard, suffers especially from June to August from the Pas de Maree (Manuel de la Navigation et la C6te o.ccidentale de l'Afrique), a tide race, supposed to result from the meeting of currents. It is a line of rollers' neither far from nor very near the shore. The hurling and sagging surf is described to resemble the surge of a submarine earthquake ; and the strongest craft, once entangled in the send, cannot escape. It would be useful to note, as at West African Lagos, the greater or less atmospheric pressure accompanying the phenomenon, and to seek a connection between it and the paroxysms of the neighbouring cyclone region. At all times sailors remark the 'shortness ' of the waves and the scanty intervals between their succession. This peculiarity cannot be explained in the usual way by shoals and shallow water causing' a ground-swell.

"With respect to the great East African ocean-current, which has given rise to so many fables gravely recorded by the Arab geographers,[1] the best authorities at Zanzibar are convinced, and their log-books prove, that both its set and drift, like the Brazilian coast-stream, are in the present state of our knowledge subject to the extremes of variation. The charts and Horsburgh lay it' down as a regular S.W. current; and so it is in the southern, whilst in the northern part it is hardly perceptible. Between Gapes Guardafui and Delgado it flows now up then down the coast; here it trends inland, there it sets out to sea. Dr Euschenberger relates that on Sept. 1,

[1] The Bahr el Kharab, or Bad Sea, the mountains El Mulattam (the lashed or beaten), El Kidameh (of repentance), and El Ajrad (the noisy); the Mountains of Magnet, and tbe 'Blind Billows ' and 'Enchanted Breakers ' which, says El Masndi, make the Omani sailor of the tribe of Azd sing—

'0 Berberah and Jafuni (Ea'as Hafun), and thy warlock waves !
  Jafuni and Berberah and their waves are these which thou
    seest! '

1835, his ship, when south of Zanzibar, was carried 50 miles in 15 hours, and was obliged to double the northern cape. The same happened to Captain Guiilain in August 1816, when he lost five days. This resulted from the superior force of the S.W. monsoon, which often drives vessels to the north 30 to 10 miles during the day and night. Lieut. Christopher (Journal, Jan. 5, 1813) reported it to be variable and violent, especially close in shore, and observed that it frequently trends against the wind. It is usually made to run to the S.W. between December and April, at the rate of 1*3 miles per hour, from It a'as Hafun to Ita'as Aswad, and two to three miles per hour between Capes Aswad and Delgado. Shipmasters at Zanzibar have assured me that when this coastal current covers three knots an hour there is a strong backwater or counter-flow, which, like the Gulf-stream, trends to the north, and against which, with light winds, native vessels cannot make way. This counter-current has extensive limits; usually it is considered strongest between Mafiyali and Pomba. The ship St Abbs, concerning which so much has been said and written of late years, was wrecked in 1855 off St Juan de Nova of the Comoro group-.(S. lat.

17° 3' 5"), and pieces of it were swept up to Brava (N. lat. 1° 6' 8"), upwards of 1000 miles. The crew is supposed still to be in captivity amongst the Abghal tribe ; and in 1865 an Arab merchant brought to Zanzibar a hide marked with letters which resembled if E B N. A writer in the *Pall Mall* opined the letters to be 'Wasm ' or tribal brands, justly observing that ͨ all the Bedawin have these distinguishing marks/ but forgetting that he was speaking of the analphabetic Somal, to whom such knowledge does not extend. As we might expect, the Mozambique stream, south of Cape Delgado, always flows southerly with more or less westing. The rate is said to vary from 20 to 80 miles a day.

Our hydrographical charts are correct enough to guide safely into and out of port any shipmaster who will sound, and can take an angle. As, however, the navigation is easy, so accidents are common. Any land-lubber could steer a ship from Bombay to Karachi (Kurrachee), and yet how many have been lost! Often, too, it is in seamanship as in horsemanship, when the best receive the most and the heaviest falls. In May 1857 the Jonas, belonging to Messrs Tidal, was sunk by mistaking Chumbi Island for its neighbour Bawi. Three of. four days afterwards the

Storm. King of Salem, Messrs Bertram, ran aground whilst hugging Chumbi in order to distance a rival. The number of reefs and shoals render it always unadvisable to enter the port at night, and in the heaviest weather safe riding-ground is found between Zanzibar Island and the continent.

Yessels from the south making Zanzibar in the N.E. monsoon, the trade-wind of December to March, leave Europa Island to the west, and the Comoro group and S. Juan de Nova on the east. Keeping well in mid-channel, they head straight for Mafiyah. They hug Point Puna, avoiding Latham's Bank,[1] and they work up hy Kwale and the Ohumbi Island. Ships from the north have only to run down the mid-channel, between Pemba and the continent, and then to pass west of Tumbatu. Those sailing southward from Zanzibar at this season pass along-shore, down the Mozambique Channel. Yessels from the south making Zanzibar in May to September, the height of the S.W. monsoon—the anti-N.E. trade—sail up the same passage. They must beware of falling to leeward; and those that neg-

[1] At Latham's Isle was found guano, which Captain Cogan, I.N., obtained permission to export. In 1847, however, it was washed away by a 'Has de Maree.'

lect 'lead and look-out ' are ever liable to be carried northwards to Pemba by the counter-current before mentioned, which may, however, now be a wind-current. At this season ship-masters missing the mark have sometimes made 3° to 4° of easting, and have preferred beating down to Mafiyah and running up again, rather than face the ridicule of appearing via the northern passage. Those leaving the Island in the S.W. monsoon stand north up channel, well out in E. Ion. 9° 42' to 43', beat south of Cape Delgado, pass between the Comoro group and the mainland, and thus catch the Mozambique gulfstream. The brises solaires blow strongest off Madagascar in June and July. They fall light in August and September.

The aspect of Zanzibar from the sea is that of coralline islands generally—a graceful, wavy outline of softly rounded ground, and a surface of ochre-coloured soil, thickly clothed with foliage alternating between the liveliest leek-green and the sombrest laurel, the only variety that vegetation knows in this land of eternal verdure. Everywhere the scenery is similar ; each mile of it is a copy of its neighbour; and the want of variety, of irregularity, of excitement, so to speak, soon makes itself felt. Zanzibar ignores the exhilaration of pure desert air, and the exaltation produced hy the stern aspect of mountain regions or hy a boundless expanse of Pampa and Sahara. Without a single element of sublimity, soft and smiling, its sensuous and sequestered scenery has no power to spur the thought, to breed an idea within the brain. The oppressive luxuriance of its growth combined with the excess of damp heat, and possibly the abnormal proportion of ozone, are the most unfavourable conditions for the masculine. The same is the case in Mazanderan, Malabar, Egypt, Phoenicia, California, and other Phre-kah—lands of the sun. And the aspect of that everlasting, beginningless, endless verdure tends, as on the sea-board of the Brazil, to produce sensations of melancholy and depression. We learn at last to loathe thee,

'gay green,
Thou smiling Nature's universal robe! '

Landing upon the island, you find a thin strip of bright yellow sand separating the sea from a curtain of vegetation, which forms a continuous wall. In some parts madrepore rock, looped and caverned by the tide, and covered with weeds and testacese, whose congeners are fossilized in the stone, rises abruptly a few feet above the wave. At other places a dense growth of tangled mangrove jungle exposes during the ebb a sheet of black and sticky mire, into which man sinks knee-deep. The regularity of the outline is broken by low projecting spits and by lagoons and backwaters, which bite deep into the land. Their pestilential, fatal exhalations veil the low grounds with a perpetual haze, and the excess of carbon is favourable to vegetable as it is deleterious to animal life.

Passing over the modern sea-beach, with its coarse grasses, creepers, and wild flowers—mostly the Ip omasa—and backed by towering trees, cocoas, mangos, and figs, we often observe in the interior distinct traces of an old elevation, marked by lines of water-worn pebbles and by coarse gravels overlying greasy blue clay. This is the home of the copal. Beyond it the land rises imperceptibly, and breaks into curves, swells, and small ravines, rain-cut and bush-grown, sometimes 40 feet deep. The soil is now a retentive red or yellow argile, based upon a detritus of coralline, hardened, where pressed, into the semblance of limestone, or upon a friable sandstone-grit of quartz and silex. The humus of the richest vegetable substance, and excited by the excess of humidity and heat, produces in abundance maize, millet, and various panicums;

tomatoes and naturalized vegetables, muhogo (the cassava), and Palma Christi; coffee, cotton, and sugar-cane; clove, nutmeg, and cinnamon trees; foreign fruits, like the Brazilian Caju, the passion-flower and the pine-apple; the Chinese Leechi; bananas and guavas, the Raphia and the cocoa, twin queens of the palms; limes and lemons, oranges and shaddocks, the tall tamarind, the graceful Areca, the grotesque calabash and Jack-tree, colossal sycamores and mangos, whose domes of densest verdure, often 60 feet high and bending, fruit-laden, to the earth, make our chesnuts, when in fullest dress, look half-naked and in rags.

The uplands, especially in the western part of the island, are laid out in Mashdmba or plantations, whose regular lines of untrimmed clove-trees are divided by broad sunny avenues. Here and there are depressions in the soil, where heavy rains slowly sinking have nursed a tangled growth of reeds and rushes, sedge and water-grass. About the Mohayra and the Bububu—the principal of the 7roraffioi πXei<rToi of the Periplus—mere surface-drains, choked with fat juncacese and with sugar-cane growing wild, there is a black soil of prodigious fertility, whose produce may, so to speak, be seen to grow. This sounds

like exaggeration; but I well remember, at Hyderabad, in Sind., that during tbe inundation of the Indus we could perceive in the morning that the maize had lengthened during the night, and the same is the case with certain 'toadstools ' and fungi in the Brazil.

Upon this waste of rank vegetation the sun darts an oppressive and malignant beam. In the driest season the 'mangrove heaviness ' of the western coast and the. cadaverous foetor announce miasma; after the rains the landscape is redolent of disease and death.

The cottages of small proprietors and slaves strew the farms. They are huts of wattle and rufous loamy dab, to which large unbaked bricks of red clay are sometimes preferred. The usual cajan pent-roof forms deep dark eaves, propped by untrimmed palm-boles. These dwellings are unwholesome, because none boast of a second storey; they are not even built upon piles, and thus their sole defence against the surrounding malaria is the shrubbery planted by nature's hand. Sickness seems generally, both in the island and on the continent, to follow turning up fresh soil, and the highlands are often more subject to miasma than the lowlands.

The lines of communication consist of mere

footpaths, instead of the hroad roads required for the ventilation of the country. When the produce of the land is valuable the lanes are lined with cactus, milk-bush (euphorbia), and succulent plants,' whose foliage shines with metallic lustre. Set in little ridges, the hedge-rows of pine-apple, with its large pink and crimson fruit, passing, when ripe, into a reddish-yellow, form a picturesque and pleasant fence. At a distance from the town the paths become rough and solitary. Nearer, they are well beaten hy negroes of both sexes and all ages, carrying fuel or baskets of fruit upon their heads, or bringing water from the wells, or loitering under shady trees to cheapen the cocoa-nut, manioc, and broiled fish, offered hy squatting negresses for their refection.

SECTION 2.

Meteorological Notes—Tbe Double Seasons, &e.

THE characteristic of meteorology at Zanzibar, as generally the case in the narrow equatorial zone, is the extreme irregularity of its phenomena. Here weather seems to be all in confusion; hardly two consequent years resemble each other. In 1853-4, for instance, the seasons, if they may so be called, were apparently inverted; heavy showers fell during the dries, and a drought occupied the place of the wet monsoon. Sometimes the rains will begin with, this year (1857) they ended with, a heavy hurst. Now April is a fine month, then the downfall will last through June.

I may also remark one great difference of climate between the eastern and western coasts of intertropical Africa. Whilst Zanzibar is supersatured with moisture, Angola, on the same parallel, is a comparatively dry, sandy, and sunburnt region. Kilwa, upon the eastern coast, and in S. lat. 8° 57', is damp and steamy. S. Paulo de Loanda, upon the opposite shore (S. lat. ,8° 48'), suffers from want of water. We find the same contrast in the South American continent. The middle Brazil is emphatically a land of rains, whilst Peru and Chili require artificial irrigation supplied by melted snow. Evidently the winds charged with moisture, the N. E. and S. E. trades and their modifications, discharge themselves upon the windward sides of continents' especially when these are fringed with cold sierras, which condense the vapour and render the interior a lee land.

In 1847 the Geographical Society of Bombay sent a barometer to Zanzibar, and requested that a meteorological register might he kept. Their wishes were not immediately carried into effect; but after a time the Eurasian apothecary in charge of the Consulate filled up in a rude way during nine months a weather-book, with observations of the barometer, of two thermometers attached and unattached, of wet and dry bulbs, of evaporation and of rainfall. In the Journal of the '.Royal Geographical Society (xxiii. of 1853), Colonel Sykes published a 'record, kept during eleven months in 1850, of the indications of several intertropical instruments at Zanzibar,' unhappily without those of pressure.[1]

The result of nine months' observations is that

---

[1] **The temperature of the island as observed by Trench travellers is—**

Max. (April 6 A.M. 2 mom.) 89° (P.)—Colonel Sykes—88° (P. in shade)
Min. (October, midnight and 0 A.M.) 73°   ditto 73°
Mean temperature of the year 79° 15   ditto 79·90 (extreme range 18°-19°)

The following are the results of the evaporating dish:—

	Total of month. Inches.	Greatest in one day of the month. inches.	Least in one day. inches.
January, 1857	2386	0099	0004
February "	2·19	010	0015
March "	2·49.49	07.09	0·00
April "	1176	0.10	0·03

THE BAROMETER.

the thermometer shows a remarkably limited range of temperature and an extreme variation of only 18°—-19°. A storm, however, will make the mercury fall rapidly through 6°—7°. The climate is far more temperate than the inexperienced expect to find so near the equator. It is within the limits of the true Trades. The land and sea breezes laden with cool moisture blow regularly, and the excessive humidity spreads a heat-absorbing steam-cloud between sun and earth. The medium temperature of January is 83° 30'; of Pebruary, the hottest month, 85° 86' (according to Colonel Sykes 83° 40'); and of March, 82° 50'. This high and little-varying mean then gradually declines till July, the coolest month (77° 10'). The mean average of the year is 79° 15'—-90'. In September and October the climate has been compared with that of southern Europe. On the other hand, the atmosphere supports an amount of moisture unknown to the dampest parts of India.

The barometer, so near the equator, is almost uniformly sluggish and quiescent. Its range diurnal and annual is here at a min. It seldom, except under varying pressure of storms or tornadoes, rises or falls above or below 30 inches at sea level, and a few tenths represent the max.

variation. It must be observed, however, on both coasts of Africa, within 6°—7° of the Line, this instrument requires especial study for nautical purposes. Here it is an imperfect indicator, because, affected from great distances, it rises without fine weather and it falls without foul. At Zanzibar the case of a whaling captain is quoted for wasting in vain precautions nearly two months. Moreover, sufficient observations have not yet been accumulated in the southern hemisphere. Where there is so little expansion in the mercurial column the convexity and concavity of the column-head must be carefully examined with a magnifying-glass, and by a reflecting instrument the smallest change could he correctly measured. The trembling of the aneroid needle, sometimes ranging through a whole inch during the gusts of the highly electrical tornado, also calls for observation. The sympiesometer is held to be even more sensitive than the mercurial barometer, especially before storms, and ignorance of its peculiarity has often 'frightened a reef in ' at unseasonable times. The same was found to be the case, in high latitudes, by Lieut. Robertson, R.N., when sailing under Captain Ross (1818), between N. lat. 51° 89' and 76° 50'.

Observations with the altitude and azimuth determined the variation of the needle in 1857 to be between 9°—10° *(W.)*. If this be correct, it is gradually easting. In 1823 Captain Owen found it to be 11° *T* (W.).[1] So, upon the opposite coast, the variation laid down in our charts of 1846 as 20° (W.) has gradually declined to between 18° 30' and 19° (W\).

Of exceptional meteoric phenomena I can speak only from hearsay, no written records existing upon the island. A single earthquake is remembered. In the early rains of 1846, at about 4 P.M., a shock, accompanied by a loud rumbling sound, ran along the city sea-front, splitting the Sayyid's palace, the adjacent mosque, and the side-walls of the British Consulate, in a direction perpendicular to the town. It was probably the result of igneous disturbance below the coralline, and it tends to prove that the island was originally an atoll: some, however, have explained it by a land-slip. Three meteors are known since 1843. In December of that year a ball of fire was visible from windows facing the north; it, disappeared without a report. The most remarkable was a bolis, which, about

[1] The Consular report of 1859 gives Captain Owen's variation.

6 p.m. on October 25, 1855, took a N.W. by W. path, burned during ten or eleven minutes, and frightened the superstitious burghers into fits. Water-spouts commonly appear during the month of April, and in the direction of the mainland: the people disperse them by firing guns. Frost and snow are of course unheard of at Zanzibar, and hail, not uncommon in the interior, never (?) falls upon the island or the coast. During the wet season generally, especially when the heats are greatest, the hills of Terrafirma are veiled with clouds, and sheet-lightning plays over the horizon. The islanders assure the stranger that storms of thunder and lightning are rare, and that few accidents happen from the electric fluid. M. Alfred May, for instance, declares that thunder is heard only three or four times a year. The same is said in West African Yoruba, in parts of the Brazil, and even in Northern Syria—Damascus, for instance. It would be curious to inquire what produces this uniform immunity under climatic conditions so different. At Zanzibar, however, the phenomenon is irregular as the seasons. I was told of several deaths by the 'thunderbolt,' and in the year 1857 the S.W. monsoon was ushered in almost daily by a tempest. Lieutenant-Colonel

Hamerton, when sailing about the island, lost by lightning his Baloch Sarhang (boatswain) ; he himself felt a blow upon the shoulder like that of a falling block. No blood appeared upon the side, but it was livid to the hip, and for some days the patient was decidedly 'shaky.' Some explained his escape by his wearing flannel; others by his standing near the davits of a longboat, which were twisted like wax by the electric fluid.

The mainlands of Zanzibar and of Mozambique are subject, as might be expected, to tornados, which much resemble those of the West African coast. Accompanying the formation and the dispersion of the nimbus, they are often violent enough to wreck small craft. Caught in a fine specimen, I was able to observe all the normal phenomena,—the building up of the warning arch, the white eye or gleam under the soffit, the wind blowing off shore, the apparent periodicity of throbs, and the frantic rage of the short-lived squall. The cyclones and hurricanes of the East Indian Islands rarely extend to Zanzibar. During 14 years there was but one tourbillon strong enough to uproot a cocoa-tree. It passed over the city about midnight, overthroAving the Mdbandani or roof-sheds, and it was followed by a burst of rain. Colonel Sykes (loco oit.) remarks, philosophically explaining the why, 'Another peculiar feature in the climatology of Zanzibar is that there is seldom any dew experienced.' The reverse is the case, as might be known by the strength of the nightly radiation. Captain Guillain (i. 2, 72) declares that the rosees which accompany the rains are sufficient for watering the ground, and observes (p. 94), I presume concerning those who remain in the open air, 'Hester a terre entre huit lieurs du soir et le lever du soleil c'est s'exposer a une mort tres probable, sinon certaine.' The sunset, never followed by twilight, is accompanied by a sudden coolness which, as in equatorial, and even sub-tropical regions generally, causes a rapid precipitation of vapour. The dews are cold and clammy, and the morning shows large beads in horizontal streaks of moisture on perpendicular surfaces. I often remarked the deposition of dew when light winds were blowing; of course it did not stand in drops, but it wetted the clothing. This I believe is an exception to the general rule. At sunset the old stager will not sit or walk in the open air, although, as in Syria, he will expose himself to it at nine or ten p. m., when the night has acquired its normal temper-attire. As in the west coast squadron, so here, there is an order that all men on deck after sunset must wear their blanket-coats and trowsers, and many an unfortunate sailor has lost his life by sleeping in the streets, thus allowing the dew to condense upon his body while under the influence of liquor. Experienced travellers have taught themselves, even in the hottest seasons of the hottest equinoctial regions, to air the hut with a 'bit of fire ' before sundown and sunrise, and it is doubtless an excellent precaution against 'chills.'

Zanzibar Island, lying in S. lat. 6°, has the sun in zenith twice a year ; the epochs being early March and October; more exactly, March 4t and October 9. Hence it has two distinct summers; the first in February, the second in September. It has double rains; the 'Great Masika ' in April to June, and the 'Little Masika' in October to November. It has two winters; the shorter in December, and in July the longer, which is much more marked than the' former. There are only three months of N.E. trade (Azyab)[1] to nine of S.E. and S.W. (Kausi).

[1] Azyab is the classical Arab term for Cascias (Kaikias) the N.E. wind—according to Eiruzabadi it is the S.E.; Sciron, the N.W., isthe Arab 'Shhrsh'; Lips, the S.W., is 'Lahash'; and EuroB, the S.E., 'Sh'luk ' (scirocco, which is in many places a

The regularity of these seasons is broken by a variety of local causes, and there is ever, I repeat, the normal instability of equinoctial climates. Theory appears often at fault upon these matters. A fair instance is Mr Cooley's assertion, that about Edlima-njaro the 'rainy season is also the hot season.' Theoretically, of course, the period of the sun's northing and of the great rains should be, north of the equator, the hot season; hut where tropical downfalls are heavy, the excessive humidity intercepting the solar rays, and the valleys and swamps refrigerated by the torrents, make the rainy season the cold weather. From June to September the natives of Fernando Po *(N.* lat. 4") die, like those of eastern intertropical Africa, of catarrh, quinsey, and rheumatism. Even in India the Goanese call the rains 'o inverno,' and Abba Gregorius makes the wet weather the winter of Abyssinia. About Kdlima-njaro the hot and dry season opens with the end and closes with the beginning of the hot monsoon.

                    The natives of Zanzibar distribute the year

due east wind). The N.E. is still commonly called 'Barrdni in vulgar Arabic, however, men would say, Bayn el Shimal w'el G-harb. At Zanzibar the east wind is called by tbe 'Washawahili Zaju—of above, and the west Pbepo Minde or TJmande—of dew or mist.

into five seasons. A far simpler division liere applicable, as in Western India, is made by those local trades the monsoons, between whose two unequal lengths are long intervals of calms and of variable winds. These are the Mausim or N.E. monsoon, and the Hippalus or S.W.

1. The Kaskazi or Kazkazi (vulgarly Kizkazi), to which the Arabs limit the term El Mausim (Monsoon),is *the* season during which the Azyab or N.E. trade blows. The wind begins about mid-November; from mid-December to mid-Eebruary its strength is greatest, and it usually ends about mid-March. In 1857, however, the Kaskazi opened with light showers, and continued in full force till March 24; usually the last vessels from Cutch and Bombay enter port about March 10. This is the first of the two hot seasons, and midsummer may be placed in Eebruary and March. A fine, cool sea-breeze from the N.E. usually prevails between 8 a.m. and late in the afternoon. When it is absent the weather is sultry and oppressive, the northerner feels suffocated; the least exertion brings on profuse perspiration, and the cuticular irritation produces boils and 'prickly heat.' The nights are close and stifling enough to banish rest and sleep. As has been shown, the thermometer

does not stand high, hut the frequent flashes of sheet-lightning playiug over the northern and western sky show a surcharge of electricity. The public health would suffer severely but for the frequent cooling showers which, especially at the end of the Kaskazi, are succeeded by several days of pleasant weather. This is the agriculturist's spring. Sesamum, holcus, rice, and other cereals, are sown upon lands previously burned for manure. It is the traveller's opportunity for visiting the interior of the island and the worst parts of the coast, but—'bad is the best.'

2. The Msika (or Masika) Mku, Greater rain or rains. About the end of March the change of monsoon is ushered in by heavy squalls from the S.E. and by tornados blowing off land. Presently the Hippalus breaks, and extends from early May into October. In May native craft make India after a run of 20 to 25 days; after the end of August they rarely attempt the voyage. This Kausi or Hippalus is usually called S.W. monsoon, but it has mostly an *eastern deflection*, possibly modified by the westerly land-breezes. The Arabs divide it, as will be seen, into three portions. Pirst, the Kaus proper,[1] in Kisawa-

[1] I can only suggest that this term is borrowed from the zodiacal sign Sagittarius.

hili Kausi Q^*), from mid-April to early August, the period of the greatest strength. Second, Kipupwe or first winter—July and early August; and third, the Dayman, which ends the Kausi.

Presently appear the rains which have followed the northing sun. The same observation was made by the Austrian mission on the White Diver in N. lat. 4° 30b On the coast we can distinctly trace their progress. In 1857 the downfall began in Peb. 15, at TJsumbara (S. lat. 5°), where the clouds are massed and condensed by a high plateau, leading to lofty, snow-capped mountains. In 1851 I found that the rainy season opened at Berberah of the Somal (N. lat. 10° 25') on April 15; and in early June they reach Bombay (N. lat. 18° 53'). Concerning the movement of the wet season in inner intertropical Africa I have already written in the Journal of the Boyal Geographical Society (sxix. 207).

The heaviest rains at Zanzibar Island begin the wet season about mid-April, and last 30 to 40 ' days; they do not end, however, till early June. Some observers remark that the fall is greatest at low water and during the ebb-tides of the Syzygies. It is, however, rare to have a week of uninterrupted rain, as in eastern India and sometimes in the Brazil. The discharge is exceedingly uncertain. Some years nnmber 85 inches, others 108. During the first eight months of 1857 and the last four months of 1858, we find a total of 120-21 inches. In 1859 it reached 167, doubling the average of Bombay (76'55), and nearly trebling that of Calcutta (56'83). We may compare these figures with those of Europe and the United States. England has 31·97 inches; Erance, 25-00 ; Central Germany, 20·00; Hungary, 16'93; Boston, 38·19 (about the same at Beyrut in Syria); Philadelphia, 45-00; and St Louis, Mo., 31-97. Of these 167 inches (1859), 104'25 fell during the Msika Mku. The number of wet days ranges from 100 to 130 per annum. According to the people, rain has diminished of late years ; perhaps it is the result of felling cocoas, and of disforesting the land for cloves. In 1857, the Great Msika was preceded by a few days of oppressive heat, which ended (March 24) in a highly electrical storm, like those which usher in the rains of western. India, and suddenly the cool S.W. began to blow. Eor some time we had daily showers, now from the N.E., then from the S.W., with high winds and loud thunderings; the rains, however, did not show in earnest before April 10.

The islanders like the Msika to open with

showers strong enough to hind the land, but not so violent as to carry off the manure deposited by the year's decayed vegetation. After this the water should fall in heavy ropy torrents, with occasional breaks of sunshine and fine weather; when this lasts thirty days, and is succeeded by frequent showers, good crops are expected. The downfall is heavier in the interior of the island than about the city, which, situated upon a point, escapes many a drenching. It must, however, be borne in mind that the phenomena of the rains, like those of the sea and air, are essentially irregular. In some seasons there will be only half-a-dozen rainy afternoons; in others as many rainy mornings. There are years of great drought, and there are seasons when the sun does not appear for six weeks in succession. Usually heavy rain is not expected after 11 a.m., and showers are rare after 2 p.m. As I subsequently remarked in the east African interior—the Tluminenses of the Brazil still preserve the tradition—there is a curious regularity and periodicity in the hours of downfall, often extending over many days. This phenomenon may have done much towards creating the 'rain-doctor.'

During the Msika the horizon is obscured,

dangerously indeed for ships : the wind veers round to every point of the compass; the sky is murky and overcast; huge purple nimbi, like moving mountains, float majestically against the wind, showing strong counter-currents in the upper aerial regions. From afar the island appears smothered in blue mist, and often the cloud-rock splits into two portions, one of which makes for the coast. Even during the rare days of sunshine the distances, owing to the continuous humidity, are rarely clear, and the exhalations make refraction extensive. A high tension of vapour is the rule. For the first three hours after sunrise the land is often obscured by ᵉ smokes,' a white misty fog, often deepening to a drizzling rain; this lasts until 10 A.M., about which time the sea-breeze begins to blow.

The Msika is much feared by the native population, and the interior of the island becomes a hot-bed of disease. The animal creation seems to breathe as much water as air. The want of atmospheric weight, and consequently of pressure upon the surface of the body, renders the circulation sluggish, robs man of energy, and makes him feel how much better is sleep than waking. Europeans, speaking from effect, complain that the 'heavy ' air produces an unnatural drowsiness—it is curious to see how many of our popular books make humidity increase the weight of the atmospheric column. During this season the dews of sunset are deemed especially fatal to foreigners. At times the body feels cold and clammy when the thermometer suggests that it should be perspiring : super-saturation is drawing off the vital heat. The lungs are imperfectly oxygenized, and, in general belief, positive is exchanged for negative electricity. The hair and skin are dank and sodden; indeed, a dry cutis is an unattainable luxury. Iron oxydizes with astonishing rapidity; shoes exposed to the air soon fall to pieces; mirrors are clouded with steam; paper runs and furniture sweats; the houses leak; books and papers are pasted together; ink is covered with green fur; linens and cottons grow mouldy, and broadcloths stiffen and become boardy.

This excess of damp is occasionally varied by the extreme of dryness. The hot wind represents the Khamasin of Egypt, the Sharki (or ShTuk) of Syria, the Harmattan of west Africa, and the Norte of the southern Brazil, Paraguay, and the Argentine Confederation. At such times the air apparently abounds in oxygen and in ozone. Cotton cloth feels hard and crisp ; even the water is cooled by the prodigious evaporation. Books and papers curl up and crack, and strangers are apt to suffer from nausea and fainting fits.

3. The Kipupwe, first winter or cold season —July and early August. The bright azure of the sky, the surpassing clearness of the water, and the lively green colours of the land, are not what we associate with the idea of the ᶜ disease of the year.' The Kausi or S.W. monsoon still blows, hut in this second or postpluvial phase its strength is diminished. As on the western coast the mornings are misty, the effect of condensation and of excessive evaporation, the sun pumping up vapour from the rapidly desiccating ground; but about four hours after sunrise a strong sea-breeze sets in, giving a little life and elasticity to the exhausted frame. When the 'doctor ' fails the heat is oppressive, and the sunsets are often accompanied by an unpleasant closeness. The beginning of the Kipupwe is held to be universally sickly. The Hindus, who declare that all cold coming from the south is had, suffer from attacks of rheumatism and pneumonia. The charms of the season induce Europeans to despise the insidious attacks of malaria: they

commit imprudences and pay for them in severe fevers. The rare but heavy showers that now fall are termed 'Mcho; ' they separate the greater from the lesser Msika.

4. Daymdn (in Kisawahili Daymdni) ends the Kausi or S. W. monsoon, and extends through August and part of October. Though the sun is nearly perpendicular the air is cooled by strong south-westerly breezes. At this time yams, manioc, and sweet potatoes grow, making it a second spring, whilst the harvest of rice and holcus assimilates it to the temperate autumn.

5. The Yuli (Puli)[1] or Msika Mdogo, second rains or Little Msika. This season lasts hut three weeks, beginning shortly after the sun has crossed the zenith of Zanzibar in the southern declination, and embracing part of October and November. It is not considered a healthy time by the islanders. The autumnal rains are sometimes wanting upon the continent, and the land then suffers as severely from drought as northern Syria does when the 'former rain ' fails. After the Vuli recommences the Kaskazi, and the

---

[1] Y and F are often interchanged, as Mpumbafu (a fool), and Mfulana (a youth), for Mpumbavu and Mvulana. Generally the Arabs of Oman and other incorrect .speakers prefer the latter, and the Wasawahili the former, a sound which does not exist in Arabic.

N. E. trade again blows. The sun is distant, the thermometer does not range high, yet the temperature of houses sheltered from the breeze becomes overpowering, and without the 'doctor' the city would hardly be habitable. At times the Trade freshens to a gale that blows through the day. The Hindus suffer severely from this ' Bdord ' (blast), and declare that it brings on fits of ' Mridi ' (refroidissement), here held dangerous. During the whole of the Azyab monsoon the people prefer hot sun and a clear, which is always a slightly hazv-blue, sky. They dislike the clouds and heavy showers called Mvua[1] ya ku pandia, or harvest rains, which are brought up at times by the N. N. West wind. On the other hand, when the Kausi or S. West monsoon blows, they hold an overcast sky the best for health, and they dread greatly the 'rain-sun.' The peasants take advantage of the dryness, and prepare, by burning, the land for maize, sesamum, and rice.

The Wasawahili, like the Somal and many other races, have attempted to conform the lunar with the solar year, a practice which may

[1] Or Mbua, the B and V being confounded, like F and V. Similarly, in the Prakrit dialects of Indra, vikh becomes bikh (poison).

date from the days when the Persians were rulers of the Zanzibar coast. They also give their own names to the lunar months of the Moslem ; and, curiously enough, they begin the year, not with Muharram, but with the ninth month (Shawwal), which they call 'Mfunguo Mosi,' or Pirst Month. The next, Zu'l Ka'adeli, is Mfunguo MMLi, Second Month, and so on till Rajab, Shaa'-ban (or Mlisho) >. and Ramazan, which retain their Arab names.[1] Amongst the Somal, five months, namely, from the second to the fifth, are known by. the old Semitic terms. The month, as amongst all savage and semi-civilized tribes, begins with sighting the moon; and the Wasawahili reckon like the Jews, the modern Moslems, and the Chinese, 12 of 29 and 30 days alternately. 'The complete number of months with God' being, says the Koran, 'twelve months,' good followers of the Prophet ignore the Ye-adar, second or embolical Adar, which the Hebrews inserted after every third year, and retain their silly cycle of 351 days. The Wasawahili add 10 to 12 days to the Moslem year, and thus preserve the orderly recurrence of the seasons. The sage in

[1] This is ignored by Captain G-uillain (Appendix, vol. iii.), who mates the *W*asawahili retain all the names of the Arab months.

charge of the local almanac is said to live at Tumbatu: he finds his New Tear's Day by looking at the sun, by tracing figures upon the ground, and by comparing the results with Arabic calendars. Their weeks begin, as usual with Moslems, on Friday (Ejuma for Juma), the Saturday being Juma Mosi, or one day after Friday, and so forth. Thursday, however, is Khamisi. This subdivision of time, though suggested by the quarters of the earth's satellite, is known only to societies which have advanced toward civilization. Thus in Dahome we find a week of four days; and even China ignores the seven-day week.

'The universal festivals,' says the late Professor H. H. "Wilson (Essays on the Religion of the Hindus, ii. 155), 'are manifestly astronomical, and are intended to commemorate the revolutions of the planets, the alternations of the seasons, and the recurrence of cyclical intervals of longer or shorter duration.' The Nau-roz *(j.jy)* or New Tear's Day, here, as in Syria, locally pronounced Nay-roz, was established in ancient Ariana, according to Persian tradition, by Jamshid, King of Kings, in order to fix the vernal equinox.[1] It is the Holi of the Hindus,

[1] In 1870, for instance, it was kept in Syria on the 11th of 'Adar' (March), old style, and on Adar 23rd, new style.

and after the East has kept this most venerable festival for 3000 years, we still unconsciously celebrate the death and resurrection of the eternal sun-god. The Beal-tinne is not yet forgotten in Leinster, nor is the maypole wholly obsolete in England. As early as the days of the Kuraysh, there was an attempt to reconcile the lunar with the solar year, and the Nau-roz, though palpably ,of Pagan origin, has been adopted by all the maritime peoples professing El Islam. Even the heathen-hating Arab borrowed it for his convenience from the Dualists and Trinitarians of Ears and Hindustan. Hence the aeras called Kadmi and Jelali. In this second solar sera the Nau-roz was transferred by the new calendar from the vernal equinox to Sept. 14, A.D. 1079, and was called Nau-roz i Mizdn   Amongst the Wasawahili it is known as Siku Khu ya Mwaka, the Great Day of the year.

Eor the purpose of a stable date, necessary both to agriculture and to navigation, and also for the determination of the monsoons, the people who ignore the embolismal month, and who have no months for the solar year, add, I have said, 10 to 12 days to each lunar year, the true difference being 16 days 9 hrs. 0 min. and

1T7 secs. Thus the contrivance is itself rude; moreover the Wasawabili often miscalculate it. Between A.D. 1829 and A.D. 1879, it would fall on 28-29 August. In 1841 they made it commence at 6 p. m., August 28, immediately after full moon: in 1850-2 they began it on August 27, and in 1856 in August 26!

Sundry quasi superstitious uses are made of the 10 embolismal days following the Nau-roz. Should rains—locally called Miongo—fall on the first day, showers are prognosticated for the tenth; if on the second, the twentieth will be wet; and so forth till the tenth, which if rainy suggests that the Kausi or S.W. monsoon will set in early. The seasons of navigation are thus reckoned. The Yuli rains are supposed to begin 30 days, counting from the twentieth, after Nau-

[1] According to Captain G-uillain, in 184G-7 it corresponded with August 29 (the New Year's Day of Abyssinia and Egypt in 1844); in 1848 with August 28 ; and in 1850, 51, 52 with August 27. He was also informed that the Yuli began 20 days after the Nau-roz, and lasted 30 (Sept. 20 to Oct. 20), that the Msika (which he writes Mouaka) begins 90 days after the 110th (Dec. 20 to March 20), and that the Mcho'o commences 20 days after the 280 (June 10 to July 1). That author, moreover, remarks that as the new Persian calendar adds to every century 22 days, instead of our 24 days, the Nau-roz thus falls behind ours 48 hours in each hundred years. Thus between 1829 and 1879, the New Year's Day should occur between the 28th and 29th August.

roz. On the eightieth (some say the ninetieth) day are expected thunder, lightning, and heavy rains at the meeting of the monsoons (mid-November), and so forth. Possibly this may he a reflection of the Hindu idea which represents the Grarbhas to he the fetuses of the clouds, and horn 195 days after conception. With us the people mark the periods hy saints' days. The Bernais say—

> Apres le jour de la Sainte Luce,
> Les jours s'allongent le saut d'une puce.

The Escuara proverb declares—

> Sanct Seim on etu Juda,
> Negua eldu da.
> ('At St Simou and St Jude, water may Le viewed.')

The basis of the following calculation is thoroughly Kisawahili—

> S'el pleut le jour de Saint Medard, (June S)
> Il pleut quarante jours plus tard.

Nor is our popular doggrel less so—

> Saint Swithin's Day, if thou dost rain,
> Eor forty days it will remain.
> Saint Swithin's Day, if thou be fair,
> Eor forty days 'twill rain nae mair.

The Wasawahili also calculate their agricultural seasons from the stars called Bulimia, a name probably derived from Ku lima, to plough.

I believe them to be Pleiades, but my sudden departure from the coast prevented my making especial inquiries. When this constellation is in the west at night the peasants say, 'Kilimia, if it sets during the rains, rises in fair weather,' and vice verst,. Also Kilimia appearing in the east is a signal for the agriculturist to prepare his land.

SECTION 3.

Climate continued—Notes on *the Nosology* of Zanzibar—Effects on Strangers.

THE climate of Zanzibar Island is better than that of the adjacent continent. Here many white residents have escaped severe fever; but upon the coast the disastrous fate of Captain Owen's surveyors, the loss of life on board our cruisers, and the many deaths of the 'Mombas Mission,' even though, finding the sea-board dangerous, they built houses on the hills which lead to the mountain region of Usumbara, prove that malaria is as active in eastern as in western Africa. Colonel Hamerton once visited the

Pangani river during the month of August: of his 19 men, three died, and all but one suffered severely. Perhaps we should not find a similar mortality in the present day, when the lancet has been laid aside for the preventive treatment by quinine and tonics. It has, however, been asserted that the prophylactic use of the alkaloid, which was such • a success in western Africa, did not prove equally valuable on the eastern coast.

Yet Zanzibar, with its double seasons and its uniformly heated and humid atmosphere, accords ill, even where healthiest, with the irritable temperament of northern races. Here, contrary to the rule of Madagascar, the lowlands over which the fresh sea-breeze plays are the only parts where the white stranger can land and live ; the interior is non habitabilis sestu. Lieut.-Colonel Hamerton, called upon in March, 1844, by Sir George Arthur, governor of Bombay, to report upon the island, wrote in September of the same year, 'The climate of the [insular] coast is not unhealthy for Europeans, but it is impossible for white men to live in the interior of the island, the vegetation being rank and appearing always to be going on; and generally fever contracted in the interior is fatal to Europeans.' Colonel Sykes (loco cit.) questions this assertion as being e contrary to all other testimony.' Every traveller, however, knows it to he correct. As in the lovely climates of the Congo River and the South Sea Islands, corporal lassitude leads to indolence, languor, and decline of mental energy, which can be recovered only by the bracing influence of the northern winter. Many new arrivals complain of depressing insomnia, with, alternations of lethargic sleep : I never enjoyed at Zanzibar the light refreshing rest of the desert. Yet the island is a favourable place for the young African traveller to undergo the inevitable 'seasoning fever, which upon the coast or in the interior might prove fatal. The highlands, or the borders of the great central basin, are tolerably healthy, but an invalid would find no comforts there—hardly a waterproof roof. He should not, however, risk after recovery a second attack, hut at once push on to his goal; otherwise he will expend in preparation the strength and bottom required to carry out his explorations. With a fresh, sound constitution, he may work hard for three years, and even if driven home by ill health he may return in comparative safety within a reasonable time.

No European, unless ■ thoroughly free from organic disease, should venture to remain longer than three or four years at Zanzibar: the same has been observed of Baghdad, and of the Euphrates valley generally. Lurking maladies will be brought to a crisis, and severe functional derangements are liable to return. The stranger is compelled to take troublesome precautions. He may bathe in cold water, sweet or salt, but he must eschew the refreshment of the mornins: walk: during the rains, when noxious mists overhang the land, the unpleasant afternoon is the only safe time for exercise. Elannel must always be worn despite the irritability of the ever-perspiring skin : even in the hottest weather the white cotton jackets and overalls of British India are discarded for tweeds, and for an American stuff of mixed cotton and wool. Extra warm clothing is considered necessary as long as the ' mugginess ' of ' msika-weather ' lasts. Sudden exposure to the sun is considered dangerous, and the carotid, jugular, and temporal arteries must be carefully protected from cold as well as from heat. Hard work, either of mind or body, is said to produce fever as surely as sitting in draughts or as wearing insufficient clothing. The charming half-hour following sunset is held dangerous, especially in hot weather-; yet most tantalizing is the cool delicious interval between the burning day and the breathless night. Natives of the country rarely venture out after dark: a man found in the streets may safely be determined to be either a slave or a thief—probably both.

Directions for diet are minute and vexatious. The stranger is popularly condemned to "lodging-house hours [5]—breakfast at 9 A.M., dinner at 3 P.M., tea at 8 P.M., bed at 10 P.M. He is told also to live temperately but not abstemiously, and never to leave the stomach too long empty. I should prescribe for him, contrary to the usual plan, an abnormal amount of stimulants, port and porter, not claret nor Rhine-wine. It is evident that where appetite is wanting, and where nourishing food, is not to be obtained, the 'patient ' must imbibe as much nutriment as he safely can. In these lands a drunkard outlives a water-drinker, despite Theodor et, "vinumbibere non est malum, sed intemperanter bibere perniciosum est '; and here Bacchus, even 'Bacchus uncivil,' is still [£] Bacchus the healer.' As usual old stagers will advise a stranger recovering from fever to strengthen himself with sundry bottles of port, and yet they do not adopt it as a preventive—" experto crede Ricardo.' The said port may be Lisbon wine fortified with cheap spirits, liquorice, and logwood—in fact, what is regimentally called 'strong military ditto ; ' yet I have seen wonders worked by the much-debased mixture. Again, Europeans are told to use purgatives, especially after sudden and strong exercise, when the £ bile is stirred up.' As an amateur chronothermalist—thanks to my kind old master, the late Dr Dickson—I should suggest tonics and bitters, which often bring relief when the nauseous salts and senna aggravate the evil. Also, in all debilitating countries, when the blood is ᶜ thin,' laxatives must be mild, othenvise they cause instead of curing fever; in fact, double tonics and half purgatives should be the rule. Above all things convalescents should be aided by change of air, if only from the house of sickness to that of a neighbour, or to a ship in port. The most long-lived of white races are the citizens of the United States: they are superior to others in mental (or cerebral) energy; they are men of spare, compact fibre, and of regular habits ; they also rarely reside more than two or three years at a time on the island. On the other hand, the small Erench colony has lost in 15 years 26 men: they lived imprudently, they drank sour Bordeaux, and when attacked with fever they killed themselves by the abuse of quinine. Swallowing large doses upon an empty stomach,, they irritated the digestive organs, and they brought on cerebral congestion by 'heroic practice ' when constipated.

According to the Arabs and Hindus of Zanzibar, ague and fever are to be avoided only by perspiring during' sleep under a blanket in a closed room—a purgatory for a healthy hot-blooded man in this damp tepid region. I found the cure-almost-as-bad-as-the-disease precaution adopted by the Spanish colonists at my salubrious residence—Hernando Po, West Africa. Only two officers escaped 'chills,' and they both courageously carried out the preventive system : on the other hand, it was remarked that they looked more aged, and they appeared to have suffered more from the climate, than those who shook once a month with 'rigors.' There is certainly no better prescription for catching ague than a coolth of skin during sleep: having purchased experience at a heavy price, it is my invariable practice when awaking with a chilly epiderm to drink a glass of water 'cold without,' and to bury myself for an hour under a pile of blankets. Every slave-hut has a cartel or cot, and the savages of the coast, like those of the Tipper Nile, carry about wooden stools for fear of dysentery. I have mentioned how our sailors dig their graves.

So much for the male sex. European women here, as in the Gulf of Guinea, rarely resist the melancholy isolation, the want of society, and the Nostalgia—Heimweh or Home-sickness—so common, yet so little regarded in tropical countries. Under normal circumstances Equatorial Africa is certain death to. the Englanderin. I am surprised at the combined folly and brutality of civilized husbands who, anxious to be widowers, poison, cut the throats, or smash the skulls of their better-halves. The thing can be as neatly and quietly, safely and respectably, effected by a few months of African air at Zanzibar or Eernando Po, as by the climate of the Maremma to which the enlightened Italian noble condemned his spouse.

The nosology of Zanzibar is remarkable for the prevalence of urinary and genital diseases; these have been roughly estimated at 75 per cent. Syphilis spreads wide, and where promiscuous intercourse is permitted to the slaves it presents formidable symptoms. The 'black lion,' as it is popularly called—in Arabic El Tayr or El Earanj ; in Kisawahili, Bubeh, Ivisvendi, or T'kego—will destroy the part affected in three weeks: secondaries are to be feared; noses disappear, the hair falls off, and rhenmatism and spreading ulcers result. Gonorrhoea is so common that it is hardly considered a disease. Eew strangers live long here without suffering from irritation of the bladder, the result, it is said, of hard lime-water: and the common effect of a cold or of stricture is severe vesical catarrh. Sarcocele and hydrocele, especially of the left testis, according to the Arabs, attack all classes, and are attributed to the relaxing climate, to unrestrained sexual indulgence, and sometimes to external injury. These diseases do not always induce impotence or impede procreation. The tunica vaginalis is believed to fill three times: as in elephantiasis the member is but a mass of flesh, a small meatus only remaining. The deposition of serum is enormous; I have heard of six quarts being drawn off. The natives punctuate with a heated copper needle, and sometimes thus induce tetanus : Europeans add injections of red wine and iodine. The latter is also applied with benefit in the early stage to sarcocele; and both complaints have yielded, it is said, to the galvanic current. Strangers are advised at all times to wear suspensory bandages.

ELEPHANTIASIS. 185

Elephantiasis of the legs and arms, and especially of the scrotum, afflicts, it is calculated, 20 per cent, of the inhabitants : Arabs and Hindus, Indian Moslems and Africans, however dissimilar in their habits and diet, all suffer alike. It is remarked that the malady has never attacked a pure white, European or American: perhaps the short residence of the small number accounts for the apparent immunity. Similarly, in the Brazil I have never seen a European stranger subject to the leprosy, or to the goitre, so prevalent in the great provinces of Sao Paulo and Minas Geraes. The Banyans declare that a journey home removes the incipient disease, or at least retards its progress : it recurs, however, on return to Zanzibar. The scrotum will often reach the knees; I heard of one case measuring in circumference 41 inches, more than the patient's body, whilst its length (33 inches) touched the ground. There is no cure, and the cause is unknown. The people attribute it to the water, and possibly it may spring from the same source which produces goitre and bronchocele.

Syphilitic and scorbutic taints appear in ulcers and abscesses. The helcoma resembles that of Aden: it generally attacks the legs and feet, the parts most distant from the centre of circulation; the toes fall of, and the limb becomes distorted. Phagsedenic sores are most common amongst the poor and the slaves, who live on manioc, fruit, and salt shark often putrid. Large and painful phlegemonous abscesses, attacking the muscular tissue, occasion great constitutional disturbance : they heal, however, readily after suppuration. Scabies, yaws (Frambsesia), psoriasis, and 'craw-craw,' inveterate as that of Malabar or the Congo River, commonly result from personal uncleanliness, unwholesome food, and insufficient shelter and clothing. That frightful malady Lupus presents pitiable objects.

The indigenous diseases which require mention are fevers, bowel-complaints, and pulmonary affections.

Fevers at Zanzibar have been compared with Aaron's rod ; at times they seem to swallow up every other disease, and generally they cause the greatest amount of mortality. As at Muhamreh, and on the swampy margins of the Shat el Arab (Persian Gulf), the constitution worn out, and the equilibrium of the functions deranged by moist heat and sleeplessness, especially during and after the heavy rains of the S. West monsoon, thus relieve themselves. Persians and northern Asiatics are even more liable to attacks than Europeans ; and, as in Egypt, rude health is rare. Some Indian Moslems have fled the country, believing themselves bewitched. Arabs born on the island, and the Banyans, who seldom suffer much from the fever, greatly dread its secondary symptoms. The 'hummeh,' or intermittent type, is remarkable for the virulence and persistency of the sequeke, which the Arabs call 'Nazlah ' (metastasis), or defluxion of humours —c dropping into the hoofs ' as the grooms say. Cerebral and visceral complications, with derangements of the liver and spleen, produce obstinate diarrhoeas, dysenteries, and a long dire cohort of diseases. Men of strong nervous diathesis escape with slight consequences in the shape of white hair, boils, bad toothaches, neuralgias, and sore tongues. The weak lose memory, or virility, or the use of a limb, the finger-joints especially being liable to stiffen; many become deaf or dim-sighted, not a few are subject to paralysis in its various forms, whilst others, tormented by hepatitis, constipation, and disorders of the bowels and of the digestive organs, never completely recover health. In this country all attribute to the moon at the 'springs' what we explain by coincidence and by the periodicity of disease. For months, and possibly for years, the symptoms recur so regularly that even Europeans will use evacuants and quinine two or three days before the new and full moons. In such cases, I repeat, change of climate is the best aid to natura curatrix.

The malignant typhus is rare at Zanzibar: it raged, however, amongst the crew of a French ship wrecked on the northern end of the island, when the men were long exposed to privations and over-fatigue. Intermittents (ague and fever) are common as colds in England. They are mild and easily treated;[1] but they leave behind during convalescence a dejection and a debility wholly incommensurate with the apparent insignificance of the attack, and often a

---

[1] In some cases an emetic will cut short the enemy. The allopathic remedies are evacuants, cooling lotions applied to the head, and sulphate of guinine (4 to 12 grains three or four times per diem), with appropriate treatment for complications. Calomel and tartar emetic must be avoided on account of their depressing effects. Liquor arsenicalis and the Tinctura Warburgii (Warburg's Drops), which is said to have failed in yellow fever, have cured malignant, inveterate, and chronic cases. The Persians at one time in Zanzibar besieged Colonel Hamerton's door for this 'Ab-i-hayyat '•—water of life. The invaluable wet sheet and the Turkish bath were unknown at Zanzibar in 1857.

periodical neuralgia, which must be treated with tonics, quinine, and chiretta.

The bilious remittent is, par excellence, the fever of the country, and every stranger must expect a 'seasoning' attack. It was inordinately fatal in the days when, the lancet being used to combat inflammation, the action of the heart was never restored. Our grandfathers, however, bled every one for everything, and for nothing: there were old ladies who showed great skill in 'blooding' cats. In 1857 men had escaped this scientific form of sudden death, but the preventive treatment so ably used on the West coast of Africa had not been tried. The cure at Zanzibar was an aperient of calomel and jalap. Castor oil was avoided as apt to cause nausea. Quinine yas administered, but often in quantities not sufficient to induce the necessary chinchonization, and the inexperienced awaited too long the period of remission, administering the drug only during the intervals. Diaphoretics of nitrate of potash, camphor mixture, and the liquor acet. ammon. were used to reduce the temperature of the skin. The most distressing symptom, ejection of bile, was opposed by saline drinks, effervescing draughts, diluted prussic acid, a mustard plaister, or a blister.

The hair was shared or closely cut, and evaporating lotions were applied to the head. The extreme restlessness of the patient often called for a timid narcotic; in these days, however, the invaluable hydrate of chloral, Sumbul and chlorodyne were unknown, and soporifics were used, as it were under protest, being believed to cause constipation. Extreme exhaustion was not vigorously attacked with medical and other stimulants ; and thus many sank under the want of ammonia and wine. I have since remarked the same errors of treatment in the West African coast; the patient was often restricted to the acidity-breeding rice water, arrowroot, and similar 'slops.' When he pined for brandy and beef-tea, the safe plan of consulting his instincts was carefully ignored.

In strong constitutions the initiatory attack of remittents is followed after a time hy the normal intermittent, and the traveller may then consider himself tolerably safe. In some Indian cases ague and fever have recurred regularly for a whole year after the bilious remittent.

The bilious remittent of Zanzibar is preceded by general languor and listlessness, with lassitude of limbs and heaviness of head, with chills and dull pains in the body and extremities, and with a frigid sensation creeping up the spine. Then comes a mild cold fit, succeeded by flushed face, full veins, an extensive thirst, dry, burning heat of shin, a splitting headache, and nausea, and by unusual restlessness, or by remarkable torpor and drowsiness. The patient is unable to stand ; the pulse is generally full and frequent, sometimes thready, small, and quick; the bowels are constipated, and the tongue is furred and discoloured; appetite is wholly wanting. During my first attack, I ate nothing for seven days; and despite the perpetual craving thirst, no liquid will remain upon the stomach. Throughout the day extreme weakness causes anxiety and depression; the nights are worse, for restlessness is aggravated by want of sleep. Delirium is common in the nervous-bilious temperament. These symptoms are sometimes present several days before the attack, which is in fact their exacerbation. A slight but distinctly marked remission often occurs after the 4th or 5th hour —in my own case they recurred regularly between 2 and 3 A.M. and P.M.—followed by a corresponding reaction. When an unfavourable phase sets in, all the evils are aggravated ; great anxiety, restlessness, and delirium wear out the patient; the mind wanders, the body loses all power, the ejecta become offensive ; the pulse is almost imperceptible; the skin changes its dry heat for a clammy cold; the respiration grows loaded, the evacuations pass involuntarily; and after perhaps a short apparent improvement, stupor, insensibility, and sinking usher in death. On the other hand, if the fever intends yielding to treatment, it presents after the 7th day marked signs of abatement • the tongue is clearer, pain leaves the head and eyes, the face is no longer flushed; nausea ceases after profuse emesis of bile, and a faint appetite returns.

After the mildest attacks of the Zanzibar remittent, the liver acts with excessive energy: sudden exercise causes a gush or overflow of bile, which is sufficient to bring on a second attack. The debility, 'which is inordinate, may last for months. It is often increased by boils, which follow one another in rapid succession, and which sometimes may be counted by scores. Besides the wet cloth, the usual remedy to cause granulation, and to prevent the sore leaving a head, is to stuff it with camphor and Peruvian bark. When boils appear behind the head, the brain is sometimes affected by them, and patients have even sunk under their sufferings. The recovery, indeed, as in the case of the intermittent type,

FEVER.

is always slow and dubious, relapses are feared, and for six weeks there is little change for the better; the stomach is liable to severe indigestion ; the body is emaciated, and the appetite is excessive, or sickly and uncertain. The patient suffers from toothaches and swelled face, catarrh, hepatitis, emesis, and vertigo, with alternations of costiveness and the reverse. As I have already said, change of air and scene is at this stage more beneficial than all the tonics and preventives in the pharmacopoeia. Often a patient lying apparently on his death-bed recovers on hearing that a ship has arrived, and after a few days on board he feels well.

Diarrhoea and dysentery are mostly sporadic ; the former, however, has at times attacked simultaneously almost every European on the Island. It is generally the result of drinking bad water or sour wine, of eating acescent or unripe fruit, and of imprudent exposure. Dysentery is especially fatal during the damp and rainy weather. It was often imprudently treated with mere astringents, and without due regard to the periods of remission, and to the low form which inevitably accompanies it. As in remittents, the patient was weakened, and his stomach was deranged, with 'slops,' when essence of meat was required. The anti-diarrhoea or anti-cholera pill of opium, chalk, and catechu has been fatal wherever English medicine has extended; witness the Crimean campaign, where the bolus killed many more than did the bullet. A complication, rarely sufficiently considered, is the hepatic derangement, from which almost all strangers must suffer after a long residence in the Tropics. At Zanzibar some Europeans were compelled to give up breakfasting, to the manifest loss of bulk, stamina, and muscular strength —vomiting after the early meal, especially when eaten with a good appetite, was the cause. Yet it was a mere momentary nausea, and when the mouth had been washed no inconvenience was felt.

Catarrh and bronchitis are common in February and in the colder months of July and August. Of endemic pulmonary diseases, pneumonia, asthma, and consumption — the latter aggravated by the humid atmosphere—are frequent amongst the higher classes, especially the Arab women debilitated by over-seclusion. The incidental maladies are tropical rheumatisms, colics, haemorrhoids, and rare attacks of ophthalmia, simple, acute, and purulent. Haemorrhoids are very common both on the Island and the coast; the people suffer as much as the Turks in Egypt without wearing the enormous bag-trowsers which have been so severely blamed.

Of the epidemics, the small-pox, a gift of Inner Africa to the world, is fatal as at Goa or Madagascar. Apparently propagated without contact or fomites, it disfigures half the population, and it is especially dangerous to full-blooded Africans. About three years ago (1857) a Maskat vessel imported a more virulent type. Shortly before my arrival, numbers had died of the confluent and common forms, and isolated cases were reported till we left the Island. All classes were equally prejudiced against vaccination. The lymph sent from Aden and the Mauritius was so deteriorated by the journey that it probably never produced a single vesicle (1857).

Until 1859 cholera was unknown even by name. Col. Hamerton, however, declared that in 1835 hundreds were swept off by an epidemic, whose principal symptoms were giddiness, vomitihg and purging, the peculiar anxious look, collapse, and death. It did not re-appear for some years; but in a future chapter I shall no-, tice the frightful ravages which it made on the East African coast at the time of my return from the interior.

Hard water charged with lime and various salts, combined with want of vegetables, renders constipation a common ailment at Zanzibar. Amongst the rich it mostly arises from indolence, and from the fact that all are greatly addicted to aphrodisiacs. The favourite is a pill composed of 3 grains of ambergris, and 1 grain of opium, the latter ingredient in the case of an 'Afvmi' (opium-eater) must he proportioned to his wants.

'Doctors' in my day were unknown at Zanzibar. Formerly, two Indians practised; since their departure the people killed and cured themselves. Amongst Arabs, and indeed Moslems generally, every educated man has a smattering of the healing art. H. H. the late Sayyid was a 'hakim' of great celebrity. A physician is valuable on the Island; throughout the African interior he is valueless in a pecuniary sense, as every patient expects to he kept and fed. The midwives are usually from Cutch; Arabs, however, rarely consent to professional assistance. The Prince kept in his establishment two sages femmes from Maskat.

SECTION 4.

Notes on the Fauna of Zanzibar.

THE list of Zanzibarian Fauna and Flora is not extensive. In the plantations the Komba or Galago abounds, and there is a small and pretty long-tailed monkey (cercopithecus griseo-viridis) with black face, green back, and grey belly: it is playful and easily tamed. This, as well as a large species of bat, is pronounced delicious by curious gourmands. The French 'tigre ' and the English 'panther ' (Felis Serval) is a leopard about 18 inches high, and of disproportionate length, with a strong large arm ; the upper part of the skull vanishes as in the cheeta, and the throat is so thick that no collar will keep its place. This felis is destructive in the interior of the Island; and in parts of the Continent the people fear it more than they do the lion •. it is trapped in the normal cage, and is speared without mercy. Two kinds of civets (Yiverra civetta, and Y. genetta). one small, the other bigger than a Persian (Angora) cat, are kept confined, and are scraped once a week for their produce. As in all Arab towns, the common cat abounds ; it has a long tail and ears, a wild look, and a savage temper. This Asiatic importation is never thoroughly domesticated in Africa, and seems always aspiring' to become a 'cat o' mountain' : on the West coast it is difficult to keep cats in the house after kittening. The feline preserves its fur in Zanzibar Island: at Mombasah there is or was a breed more grotesque than the Manx, and completely bald like the Chinese dog. The so-called 'Indian badger ' (Arctonyx collaris, Cuv.) digs into the graves and devours the dead. The rodents are grey squirrels, small rabbits (?), large rats, some of peculiar but not of unknown species, and mice, probably imported hy the shipping. The 'wild boars ' are pigs left hy the Portuguese : strangers mistaking the tusks often describe them as 'horned' (choeropotamus). The Saltiana antelope is common : it smells strongly of musk, and its flesh resembles the rat's.

A fine large fish-hawk, with gold-fringed eye and yellow legs, bluish-black plume, and grey neck-feathers, haunts the Island and the coast: the other raptores are the brown kites (F.

chilla), the scavengers of Asia and Africa. As at Aden, so here, there are no common crows or sparrows ; the place of the former is taken by the African species (corvns scapulatus), with white waistcoat, popularly called the 'parson crow,' and the latter appears in the shape of the Java variety, which, introduced about thirty years ago (1857) by Captain Ward, a Salem ship-captain, has multiplied prodigiously. Green birds, like Amedavats, muscicapae of sorts, especially the 'king-crow' of India, here called' 'Drongo,' abound ; and visitors, like the Trench savant on the Dead Sea, speak of a humming-bird, a purely New World genus, probably mistaking for it a large hawk-moth. The parroquet resembles the small green species of India: it is tamed and taught to talk. Zanzibar cannot boast of the Madagascar parrot, a plain, brown, thick-bodied bird, celebrated for distinct articulation.[1] Martens do not build at Zanzibar (?) : they halt at the Island in their migrations ; and one kind, it has been remarked, never remains longer than four to five days. After the rains the lagoons are covered with wild-duck, mallard, and widgeon. The snipe (jack, common, and solitary),

[1] Mr Lyons M'Leod says (vol. ii. 34V) that a 'very handsome jet-black parrot ' is to be procared there.

a bird which everywhere preserves its fine game flavour, is found on the Island and in the central Continent. Sandpipers (charadrius hiaticula) run on the beach, and the waters support various kinds of cranes, gulls, and terns.

When fewer ships visited the port, the sand-spit projecting from 'Frenchman's Island' was covered with bav-turtle[1] (chelone esculenta or Midas), which the negroes were too indolent or ignorant to catch. The iguanas or harmless crocodiles '(oubeva. Se avSpa>7rcov aStxoucriv) of the Periplus, have not yet been killed out of Zanzibar—and there are several species.[2] Until lately the true crocodile was found in a small sweet stream about eight miles south of the town, and the monsters swarm in every river of the mainland.

Snakes are neither numerous nor deadly: possibly the climate, as in Ireland and Bermuda, is too damp for them. I heard of a python[3] resembling that of Madagascar and

[1] The ^eXwvt] dptivrj, or mountain-tortoise of the Periplus (chap. i. 15), may have been a turtle or terrapin. A small quantity of tortoise-shell is sold on the island by Malagashes (Madagascarians) and Comoro men.

[2] The iguana abounds on the West Coast of Africa, and in the Bonny Biver, where the huge hideous lizard is Ju-Ju—obnoxious to the honours of divinity.

[3] So Dr Boschenberger mentions at Zanzibar a coluber called boa-constrictor, and peculiar to America.

Iaclia; it is 18 feet long, and tliick as a man's thigh. Its favourite habitat is in sugar-cane patches near water, and it is occasionally fatal to a dog. There are water-snakes in the harbour, like those once supposed to be peculiar to Western India. The people speak of a green 'whip-snake'—vaguest of terms—whose vertebrae appear through the skin, and there are the usual legends of a venomous tree-serpent which can shoot itself like an arrow. The pagan Mganga or Medicine-man ties above the snake-wound a circle of wire with two small bits of wood strung upon it. This, he says, prevents the venom ascending; and doubtless the ligature is for half - an hour or so effective. The people have 'Eiss ' or serpent-stones, which suggest the Irish murrain-stones. Englishmen of undoubted character have recounted cures effected by this remedy, which was so mysterious before capillary attraction robbed it of its marvel.

There is a variety of small tiliquse, and of large black earth-lizards. One species, with melancholy chirrup and unpleasant aspect, supplies the people with Herodotean tales. It is, they say, a hermaphrodite, and its flanks are torn by its young during parturition. The chameleon also suffers from the popular belief that it kills men with its breath. Scorpions are small, and not so common as in the interior: the animal is mashed and applied as a poultice to its own wound, which may derive some benefit from the moisture. Centipedes haunt houses that are not cleaned and whitewashed, and millipedes abound in every plantation.

The fish supply is variable[1] as the climate. Sometimes it is excellent; at other times none but the poorest will eat it, and there are many species considered always poisonous.[2] It is most abundant in the S. West monsoon, when small fry may be caught in the still waters of the harbour. Sharks are large and numerous, especially near Chumbi (La Passe) Island, where all the best fish is netted ; but these tigers of the sea do not injure the bathers on the beach. Though the shark is easily hooked in the very harbour, many cargoes of its salted meat are annually imported from Oman. The liver-oil is used to anoint the body : and when Europe requires a

[1] have not seen the 'Pishes of Zanzibar,' published in 1867 by Lieut.-Col. Playfair, H.M.'s Consul, and Dr Gunther (Van Voorst, 1, Paternoster Eow).

[2] The eel-shaped fishes with green bones have the reputation of causing stomach-pains and vomiting. I may observe that the Oriental mind readily connects venom and verdant colours.

succadeneum for huile de nxorue, I shall recommend to her this shark-oil as an article of superior nauseousness.

The whale fishery reminds us of what it was on the Brazilian coast a century ago. The mammals are sometimes found in soundings, and a wounded sperm-whale lately entered Zanzibar harbour. In May, June, and July, ships of 200 to 600 tons visit the waters south of Mafiyah Island ; if the capricious leviathan he not found there and then, it is waste time to cruise about. In July, and at the beginning of the N. East monsoon, schools migrate up the coast in search of food as far as the Bed Sea. Erom 30 to 60 lbs. of ambergris have been brought in one year to the island, and a little of it is exported to Europe. This high-priced article (1 lb. = £14) is taken from the rectum of the spermaceti whale : it seems to have caused constipation and disease, and the oil drawn from these fish is yellow and bad. The Arabs burn it in pastiles, and use it not only internally but externally like musk. Old travellers report that the Somal taught camels to hunt for it by the scent, in the same way as pigs learn to find truffles ; and the tale has been told to modern travellers. The main virtue of ambergris is probably its heavy price.

The celebrated 'Sir' (Seer) fish, a corruption from Shir Mahi (^l.   or £ tiger fish/ so called' on account of its armature, known to the Arabs as Kunad (oA) and in parts of India termed 'Surma,' appears, for about a fortnight, at Zanzibar during its period of migration northwards in May and June. There are also £ pomfrets,' scates, soles which are small and not prized, and red and grey mullet, excellent in July, August, and September. The remora and the flying-fish enter the harbour; the hippocampus is known ; there are mangrove-oysters, £ oysters growing on trees '—a favourite subject with all old and with many new African travellers—and a small well-flavoured, rock oyster, a favourite relish with Europeans, caught about Chumbi Island. I saw no lobsters, so common in the Camaroons river of Western Africa. The sands abound in Medusse, or jelly-fish, and in a large cray-fish, which the Arabs consider wholesome for invalids : it makes a rather insipid salad, but it is excellent when dressed after the fashion of the Slave Coast. The receipt is worth giving, and may be found useful in England. The meat, taken out after boiling, is pounded and mixed wdth peppers and seasoning. It is then restored to the shell, the whole is baked in the oven, and, served up piping hot, it forms an admirable 'whet.' Another kind of shell-fish is indeed a 'soft crab ; ' when cooked it seems to melt away, no meat remaining within : a third, also soft, is red even before being boiled. On every unfrequented strip of sand or weed small crabs gather in thousands ; most of them have only one large claw, and their colours are a brilliant pink, pearly white, violet, and tender red.

The seas are little explored (1857), and there are legends of ichthyological marvels which remind us of European romantic zoology. I was told by Lieut.-Colonel Hamerton of a fish, possibly one of the Mursenidse, measuring nine feet long by three in diameter : the shape was somewhat like a leech, both extremities being similar; the *ribs* resembled, but were rather flatter than, those of a bullock, and the flesh had the appearance of beef. A specimen, he said, had lately been brought from Kipombui, a small harbour opposite Zanzibar ; the prey, however, is always cut up as soon as caught. This reminds us of the 'full-sized devil-fish ' of the West Indian seas. The Arabs describe a monstrous polypus, with huge eyes and arms 10 feet long: they declare that it has entangled bathers and pulled them down close to shore. It is, in fact, the 'piuvre,' so famed of late; and since I left Zanzibar a French illustrated newspaper showed one of these horrors grappling with a man of Avar's gig. Thus Oppian described a fish that smothered mariners with its monstrous Avings, and drew them under water wrapped in a lethal embrace. Nieuhoff (Brazil, 1640) mentions a 'lamprey ' at Pernambuco that 'snatched all that fell in this Avay (both men and dogs that swam sometimes after the boat) into the water.' Finally, Carsten Niebuhr (Arabia, chap. i. p. 140. 1762) declares that 'the cuttle-fish is dangerous to swimmers and divers, of whom it lays hold with its long claws; these do not wound, but produce swelling, internal pains, and often an incipient paralysis.'

Sponge is found in abundance, but when dry it decays. Fine conchological collections were chiefly made in former years. The merchants spoiled the market by supplying whole cargos for Avatch-dials and for polishing porcelain. Slaves still fasten their canoes to the several banks in the roadstead, and find in the transparent waters the murex and other prized specimens. The harp-shell and £ double-harp' are found upon the softer sands enveloped in the folds of their OAVU-ers; thus parasites cannot ruin their beautiful and brilliant hues. The 'Kheti,' or common cowrie, is picked np when the tide is ont in vast quantities by the coast people, from Ra'as Hafun to Mozambique. Lieut.-Colonel Hamexton was fortunate enough in .those early days to obtain two specimens of the Cyprsea Broderipii, or orange-cowrie, with a stripe down the dorsum. Exaggerated ideas of its value had been spread, and it was reported that £500 had been offered for a single shell. The cowrie trade of Zanzibar was begun by M. E. P. Herz, of Hamburg. He made a daring speculation, and supplanted in Western Africa the rare and expensive Hindostan shell by the coarse, cheap Cyprsea of this coast. During the last century the Portuguese used to export cowries for Angola from the Bio das Caravelhas, in Brazilian Porto Segura. The success of M. Herz's investment opened a mine of wealth. M. Oswald (senior), afterwards Prussian Consul-general at Hamburg, commenced as half-owner of a small vessel which shipped cowries at Zanzibar, and traded with them for palm-oil at Appi Vista, Whydah, Porto Novo, and lastly Lagos, on the Slave Coast. As the sack was bought for SO.50 to $1.44, and sold for $8 to $9, the trip cleared $2d,000 (£4800), paid half in coin, half in 'oil; ' and the single vessel soon increased to three. The owner was an excellent ship-master, who carefully supplied his employees with maps, charts, and sailing directions. He died in 1859, leaving a self-insuring fleet of 18 sail. In 1863 his sons had raised the number to 24, and they kept up large establishments at Lagos and Zanzibar.

The retail cowrie trade was solely in the hands of Moslems; the Banyans would not sanction the murder of their possible grandmothers. On the Continent, as on the Island, the shells are sunned till the fish dies and decays, spreading a noxious foetor through the villages. The collection is then stored in holes till exported to Zanzibar. There the European wholesale merchant garbles, washes, and stows away the shells in bags for shipment. They are sold by the 'Jizleh,' a weight varying according to the size of the shell : from 3 to 3.50 sacks would be the average. The price of the Jizleh presently rose to $7, to $8, and in 1859 it was about $9. Seven vessels were then annually engaged in carrying cargoes from Zanzibar to Lagos and its vicinity. This rude money finds its way to Tinbuktu (Timbuctoo) and throughout Central Africa, extending from the East to places as yet unvisited by Europeans. Of late years, however, the increased metallic currency lias caused the cowrie trade to fall off, and the steady rate of decrease shows that shell money is doomed.

Here, as in Western India, the rains, bring forth a multitude of pests. The rooms when lighted at night are visited hy cockroaches and flying ants; scarab sei and various mantidse; moths and 'death's heads' of marvellous hideousness. Giant snails (achatinse), millepedes, and beetles crawl over the country, and the firefly glances through the shade. Mosquitos are said not to he troublesome, but in an inner room I found curtains necessary; the house-fly is a torment to irritable skins. Pleas, and the rest of the 'piquante population,' are most numerous during the north-east monsoon. The bug, which was held to be an importation, is now thoroughly naturalized upon the Island ; in the interior it is as common as in the cities of Egypt and of Syria, where a broken rafter will discharge a living shower. I could not, however, hear anything of the 'Pasi bug,' which, according to Hr Krapf, causes burnings, chills, and fever. He made it to rival the celebrated Meeanee (Muganaj) bug, the Acarus Persicus, whose exceedingly poisonous bite was supposed to be fatal. In the Lake Ptegions of Central Africa (1.371) I have conjectured that the word is a corruption for Papazi, a carrapato, or tick. So Dr Krapf writes in the German way 'Sansibar' for Zanzibar.

The ants in Zanzibar, as in the Brazil, require especial study, and almost every kind of tree appears to have its peculiar tenantry. Upon the clove there is a huge black pismire whose nip hums like fire; as it has a peculiarly evil savour, tainting even the unaromatic 'hush,' it is mashed and stuffed up the nostrils as a cure for snake-bites. The Copal is colonized by a semi-transparent ginger-coloured formica, whose every bite draws blood, and the mango-leaf is doubled up by a smaller variety into the semblance of a bird's nest. The horrible odour in parts of the bush, which young African travellers attribute to malaria and which often leads them to suspect the presence of carrion, generally proceeds from ants : I remarked this especially w^rhe,n visiting Abeokuta and other places in West Africa. Throughout the interior ' drivers,' as they are sensibly termed on the Guinea Coast, visit the huts in armies, and soon clear them of all offal. A small black ant attacks meat,, and the best way to procure a clean skeleton is to expose the body near its haunt; beware, however, of cats and dogs. As in Africa generally, the termite is a plague; this small animal greatly obstructs civilization by the ravages which it commits upon books and manuscripts.

Few, if any, domestic animals are aborigines of the Island, and of those imported none thrive save Bozal negroes and asses. Cattle brought to Zanzibar die after the first fortnight, unless protected from sun, rain, and dew, and fed with dry fodder. The fatality resulting from the use of green meat leads here, as in the Con can and at Cape Coast Castle, to the impression that the grass is poisonous. At some places in the mainland, Pangani for instance, cattle will not live— this is certainly the .effect of tsetse. At Cape Coast Castle liorses always die ; at Accra they survive, if not taken away from the sea-board: in 1863, during a short march through the country, I found an abundance of the tsetse, or 'spear-fly.' The specimens sent by me to England were lost with other collections in the ill-fated £ Cleopatra.' As has lately been shown, the tsaltsal of Bruce is mentioned in Deut. xxviii. 42, in Isa. xviii. 5, and in Job xii. 7. Tbe word is translated fish-spear, harpoon, locust; but it is not proved that, tsaltsal and tsetse are the same fly, and the similarity of the two words may be the merest coincidence. The Banyans of Zanzibar, who, having no local deity like their more favoured brethren of Aden and Maskat, keep cattle for religious purposes, never sell their beasts, and energetically oppose their being slaughtered. Bullocks cost from $8 to $16, and are generally to be bought.

Sheep are principally the black-faced *Somali,* with short round knotted tails, which lose fat from rich grazing: in their own desert country they thrive upon an occasional blade of grass growing between the stones. The excessive purity of the air doubtless favours assimilation and digestion, and as the diet of the desert Arabs proves, life under such circumstances can be supported by a minimum of food. I believe that in early times the Persians introduced this animal into Somali and Galla-land. The Wakwafi, who are rich in black cattle, contemptuously call their Galla neighbours 'Esikiriesbi,' or 'short-tailed sheep,' from the article forming their only wealth. The Somali muttons are the cheapest, averaging from $1 to $3. There is also a 'Mrima' race, with rufous ginger - coloured, hairy coats, and lank tails like dogs: others, again, have a long, massive caudal appendage like Syrian or Cape wethers. These cost $2 to $5, and are considered a superior article. The most expensive are from the Island of Angazljah,

GOATS. 213

or Great Comoro, and they are often worth from $8 to $9. As a rule, Zanzibar mutton, like that of the Brazil, is much inferior to beef, and presents a great contrast with the celebrated 'gramfeds' of India.

Caponized goats in these regions are larger, fatter, and cent, per cent, dearer than sheep : I have heard of $15 to $16 being paid for the Comoro animal. The meat is preferred to mutton: my objection to it is the want of distinct flavour. Yet goats are always, offered as presents in the interior. Some of the bucks brought from the Continent have a peculiarly ungoatly appearance, with black points and dark crosses upon their tan - coloured backs and shoulders, and with long flowing jetty manes like the breast hair of a Bukhti or Bactrian camel. They must be kept out of the sun, and fed on vetches as well as grass, otherwise they will die during the rains from an incurable nasal running.

A stunted Pariah dog is found upon the Island and the Continent: here, as in Western Africa, it is held, when fattened, to be a dish fit for a (Negro) king. Some missionaries have tasted puppy stew — perhaps puppy pie — and have pronounced the flesh to be sweet, glutinous, and palatable. The horse is now a recognized article of consumption in Europe; the cat has long served its turn, as civet de lapin, without the honours of publicity; and the day may come when '£ dog-meat' will appear regularly in the market. I have often marvelled at the prejudices and squeamishness of those races who will eat the uncleanest things, such as pigs, ducks, and fowls, to Avhich they are accustomed, and yet who feel disgust at the idea of touching the purest feeders, simply because the food is new. It is indeed time to enlarge the antiquated dietary attributed to the Hebrew lawgiver, and practically to recognize the fact that, in the temperates at least, almost all flesh is wholesome meat for man.

European dogs at Zanzibar require as much attention as white babies, but these die whilst those live. They must be guarded from heat and cold, sun and rain, dew and wind. Their meals must be light and regular, soup taking the place of meat. They must be bathed in warm water, their coats should be carefully dried, they are sent to bed early, and their smallest ailments require the promptest treatment with sulphur, 'oil,' and other specifics, otherwise they will never live to enjoy the honourable status of peres et m&res de families. The great object is- to breed from them as soon as possible, and the Creoles thrive far better than even the acclimatized strangers. Arabs have been known to pay $50 for a good foreign watch-dog, hoping thus to escape the nightly depredations of the half-starved slaves. They are kind masters, great contrasts to the brutally cruel Negro, whose approximation to the lower animals causes him to tyrannize over them. On the West Coast of Africa the black chiefs often offer considerable sums for English dogs; but none save the lowest 'palm-oil rough ' would condemn the [c] friend of man ' to this life of vile African slavery. It is really pathetic to meet one of these unfortunate exiles in- the interior, where a white face is rarely seen : the frantic display of joy, and the evident horror at being left behind, have more than once made me a dog-stealer.

At Zanzibar, as upon the Continent, fowls may he bought in every village, the rate being 6 to 12 for the dollar, which a few years ago procured 36. They are lean, for want of proper food; ill flavoured, from pecking fish; and miserably small, the result of breeding in—the eggs are like those of pigeons. Yet they might be greatly improved; the central regions of Africa show splendid birds, with huge bodies and the shortest possible legs. This variety is found in the Brazil; and at Zanzibar the mixture of blood has produced a kind of bantam with a large foot. The black-boned variety of poultry, and that with the upright feathers—the 'frizzly fowl ' of the United States—are also bred here. Capons are manufactured by the blacks of Mayotte and Nosi-bdh (Great Island). How is it that the modern English will eat hens, when their great grandfathers knew how to combine the flavour of the male with the tenderness of the female bird ?

Peacocks are brought, as in the days of the Ophir trade, from Outch. Madagascar sends hard, tasteless geese and common ducks, and Mozambique supplies turkeys which are here eaten by Arabs. A local superstition prevents pigeon-breeding in the house: the birds are found wild on the opposite coast, but Moslems will not use them as food. The Muscovy duck, aw aborigine of the Platine Yalley, has of late years been naturalized—it is a favourite with Africans, who delight in food which gives their teeth and masticatory apparatus the hardest and the longest labour. The only gallinaceous bird which Africa has contributed to civilization, the Gwinea-hen, here called the 'Abyssinian cock,' is trapped by slaves upon the mainland, and is brought to the Island for sale. As might he expected so near their mother-country, there are seven or eight varieties of this valuable fowl, and until late years some of the rarest and the most curious have been unwittingly used for the table. In every part of the Arab world the Guinea-fowl has a different name : in Syria, for instance, it is called Dik el Rumi (not Dik el Habash) or Roman (Greek) cock, a term generally given to the turkey. It is curious on a coast of estuaries and great river-mouths that the flamingo was not seen hy us.

SECTION 5.

Notes on the Flora of Zanzibar.

THE prosperity of Zanzibar, the Island, has hitherto depended upon the cocoa and the clove-tree. The former grows in a broad hand around the shore: on the Continent it follows the streams as far as 60 miles inland. In Zanzibar the Arab saying that ᶜ cocoa and date cannot co-exist,' is literally correct; near Mombasah town, however, there is a fruit-bearing phcenix, and on the promontory, fronting the fort, there is a plantation of small stunted trees. Everywhere on the Pangani river we found the ' ᶜ brab,' a wild phoenix, as the word derived from the Portuguese ᶜ brabo,' corrupted from 'bravo,' or rather in the feminine (palma) 'brava,' suggests ; and it would appear that the cultivated variety might be induced to thrive. The country was almost denuded of the cocoa to make room for cloves, when the late Sayyid threatened confiscation to those who did not plant in proportion of one to three. There are now (1857) extensive nurseries in the MashambA (plantations), and as this palm hears after six or seven years, it soon recovered its normal status. Many trees are prostrated by gusts and tornados : the Hindus replant them by digging a hole, and hauling up the bole with ropes made fast to the neighbouring stems—this simple contrivance is here unknown.

The Wasawahili have many different names for the nut, viz. Kidaka, too green when it falls to the ground for any use but fuel; I)afu, or Kitdle, when the milk is drinkable, the husk is burned, and the shell is made into a ladle (maghraf) ; the Kordma, when the meat is fit to eat, and Nazi,[1] the full-grown nut ready for oil-making. This most useful of plants supplies, besides ?neat, wine and spirits, syrup and vinegar, cords, mats, strainers, tinder, firewood, houses and palings, boats and sails — briefly, all the wants of barbarous life. Every part of it may be pressed into man's service, from the sheath of the first or lowest leaf, used as a sieve, to the stalk of the young fruit, which,

[1] Nazi, in Kisawahili, is tlie fruit, Mnbzi the tree : in this case the initial letter is evidently a contraction of Mti, a tree. The name for the sun-dried meat, 'kobra,' is borrowed from, the Hindustani 'khopra.'

divested of the outer coat, is somewhat like our chestnut. During the hot N. East monsoon the refrigerating, diuretic milk is a favourite with strangers, and much feared by natives. A respectable man is derided if seen eating a hit of ripe cocoa-nut, a food for slav.es and savages from the far west, hut he greedily consumes the blancmange-like pulp of the Dafu, which is supposed, probably from its appearance, to secrete virility. Rasped, the ripe kernel enters into many dishes; the cream squeezed from it is mixed with boiled rice, and the meat, kneaded with wheat-flour and clarified butter, is made, as at Goa, into scone-like cakes. No palm-wine is so delicious as that of the cocoa-tree, and the vinegar is proportionally good. The Zerambo, or distillation from 'toddy,' is adulterated with lime, sugar, and other ingredients, which render it unpalatable as it is pernicious.

Eormerly there were many cocoa-nut oil-mills in the town ; now (1857) they are transferred to the plantations where Sesamum (Simsim) is also crushed. The 'Engenho' is ruder than in the Brazil. A camel, blind-folded to prevent it eating the oil-cake or striking work, paces slowly round the 'horse-walk,' moving a heavy beam; this rolls a pestle of 6 inches in diameter in a conical wooden mortar, flat-rimmed above, and 1 feet deep, by 3 wide. Formerly as many as 70,000 lbs. were exported in a single vessel. Now the people save trouble by selling' the dried nut, and when oil is wanted for home use they press and bruise it in water, which is then boiled; consequently, though the tree again begins to cover the Island Coast, the oil is three times dearer than at Bombay. It is calculated that 12,000,000 nuts were exported last year (1856) for the soap and candle trades, and a single French house has an establishment capable of curing 50,000 per diem. Demand has prodigiously raised the price of this article. In 18-12 the thousand cost from $2 to $2.50; in 1857 it was $12.50. Though the coir of Zanzibar is remarkably fine and was much admired at Calcutta, little use is made of it: some years ago certain Indian Moslems tried to obtain a contract from the local Government, and did not succeed, prepayment being the first thing insisted upon.[1]

The constitutional indolence of the people, their dislike to settled and regular work, and their Semitic unwillingness to venture money, have, despite cheap labour and low ground-rents, prevented the Island from taking to its most ap-

[1] I shall speak of the clove in a subsequent chapter.

propriate industry — sugar-growing. Refiners are agreed that the cane in Zanzibar and Pemba is equal to that in any part of Asia. About three years ago (1857) the late Sayyid established a factory at his estate of Mohayra under a Frenchman, M. Classun, an assistant, and 32 supervisors. Compelled to live in the interior, they sickened, and died off, and thus Mauritius lost another dangerous rival. A superior article was also made by the Persians, hut they all caught fever, and either perished or disappeared. The sugar now grown is consumed on the Island, and there is only one steam-mill belonging to the Sayyid.

Cotton is said to thrive upon the Island, but the irregular rains must often damage the crop. At present a small quantity for domestic use is brought from the coast, where there .are plots of the shrub growing almost wild. In the drier parts of the Benadir, however, the material for hand-made cloth must be brought from India, mostly from Surat.

The virgin soils of Zanzibar, in fact, labour under only one disadvantage,—the faineantise of the people, but that one is all in all, hence complaints concerning the expense. In the "West India plantations 1 head was allowed per acre of cane, per 2 acres of cotton, and per 3 acres of coffee. Here 4 head would hardly do the work; slave labour is bad, and free labour is worse.

Coffee was once tried in tbe Island, but the clove soon killed it; now not a parcel is raised for sale. The berry, which was large and flavourless, was not found to keep well. The over-rich soil produces an undue luxuriance of leafage, and the shrub lacks its necessary wintering.

In the Brazil the richest lands are given to coffee, the next best to sugar, and the worst to cotton and cereals. The Zanzibar coast from Mombasah to Mozambique produces small quantities of coffee. Here great care is given to it; the berry has a peculiarly dry and bitter flavour, pleasant when familiar, and producing when first taken wakefulness and nervous excitement. At present the Island imports her supplies from Malabar and Yemen. The consumption is not great; the Arabs, who hold it a necessary of life at home, here find it bilious, and end by changing it for betel-nut. The coast growth sells in small lots, at various prices, and may become an article of export. In the African interior the shrub is indigenous between Northern TJnyamwezi (S. Lat. 1° O') and Southern Abyssinia (N.

Lat. 10°); and, as it is found on the Western Coast growing wild about the Rivers Nunez and Pongo (N. Lat. 10° 1'), it probably extends in a broken band across the Continent. There appear to be many varieties of the shrub. In Karagwah the wild bean is little bigger than a pin's bead. Harar exports a peculiarly large species, which sells as Mocha, and the Mozambique coffee does not at all resemble in flavour that of West Africa. Dr Livingstone (Missionary Travels, chap. x.) tells us that coffee brought from Southern Arabia to Angola by the Jesuits was spread probably by agency of birds to 300 leagues from the coast. It has long been £ monkeys' food,' but it is now worked by the ex-slavers.

Indigo bere, as well as in most parts of intertropical Africa, grows wild. The great expense of establishments, with the time and trouble, the skill and attention required for the manufacture, will leave it in the hands of Nature for many years to come.

Tobacco might be raised : the plant extends thoughout Eastern and Central Africa, wherever the equinoctial rains fall. Usumbara exports to Zanzibar stiff, thin, round cakes which have been pounded in wooden mortars, and neatly packed in plantain leaves. It is dark and well-flavoured :

sailors pronounce it to be very 'chawable.' Here it sells at two pice,[1] or f *d.*, per cake; at Usumbara it commands about one-fiffck of that price, paid in cloth and food.

The oil palm (Elseis Guineensis), whose produce has done so much for the Guinea Coast and the fatal Bight of Biafra, is found, I am told, on the Island of Pemba, and at other places near Zanzibar. About the Lake Tanganyika it grows in abundance; the fruit, however, is a raceme, like the date's, not a spike, as in the Bonny river. The 'Mchikichi ' is, therefore, a different and probably an unknown species. Like that of West Africa, it supplies wine as well as oil (The Lake Begions of Central Africa, vol. ii. p. 59). The palm-oil might easily be introduced into Zanzibar, and would doubtless thrive ; but the people have enough to do without it.

The Mbono or Palma Christi springs up spontaneously, as in most tropical regions, throughout Zanzibar Island and on the coast. The Hindus say of a man with more vanity than merit, 'The castor shrub grows where other plants can't.' The seed is toasted in iron pots, pounded, and boiled to float the oil. After

[1] The Hindu anna, which contains four pice, is here reckoned at eight.

aloes it is tlie popular cathartic, and it is rubbed upon the skin to soften the muscles, with an effect which I leave to the nasal imagination. Cinnamon and nutmeg trees were planted by the late Sayyid, and flourished well on some soils. The latter takes nine years, it is said, before bearing fruit, and gives trouble—two fatal objections in Arabs' eyes. Tbe spice is now imported from India. When at Kazak of Unyamwezi I saw specimens brought, it is said, from the Highlands of Karagwah, but the plentiful supply from the farther East would prevent this trade being here developed. The cacao shrub (chocolate), which thrives so well at Prince's Island and Eernando Po in the Biafran Bight, has never, I believe, been tried in Zanzibar.

The Mpira, or caoutchouc tree, flourishes in the Island, and on the adjacent Continent. The people of Eastern Madagascar tap it in the cold season, and have sent large cargoes to America. Mr Macmillan, U. S. Consul, Zanzibar, offered $1000 for good specimens, but the Wasawahili would not take the trouble to make a few incisions. I heard of two varieties, a ficus and a lliana; there are probably many more: about the Gaboon river the valuable gum is the produce of a vine or climber, with an edible fruit, and the people have learned to extract a coarse article, and to adulterate it till it is hardly tradeable. Here they use the thinner branches, well oiled for suppleness, as 'bakurs '—the policeman's truncheon, the cat-o'-nine-tails, the [6] Chob,' and the 'Palmatorio ' of E. Africa. I may here remark that our gourd-shaped articles resist the climate of Zanzibar, whilst the squares and the vulcanized preparations become sticky and useless. The London-made blankets of smooth and glazed caoutchouc are so valuable that no traveller should be without them : those that are not polished, however, cannot be called waterproof; becoming wet inside, they are unpleasantly cold. Eor exposure to the sun white impermeables must be preferred to black, and a first-rate article is required; our cheap boots and cloaks soon opened, and when exposed to great heat they were converted into a viscid mass.

The tamarind, as in India, is a splendid tree, but the fruit, though used for acidulated drinks, is not prepared for exportation. A smooth-rooted sarsaparilla, of lighter colour than the growth of the Brazil and Jamaica, is found wild upon the Island and the coast. The orchilla, which gives its name to the Insulse Purpurarise, has been

tried, and, resembling that of the Somali country, it gives good colour. This lichen chooses the forks of trees in every lagoon. In the Consular report by Lieutenant-Colonel Playfair on the trade of Zanzibar for the year 1863, I find—
'Orchilla is obtained from the more arid parts of the coast to the north: none grows on the Island.'

The people of Zanzibar are fond of fruits, especially the mango, the orange, the banana, and the pine-apple. All of these, however, except the plantain—the bread-fruit of Africa—are seedlings, and engrafting is not practised. Wall-fruit is of course unknown.

The mango, originally imported from India, and as yet unplanted in the central regions, is of many varieties, which lack, however, distinguishing names. Two kinds are common—a large green fruit like the Alphonse (Affonso) of Western India, and a longer pome, with bright red-yellow skin, resembling the Goanese £ Kola.' These, with care, might rival the famous produce of Bombay: even in their half-wild state the flavour of turpentine is hardly perceptible. The fruit is said to be heating, and to cause boils. The Arabs spoil its taste by using steel knives : with the unripe fruit they make, however, excellent jams, and pickles[1] eaten in broths of fowl or meat. The pounded kernels are administered in dysenteries, hut the relish or sauce of which the Gaboon people are so fond is unknown here and even in India. The fruit is most plentiful during the N. East monsoon.

There are many varieties of the orange, all, however, inferior to the produce of the Azores and the Brazil, of Malta and the Mozambique. The 'native' fruit, supposed to be indigenous, is green, not so sweet as the kinds grown by the Portuguese, and the coat must be loosened by two days' exposure to the sun or it can hardly be removed. It seldom ripens before the beginning of July, and it is best in August. The Persian variety, from about Bandar Abbas, comes to market in early May; it has grown common since 1842, and it has excelled its original stock. The peel is loose and green, and the meat, when cleared of pips, tastes somewhat like currants. The small brick-red Mandarin is good, and resembles the African and Brazilian Tangerine. The trees want care, they run to wood, the fruit is often covered with a hard, rough, thick, and almost inseparable rind, and

[1] The mango pickles of Makdishu are described by Ibu Batutah in. A.D. 1331.

the inside is full of bitter seeds, pithy placenta, and fluffy skins. The wild oranges upon the Island and the Continent resemble those which we call Seville. As a rule the 'golden apple' abounds from May to October. It is considered cooling, antibilious, and antiseptic, especially when eaten before other food in the early morning. Thus it was a saying in the Brazil that the physician does not enter that house where orange-peel is strewed about. In "West Africa the Bev. Mr Brown [1] of Texas judged the fruit harshly, and predicted the death of a brother missionary who was too fond of it. Many boxes and bags of oranges are carried as presents from Zanzibar to the northern ports (Banadir), Aden, and even Bombay; 'Gulf-Arabs,' who have not such luxuries at home, will here devour a basket-full at a sitting. The sweet limes of Zanzibar are considered inferior to none by those who enjoy the sickly 'mawkish' flavour: the acid limes are cheap, plentiful, and aromatic; they are second only to those grown about Maskat, the ne plus ultra of perfume and flavour.

. [1] Missionary of the Southern Baptist Connexion. He published a book of Travels in Western Africa, and a Grammar and Dictionary of the Yoruba language, printed by the Smithsonian Institution (May, 1858).

FRUITS. 231

Tlie Pamplemouse or Shaddock, the Pummalo of Bombay (Citrus Decumana), has been planted upon the Island, but the people declare that it will not ripen: the same is said of the citron, and the Zan'zibarians ignore the Persian art of preserving it.

Bananas at Zanzibar are of two varieties, red and yellow: they are not remarkable for delicacy of taste. In the highlands of the interior, as Usumbara and Karagwah, the 'musa ' may be called the staff of life. The plantain, in India termed ᶜ horse-plantain,' is a coarse kind, sometimes a foot long, and full of hard black seeds: Europeans fry it in butter, and the people hold it to be a fine ᶜ strong ' fruit. The musa bears during all the year in Zanzibar, but it is not common in May and June.

The pine-apple of the New World grows almost wild in every hedgerow and bush : cultivation and planting near running water would greatly improve it. At present the crown is stuck in the earth, and is left to its fate wherever the place may be. Strangers are advised to remove the thick outer rind, including all the 'eyes,' which, adhering to the coats of the stomach, have caused inflammation, dysentery, and death. The ananas ripens in the cold season : when it is found throughout the twelve months the people predict that next year it will fail. It is, in fact, a biennial, like the olive in Palestine.

The especial fruits of the-poor are the Panas or 'Jack ' of India, and an even more fetid variety, the 'Doriyan,' which certain writers call the c Aphrodisiac dorion.' Some Europeans have learned to relish the evil savour, and all declare the Jack to he very wholesome. Hindus refuse to touch it, because it is 'heating food:' they say the same, however, of all fruits with saccharine juices. The nuts are roasted, and eaten with salt, as in India, and the villagers fatten their poultry with 'the rind and the rotten.'

The bread-fruit, and the curious growth (Ravenala) known as the 'Travellers' Tree,' were introduced from the Seychelles Islands: the young plants, however, were soon uprooted and strewed about the fields. Grapes, both white and red, look well, but, as in the Tropical Brazil, the bunches never ripen thoroughly; in fact, the same cluster will contain berries of every age, from the smallest green to the oldest purple. This is a great disadvantage when making wine, and requires to be corrected by syrup. The grape can hardly he expected to thrive where the hot season, as in parts of the New World, is also the rainy season. Like the produce of the Gold Coast, the stones are large and hitter, and the skin is tart, thick, and leathery. Bacchus, though he conquered India and founded Nysa, seems to disdain the equinoctial regions. According to the French another variety should he introduced, and perhaps the ground-grape of the Cape might succeed better. There are many varieties of the vine in the Central Continent, hut the people have hardly learned to eat the fruit : at Zanzibar certain Arabs tried it with sugar and rose-water, and suffered in consequence from violent colics. We read in 'El Bakui ' (A.D. 1403) that some vines bear three crops per annum.

The water-melon, most wholesome of fruits in warm climates, is found in Zanzibar and in the Lake Legions of the interior: the best are said to grow' about Lamu and Brava. It is a poor flavourless article, white-yellow (not white and pink) inside, dry, and wanting the refreshing juice; it is fit only for boiling, and its edible seed is the best part. The growth of the papaw • is truly tropical; a single year suffices to hang the tree with golden fruit, which is eaten raw and boiled. Hindus, as usual, object to its £ beat; ' tbe Arabs make from tbe pips, which taste like celery, a sberbet, -wbicb is said to have peculiar effects.[1]

Tbe 'Khwemwe ' tree bears a nut with a bard reticulated skin: tbis is roasted like tbe chestnut, and it affords a small quantity of oil. The Sita-phal (Annona squamosa) and its congener, the Jam-phal, or sour-sop (A. reticulata), grow wild over the Island and tbe Coast; as in tbe Brazil, little attention is paid to them ; tbis c custard-apple ' is here considered to be a wholesome fruit. Tbe guava is popularly called Zaytun, which means 'olive,' a quasi-sacred fruit, possibly on tbe principle that in England many growths become palms about Easter-time. It runs wild around Mombasah, and spreads over much ground by a peculiar provision of nature :[2] tbe guavas are said not to ripen well; yet on the West coast they are excellent. The Jamli, a well-known Indian tree (Eugenia Jambu), whose somewhat austere, subacid fruit resembles tbe damson or bullace, is everywhere common. In

[1] The 'hot amourist ' pronounces this drink to he *CJ*

[2] The seeds cannot easily he digested. Thus the lo-wer regions of Fernando Po are a thicket of guava, suggesting the Jackal-coffee of the Neilgherries.

A.D. 1331 the traveller Ihn Batutah found El Jammiin (^AA) at Mombasah.

The interior of the Island produces the 'Eursad,' a small stunted variety of the Persian red mulberry ; the 'Tut,' or white species, grows in every jungle from the shore of the Mainland to Euga, in Bsumbara, and suggests the possibility of rearing silk-worms. The pomegranate here, as on the Coast, gives a fruit which is hardly eatable : during the season Omani ships bring a supply of the very best description from the Jebel el Akhzar (the Green Mountain), near Maskat, and apples from the Persian Gulf. The Badam, locally called Bidam (the Persian almond), is here barren; the broad polished leaves are used as platters by the vegetarian Hindus. The Chinese Bambotang or Leechee is neglected, and the fruit is poor. The Ber (jujube) is unusually well-flavoured; according to Moslem custom, the Arab dead are washed with an infusion of the leaves. That South American growth the Mbibo or Cashew (Caju) tree abounds here and on the continental sea-board: the nuts are roasted, the pulp is eaten, though its astringent quince-like flavour is by no means pleasant, and the juice is distilled, as at Goa. After pressure, the yield, exposed two or three days for fermentation, produces the celebrated 'Cauim' (Caju-ig) of the Brazilian Tupy-Guarani race, a wine here unknown. The still yields at first a watery spirit, which by cohobation becomes as fiery and dangerous as new rum. The lower orders like it; the effects, they say, last out the week.

The principal wild trees are the following. The fan palm, a native of the Island and the Continent, supplies the chief African industry—mat-making. The 'Toddy palm' is found everywhere ; the fruit is eaten, but no one cares to draw off the beverage. The Dom, or Theban palm (Hyphene Thebaica), is a rare variety, and the wood is used chiefly for ladder rungs. Gigantic Baphias, called by the Arabs Nakhl el Shaytan, 'the Devil's palm,' throw over the streams fronds 30 and 40 feet long: these, cut, stripped, and bound into rafts, are floated down and exported from the Mainland to the Island ; the material is soft and good for hut-making. The graceful Areca palm flourishes everywhere, especially upon the banks of the Pangani river : at the mouth of this stream a saw-mill might be set up for a few dollars, and I have no doubt that it would yield large profits, and extend its business as far as the Red Sea.

The Bombax, or silk-cotton tree (Eriodendrum anfractuosum), the Arab Dibdj and the Ivisawahili Msufi, common in East as in West Africa, affords a fibre usually considered too short and brittle for weaving, but I have seen Surat cotton very nearly as bad. The contents of the pericarp have been used for pillow stuffings : the only result *(dicunt)* was a remarkable plague of pediculi. The Kewra, or frankincense tree of India, abounds. The red beans of the Abrus Precatorius are used by the poor and by the wild people as ornaments ; even the mixed Luso-African race of Annobom will wear huge strings of this fruit, our original 'carat.' The soft-wooded Baobab, Mbuyu or calabash tree (Adansonia digitata), grows rapidly to a large size upon the Island as upon the Eastern and Western coasts. It is a tree of many uses. The trunk, often girthing 40 feet, forms the water-tank, the trough, the fisherman's Monoxyle ; the fibrous hark is converted into cloth, whose tough network is valued by the natives; the fruit pulp is eaten, and the dried shells serve as Brxyu, or gourds. I have repeatedly alluded to this tree in the Lake Regions of Central Africa, and I shall offer other notices of it in the following pages. Of late the Mbuyu or Baobab has brought itself into notice as affording a material more valuable for paper than straw, esparto or wood pulp, and its superiority to other African basts, has been acknowledged in England.[1] The Mpingo (Dalbergia Melanosylum) gives a purple timber, not a little like rosewood. The 'African oak,' a species of teak, is reported to exist; but this tree does not extend far north of Mozambique. The 'P'hun' is a stately growth, whose noble shaft, often 80 feet high, springs without knot or branch, till its head expands into a mighty parachute. It is more ornamental than useful,—the wood is soft, full of sap, like our summer timber, and subject to white ants. In these hot, wet, and windy tropical regions some trees, especially those without gum or resinous sap, grow too fast, and are liable to rot, whilst others take many years to mature, and are almost unmanageably hard and heavy. Hence we have had timber-cutting establishments set up hy our Government. at a large expense in the Brazil and in West Africa, but the produce never paid the voyage to England.

[1] According to my friend Mr P. L. Simmonds (The Journal of Applied Science) this bast fetches readily £14 to £15 per ton., and 'although the paper makers will buy any quantity brought to market, it is to he regretted that they will offer no combined assistance to facilitate the obtaining larger supplies of this important product.'

The woods known to commerce are the 'LiwcV a white-veined, faintly-perfumed, bastard sandal from Madagascar: it is used for the sacred fire hy the poorer Parsees. Granadille wood is exported from the Mainland to Europe, where it is worked for the bearings of mills and for the mouth-pieces and flanges of instruments. The Arabs call it 'Abnus,' and the Sawahili 'Mpingo,' both signifying ebony, which it resembles in appearance, though not in qualities. Less brittle than ebony, and harder than lignum vitae, it spoils the saw; and being very heavy, it refuses to absorb grease or water. It makes good ram-rods, and the Usumbara people have cut it into pipe-bowls long before our briar-root was dreamed of.

The sweet-smelling £ Kalambak' (Yulg. Columbo), once common upon the Island, is now brought from Madagascar. There are two kinds,
■—one poor and yellow, like our box, the other hard, heavy, and dark red. Its fine grain takes the high polish of mahogany, and it would make good desks and work-boxes. Comoro men and Indian carpenters turn out rude furniture of this wood, which is wilfully wasted: in felling and shaping it the plantation-slaves, who ignore the saw, chip away at least half. The smoke is

said, to keep off mosquitos. The mango, the jack, the copal tree, and many others, give fine hard woods for cabinet work.

Planks and scantling, cross-beams and door-panels, are made of two fine trees, the 'Mtimbati ' and the c Mvule.'[1] The negro carpenters always sacrifice, I have said, a tree to make a plank, and the latter is so heavy that for all light erections, such as upper rooms, boards must be imported from Europe. The Mtimbati is the more venous ; rungs of ladders, well kept and painted, will last 15 years. The enduring Mvfile, a close-grained yellow wood, is rare upon the Island, but common in the Coast jungles. As is the case with the Kalambak, there is no tariff for these trees : what to-day is sold at a bazar auction for $1 may in a week fetch $8. A good practical account of the medicinal plants and timbers of Madagascar and Mozambique, Zanzibar and the Seychelles, will be found in appendices A. B. vol. ii. of Mr Lyons McLeod's 'Travels in Eastern Africa, with a Narrative of a Residence in Mozambique.' Captain Guillain may also be consulted, vol. i. p. 23—25.

The Bordi or Zanzibar rafters are felled by

[1] The Inzimbati (a leguminosa) and Invouli of Capt. G-uillain.

slaves on the Mainland, and are brought over by Arabs and other vessels. The material is the useful mangrove, of which we here find the normal two species ; the Arabs call both 'Gurum,' and prefer the Makanda, or red kind. At Zanzibar the posts which become worm-eaten, and are reduced to powder by white ants, must he changed every five years. In arid Maskat they will last out the century, and they find their way to Aden, to Jeddah, and even to Meccah. The usual price in the Island is $2 to $3 per [c] Korjah,' or score.

The Mti wa Muyt.u (wild wood), or white mangrove, is found growing not in brackish water, and upon the mud, like the red variety, but chiefly upon the higher sandy levels, The wood is small, it shrinks when dried, it splits easily, and snaps; it is worm-eaten at once, and its porous nature causes it easily to absorb water. In Zanzibar it is used for fuel in lime-burning, and it makes a hot and lasting fire ; the people also turn it into caulking mallets, which do not crack or spread out. The usual price (1857) is half a German crown per Korjah.

Yegetables are little prized at Zanzibar : the list is rather of what might be than of what exists. A local difficulty is the half-starved slave who plunders every garden; nothing less than a guard of Baloch would preserve edible property from his necessities and from his truly African wantonness of destruction.

Almost all European vegetables will grow in the Island; they require, however, shade, and they should be planted, as at Bourbon and the Mauritius, between rows of cool bananas. The best soil is the dark vegetable mould near the streams. Here lettuces, beet-root, carrots, potatoes, and yams would flourish—cabbages and cauliflowers have never, I believe, been tried. The 'Jezar,' an excellent sweet potato from Comoro and Madagascar, has been neglected almost to extinction. Thirty barrels of many sorted beans were sent from the Cape and grew well: they are good and abundant in the African interior, but the Island has allowed them to die out. The 'egg-plant' is remarkably fine, and the wild species thrives everywhere on the sea-board between Somali land and Zanzibar. The Continent sends sundry kinds of pumpkins and gourds. Cucumbers of many varieties grow almost without sowing,—the people declare that they become bitter if touched by the hand whilst being peeled. The Arabs make from the seed an oil of most delicate flavour, far superior for salads than the best Lucchese olive. In London I bave vainly asked for 'cucumber-oil: ' the vegetable is probably too expensive, and the seeds are too small to be thus used at home. About Lagos on the Slave Coast, however, there is a cucumber nearly a foot long, with large pips, which might be sent northwards, and I commend the experiment to the civilized lover of oil. All kinds of 'Chilis,' from the small wild 'bird-pepper ' to the large variety of which the Spaniards are so fond, thrive in Zanzibar, which appears to be their home. There are extensive plantations of betel-pepper on the Eastern coast of the Island.

Wheat, barley, and oats here run to straw. Eice is the favourite cereal. The humid low-lands are cleared of weeds by burning, and the seed is sown when the first showers fall. To judge from the bazar-price, the home-grown article is of a superior quality ; but nowhere in East Africa did I find the grain so nutritious as that of the Western Coast. The hardest working of all African tribes, the Ivru-men, live almost entirely upon red rice and palm-oil. The clove mania has caused the cereal to be neglected ; formerly an export, it is now imported, and-in 1860 it cost the Island £38,000. Jowari (Holcus Sorghum), here called by the Arabs Ta'am (food), and by the Wasawahili Mtama,—an evident conniption,—is sown in January and February, and ripens 6 months afterwards. The wheat of the poorer Arabs, and the oats of horses, it grows 18 feet high, but the islanders have little leisure, except in the poorest parts, to cultivate. Banyans, Arabs, and Wasawahili buy it in the Brava country, the granary of Southern Arabia, on the sea-board from Tanga to Mangao, and in some districts of the near interior ; they retail it in Zanzibar at large profits. Sesamum (the Hindustani Til or Gingil, the Arabic Simsim), the commonest of the oleaginous grains, of late demanded by the French market, where the oil becomes huile d'olives, is also brought from the Mainland, especially from the northern ports, Larnu and its neighbours, the Banddir or Haven-land. In 1859 the Island of Zanzibar exported 8,388,360 lbs, = £20,000. Besides this, the coast ports shipped several cargos directformerly, East Africa used to supply the Bed Sea with this article.

Maize (Muhindi) is a favourite article of consumption, and a little is grown on the Island. Bajrl (Mdwele, Panicum spicatum, Boxb.), the small millet, a thin grain, inferior to that of Cutch and Western India, is little cultivated.

The gram[1] of Hindustan (in Arabic, Hummus ; in Persian, Nukhud; and in Kisawahili, Dengu, Cicer Arietinum) is of several varieties, white and red. The Lubiya pulse is also of many sizes and colours ; the black flourishes everywhere, the red is common, and the white, which the Portuguese of Goa import from the Mozambique regions, is rare: The best and largest comes from Pemba Island; it is also grown on the Continent. The leguminous T'hur (the Arabic Turiyan, and the Kisawahili Baradi, Cajanus Indicus) is almost wild: the Banyans mix it with rice, and make with it the well-known * I)all ' and 'Kicbri.' The small green pea, known in India as Mung (the Persian Mash, and the Kisawahili Chiroko, or Toka, Phaseolus Mungo, Koxb.),is boiled and eaten with clarified butter (Ghi) like T'hur. The people also use the little black grain resembling poppy-seed, known in India as IJrat; in Cutch, Papri; and here, P'hiwf (Phaseolus radiatus).' The Muhogo, in the plural 'Mihogo,' or White Cassava (Manihot Aypim), resembles in appearance the sweet Manioc of the Brazil (Aypim or Macaxeira). The knotted stem, about six feet

[1] Palpably : corruption of tbe Portuguese Grao—grain generally.

long, is crowned with broad digitated leaves; the conical root, however, has a distinct longitudinal fibre the size of small whipcord, which is not found in the 'black, or poisonous, Manioc ' (Jatropha Manihot, or Manihot utilissima). The people have not attempted to masticate it into a means of intoxication, the Caysuma of the Brazilian Tupy.[1] The Muhogo grows everywhere in Zanzibar Island: it is planted in cuttings during the rains, and it ripens six or eight months afterwards. In the Consular reports for 1860 we are told that 'the Manioc or Cassava, which forms the chief food of the slaves and poorer classes, yields *four* crops a year.' This is not probable: the longer all Jatropha is kept in the ground, within certain limits, the larger and better is the root. Manioc is carried as an acceptable present by travellers going into the interior.

At Zanzibar the traveller should train his stomach to this food, and take care not to call it 'Manioc.' When raw it resembles a poor chestnut, but in this state none save a servile stomach can eat it without injury. Europeans compare

[1] I have read in some book that the 'Pywaree ' of Guiana is made from the masticated and fermented juice of the cassava-[1] flower '—probably for—'flour.'

it with, parsnips and wet potatoes : the Hindus declare it to be heavy as lead, and so ' cold ' that it always generates rheumatism. The Wasawahili have some fifty different ways of preparing it. Boiled, and served up with a sauce of ground-nut cream, it is palatable: in every bazar sun-dried lengths, split by the women, and looking like pipe-clay and flour, are to be bought: a paste, kneaded with cold water, is cooked to scones over the fire: others wrap the raw root in a plantain-leaf and bake it, like greeshen, in the hot ashes. The poorer classes pound, boil, stir, and swallow the thick gruel till their stomachs stand out in hold relief. Bull of gluten, this food is by no means nutritious; and after a short time it produces that inordinate craving for meat, even the meat of white ants, which has a name in most African languages.

. The Bhang (Cannabis Sativa), which grows plentifully, though not wild, in the interior of the Continent, is mostly brought to Zanzibar from India. In Mozambique the Portuguese call it Bange or Canhamo de Portugal (Portugal hemp), and in the Brazil it is also known as Bange, evidently the Hindustani 'Bhang.' The negroes smoke it for intoxication, but ignore the other luxurious preparations familiar to Hindustan, Egypt, and Turkey.

Wanga or arrow-root, globular like a variety found in the Concan, is much less nutritious than the long kind. Here the best is brought from Mombasah, and after the rains the southern coast could supply large quantities. The people levigate the root, wash, and sun-dry it: the white powder is then kneaded with Tembu (palm-wine) into small balls, which are boiled in the same liquid. It is ᶜ cold ' and astringent: the Arabs use it as a remedy for dysentery, and the Hindus declare that it produces nothing but costiveness. Ginger thrives in the similar formation of Pemba, and yet it will not, I am assured, grow at Zanzibar, where it is imported from Western India, the tea being in this climate a good stomachic. The Calumba or Colombo root is largely exported to adulterate beers and bitters. Curious to say, the ground-nut, which extends from Hnyamwezi to the Gambia, is rare at Zanzibar.

The corallines of the coast are of course destitute of metals. A story is told of an ingenious Erenchman who, wishing to become Director of Mines in the service of H. H. the Sayyid, melted down a few dollars, and ran a vein of silver, most unfortunately, into a mass of madrepore : the curious 'gangue ' was shown to Lieutenant-Colonel Hamerton, and thus the 'cute experiment failed. The African interior heyond the mountains is rich in copper and iron. I have described the copper of the Taganyika Lake Region: it is said to he collected in small nuggets from torrent-beds, and the bars have evidently been cast in sand. The iron of the Umasai country makes the finest steel.

Gold has undoubtedly been brought from the mountains of Chaga; and the eastern plateau promises to rival in auriferous wealth the Gold Coast. The great fields north of and near the Zambeze, and N. West of Natal, beyond the Transvaal Republic, discovered in 1866-7 by the German explorer, M. Mauch, a country consisting of metamorphic rocks and auriferous quartz, will probably be found extending high up in East Africa throughout the rocks lying inland of the maritime and sub-maritime corallines. It is also likely that the vast coal-beds, explored by the Portuguese, and visited by Dr Livingstone, in the vicinity of Tete on the Zambeze, and afterwards prolonged by him to the Rufuma river, a formation quite unknown to our popiular works, will be extended to the Zanzibar coast. The valleys of rivers falling into the Indian Ocean should be carefully examined. The similarity of climate and geographical position which the province of Sao Paulo, and indeed the maritime regions of the Brazil generally, present with Eastern Africa, first drew my attention to its vast and various carboniferous deposits, and they are found to correspond with those of the Bark Continent. Messrs Rebmann and Pollock visited a spot near the 'Water of Doruma,' in the Rubai Range, near Mombasah, where antimony [1] is dug. They found no excavations, but the people told them to return after the rains, when the ground would be soft. The holes, they say, were rarely deeper than a foot and a half. Captain Guillain (iii. 277) was told that near the village 'M'tckiokara' 'il existe, presque a fleur de terre, des amas d'une substance metallifere, qui semblerait etre un antimoniure d'argent, autant qu'il a été permis d'en juger par les eckantillons donnes a nos voyageurs.'

The valuable corals are not found at Zanzibar, hut the people sell a thin and white-stem-

---

[1] I heard also of antimony on the Brazilian coast, opposite the Island of S. Sebastiao, in the Province of S. Paulo, but I have not seen any specimens of it.

rned madrepore, with brocoli-shaped heads of the liveliest red (TiibiporaMusica?). Gypsum abounds at Pemba and other places. Ships bring from Maskat a line hydraulic mortar called Saraj, the result of burning shells in small kilns (Tandur for Tanmir). The material is then stored in bags, pounded, and made into paste when required : it sets to stony consistency like the Pozzolana used by the Romans for under-water buildings. I presume that they mix with this calcaire a certain proportion of sand. The natives do not use shell-lime when chewing betel-nut and leaf: they spoil their teeth with the common stuff.

The disadvantage of coralline as building material is that it retains for a long time its ' quarry-water.' The Arabs dry it involuntarily, and humour their indolence by expending a dozen years in constructing a house—the home, as at Damascus, being rarely finished during the owner's life. The remedy is to expel the salts of lime and the animal gelatine by baking the stone, as is practised in the South Sea Islands. Kilns would make good lime at Zanzibar: on the island and coast the people now burn the gypsum and polypidoms in heaps piled upon a circle of billets, and the smoke, which fills half the town, is considered wholesome. Instead of being kept unslaked in sacks, it is wetted with sea-water, which prevents it drying, and it is then heaped up in the moist open air. Moreover, it is mixed with sea-sand, which is washed in fresh water, but its salt 'sweats out ' for many a long year. Thus the best houses are liable to cuticular eruptions during the wet season : the mortar cracks, and is patched with a leprosy of blue, yellow, and green mould. The flat roofs are protected from the rain with thick coatings of this material, pounded to the desired consistency by rows of slave-women and boys, armed with long flat tamps and rude mallets. During the last 15 years the price of lime at Zanzibar has increased five-fold, $11 being now (1857) paid for a small heap ; and, as usual, when Europeans are the purchasers, it rises 50 per cent.

SECTION 6.

The Industry of Zanzibar.

THE industry of Zanzibar is closely akin to nil; the same may be said of the coast—both are essentially exportihg, and cannot become manufacturing centres, at least as long as the present race endures.

The principal supply is of matting and bags for merchandise: the labourers are mostly women, who thus spend the time not occupied in domestic toil. The best mats are those sent by Madagascar: the 'native ' Simim (in Kisawahili termed Mkeka), an article upon which none but Diwans may sit, is neatly made of rush and palm-fronds from the river-side and from the low grounds of the coast; it is dyed in red patterns with madder, and the root of the Mudaa-tree boiled in water gives it a dark purple variegation. The housewives also make a rude fan, imitating that of Maskat. Materials for common mats and grain-bags are found in strips of palmated and fan-shaped leaves, cut in the jungles of the mainland, sun-dried, carefully scraped with knives, and plaited by men, women, and children. The Maskat traders buy these lengths, and sew them together with Khus, or thread made from the cocoa-leaf. The large Jambi (mat), varying from 8 to 10 cubits long, costs about a quarter of a dollar: this is employed in bagging (in Arabic, Kafa'at, and in Kisawahili, Makanda) to defend from rain the cottons, beads, and other articles which are carried by traders into the far interior.

Cloth is fringed by Wasawahili and slaves. Many tribes, those of Chaga for instance, will not take a 'Tobe' without its 'Tardzd,' and generally when a piece of stuff is given to a wild man, he sits down and first unravels the edge. The selvage also constitutes a highly-prized ornament.

Bill-hooks (mnnda), coarse sword-blades (upanga), and knives (kesu); hatchets (skoka), and hoes (jembe)—the latter two diminutive, and more like playthings than working-tools— are made of imported iron, and form a staple of trade with the mainland. The European spade and the American broad axe still await introduction. Those who would explore E. Africa should supply themselves with a large stock of such hardware, and be careful not to waste them—to savages and semi-barbarians they are everywhere more precious than gold.

Split bamboo forms the brooms, and the hard material tears the plaster from the walls. A coarse pottery, which the saltness of the clay renders peculiarly brittle, is fabricated by the Wasawahili at Changani Point, and supplants the original lagenarias. Some Kumars, or Hindustani potters, came to Zanzibar a few years ago; they suffered so severely from fever that, fancying themselves bewitched, all ran away.

CHAPTER VI.

VISIT TO THE PRINCE SAYVID MAJID.—THE GO-VERNMENT OE ZANZIBAR.

¹ Zanzibar is an island of Africa, on tbe coast of Zanzibar, governed by a king -who is a tributary to the Portuguese.'
REECE'S CYCLOPAEDIA.

■WE now proceed to wait npon H. H. the 'Sayyid of Zanzibar and the Sawahil,' who would be somewhat surprised to hear that he is 'tributary to the Portuguese.'

Tbe palace lies east of, and close to, the fort. It is fronted by a wharf, and defended by a stuccoed platform mounting eight or nine brass guns en barbette, intended more for show than use. Tbe building is a kind of double-storied, wbite-wasbed barrack, about 110 feet long, roofed with dingy green-red tiles, and pierced with a few windows jealously raised high from the ground; shutters painted tender-green temper

the sun-glare, and a few stunted, wind-wrung trees beautify the base. Seaward there is a verandah, in which levees are held, and behind it are stahles and sundry outhouses, an oratory and a graveyard, where runaway slaves, chained together by the neck, lie in the shade. In this oratory, as in other mosques, are performed the prayers of the two Great Festivals which, during the late prince's life, were recited at the Mto-ni ' Cascine.' Here, too, is the large, gable-ended house commenced in his elder age by the enterprising Sayyid Said, and built, it is said, after the model of the Dutch factory at Bander Abbas. It was intended for levees, and for a hall of pleasure. Unhappily, a large chandelier dropped from the ceiling, seventy masons were crushed by a falling wall; and other inauspicious omens made men predict that the prince would never enter the 'Akhir el Zaman ' (End of Time). It has since been shut up, like one of our ghost-haunted houses, which it not a little resembles.

In the centre of the square, opposite the palace, stands the Sayyid's flag-staff, where the ' Bakur ' is administered, where executions take place, and where, according to an American traveller,[1] distinguished criminals are fastened to a

[1] **Recollections of Majunga, Zanzibar, Muscat, Aden,** vol. i.

pole, and are tied from the ankles to the throat, * till the sonl of the dying man is literally squeezed out of its earthly tenement.' The author, who visited Zanzibar in 'the mercanteel,' was grievously hoaxed by some kind friend. Under Sayyid Said torture was unknown, death was inflicted according to Koranic law, and only one mutilation is recorded. I may remark, en passant, that in this part of the world the two master romancers, Ignorance and Interest, have been busily at work; and that many a slander rests upon the slenderest foundation of fact. Adventurers have circulated *the* most ridiculous tales. We hear, or rather we have heard, of 300,000 Arab cavalry, and hordes of steel-clad negroes, possibly a tradition of the 'Zeng ' (Zanzibarians), who, in the days of the Caliphs, plundered Basrah. We read of brilliant troops of horse artillery, whose only existence was in the brain of some unprincipled speculator ; and yet this report sent a battery from Woolwich as a present for the late Sayyid. To the same category belong the Amazons bestriding war-bullocks, doubtless a revival of El Masudi, who in our tenth century reported that the 'King of Zeng ' commanded, Dahoman-like, an army of

Mokha, Aden, and otter Eastern Ports. Salem : George Creamer, 18 54.

soldieresses, mounted, as are the Kafirs, upon oxen —the Portuguese 'boi-cavallos.' Some travellers have asserted that the Cape tribes learned cattle-riding from Europeans : but Camoens, making his hero land at the Agnada de S. Braz, after sailing from the Angra de Santa Elena, expressly states—

> 'Embrown'd the women by the burning clime,
> On slow-paced oxen riding came along.'—Canto V. 63.

Durbars, or levees, are held three times a day, after dawn-prayers, in the afternoon, and at night. The ceremonial is simple. The lieges, passing the two Sepoys on guard at the gate, enter with the usual Moslem salutation, and after kissing hands take their appointed places. There is no lord of the basin, lord of the towel, or lord of the pelisse, deemed indispensable by every petty Persian governor. The ruler is addressed, Ya Sidi, my lord, and is spoken of by his subjects as Sayyidna, our prince. Coffee is served, but only at night; and all forms of intoxicants are jealously banished. The long, bare reception-hall, ceilinged with heavy polished beams, and paved with alternate slabs of white and black marble brought from Marseille, boasts only a few dingy chandeliers, and three rows of common wooden-bottomed chairs. It is, however, unencumbered with the usual mean knicknaoks, French clocks and bureaux, cheap prints, gaudy china, and pots of neglected artificial flowers, supposed to adorn the window-sills; nor, after the fashion of Zanzibarian grandees, are the sides lined with seamen's chests, stuffed full of arms, watches, trinkets, cashmere shawls, medicines, and other such c chow chow.'

The Prince received us at the Sadr, or top of the room, with the usual courtesy. He was then a young man, whose pleasing features and very light complexion generally resembled those of his father. This is said to have been the case with the whole family. We found the 'divan' of Egypt and Turkey unaccountably absent, banished by the comfortless black-wood 'Kursi' of Bombay. After a few minutes' conversation two chairs were placed before us, bearing a tray of sweetmeats, biscuits, and glasses of sherbet; of these we ate and drank a mouthful in acceptance of hospitality, and we were duly pressed to eat. Lemonade and confitures take the place of strong waters amongst Europeans, and of the cocoa-nut milk, the mangoes, and the oranges of humbler establishments. Pipes, however, though offered by the late Sayyid to distinguished European guests, are never introduced, in deference to Wahhabi prejudice; nor did we suffer from tlie rose-water ablutions of which M. Guillain complains. Feminine eyes did not peep at us from the inner apartments; but we were fronted by well-dressed slaves who, as we pass through the crowded outer hall, will steal, if they can, the gilt tassels from our sword-knots, and who have picked the pockets of guests, even when dining with their Prince. H. H. the Sayyid Majid took considerable interest in our projected journey, and suggested that a field-piece might be useful to frighten the Washenzi (wild men). We left the palace much pleased with the kindness and cordiality of its owner, into whose ear, moreover, evil tongues had whispered the very worst reports.

The Government of Zanzibar is a royal magistracy, the only form of rule to which the primitive and undisciplinable Eastern Arab will submit. Whenever a new measure is brought forward by the Sayyid it is invariably opposed by the chiefs of clans, who assemble and address him more like an equal than a superior. One of the princes of Maskat corrected this turbulent feudality after the fashion of Mohammed Ali Pasha and his Mamluk Beys ; even now a. few summary examples might be made to good purpose. In the days of the late Sayyid's highest fortunes the most tattered of Suris would address him, ᶜ O Said ! ' and proceed to sit unhidden in his presence. Similarly, Ibn Batutah, when describing the Sultan of Oman, Abu Mohammed bin Nebhan, tells us, ᶜ he has the habit of sitting, when he would give audience, in a place outside his palace; he has neither chamberlain nor wazir, and every man, stranger or subject, is free to approach him.' Sometimes a noble, when ordered into arrest at Zanzibar, has collected his friends, armed his slaves, and fortified his house. One Salim bin Abdallah, who had a gang of 2000 musketeer negroes, used to wage a petty war with the Sayyid's servile hosts. It is, perhaps, the result of climate that these disturbances have never developed into revolutions.

The ᶠ ministers ' spoken of by strangers are the Nakhodas of the fleet: by virtue of a few Trench or English sentences, they are summoned when business is to be transacted with Europeans who are not linguists. The late Sayyid's only secretary and chief interpreter was Ahmad bin Aman of Basrah (Bussorah), a half-cast Arab, popularly called by the lieges 'Wajhayn ' or 'two faces.' According to some he was a Sabi or Sabsean, commonly known as a Christian of Saint John; and men declare that he began life as a cabin-boy and rose by his tmusual astuteness. When any question of unusual gravity occurs the Sayyid summons the Ulema, the Shaykhs, and especially the two Kazis, Shaykh Muhiyy el Din, a Lamu doctor of the Sunni school, and Shaykh Mohammed, an Abdzi. Causes tried by ecclesiastics generally depend upon the extent of bribery; but there is always an appeal to the Prince, or in his absence to the Governor. The Kazis punish by imprisonment more or less severe. The stocks are set up in every plantation ; the fetters are heavy, and there is, if wanted, a ponderous iron ring with long spikes, significantly termed in Persian the 'Tauk i Ta'at,' collar of obedience. Instant justice is the order of the day, and the crooked stick (bakur) plays a goodly and necessary part; how necessary we see in the present state of Syria, whence the 'Tanzimat ' constitution has banished the only penalty that ruffians fear. Prom ten to fifty blows are usually inflicted : in the Gulf, when the bastinado is to be administered with the Nihayet el Azab (extreme rigour), half-a-dozen men work upon the culprit's back, belly, and sides, and a hundred strokes suffice to kill him. Severe examples are sometimes necessary, though, chastisement is on the whole wild and unfrequent. Zanzibar town is subject to fires, originating with the slaves, often in drunkenness, more often for plunder; and this induced the late Sayyid to forbid the building of cajan 'tabernacles ' (Makuti or Banda-ni) upon the house-tops. His orders were obeyed for four months, an unusually long time; and at last Europeans, in consequence of the danger which threatened them, were compelled personally to interfere with the severest preventive treatment. The Prince alone has the power of pronouncing a capital sentence; and, as usual in Moslem countries, where murder is a private, not a public, offence, the criminal is despatched by the relatives of the slain. Death may be inflicted by the master of the house upon a violator of domicile, gallant, or thief; the sword is drawn, and the intruder is at once cut down. Eines and confiscations, which have taken the place of the Koranic mutilation, are somewhat common, especially when impudent frauds are practised upon the Prince's property. Confinement in the fort, I have said, is severe, but not so much feared as at Maskat, whose rock dungeon is an Aceldama; I saw something of the kind at Pernando Po. Criminals have a wholesome horror of being the ruler's guest, yet they sometimes escape by the silver key, and, once upon the mainland, they may laugh at justice. I heard of a Banyan who, despite being double-ironed, managed to 'make tracks.'

The military force of Zanzibar is not imposing. In 1846, throughout the African possessions of the Sayyid, the permanent force was only 100 men, namely, about 80 at Zanzibar, 250 at Mombasah, 30 at Lamu, 25 at Patta, 6 to 10 at Kilwa, and sundry pairs at Makdishu and other places; after that time they were doubled and even trebled. The 'regulars ' consist of a guard of honour, a 'guardia nobile ' of a dozen serviles habited in cast-off Sepoy uniforms, collected from different corps of the Bombay army : one musket carries a bayonet, the other a stick. The cost of new equipments was once asked by the late Sayyid; after glancing at the total, he exclaimed that the guard itself would not fetch half that sum. The irregular force is more considerable, and represents the Hayduques of old Eastern Turkey, the Arnauts or Albanians of Egypt, the Bashi-Buzuks of El Hejaz, and the Sayyareh and Zabtiyyeh of modern Syria. The so-called Baloch are vagrants and freebooters collected from Northern

Arabia and from the southern seaboard of Persia, Mekran, and Kilat: when the Prince required extra levies he rigged out a vessel and recruited at Guadel or at Makallali. He preferred the Aryan,[1] as being more amenable to discipline than the Semite : *moreover,* the Arab clansman, like the Highlander of old, though feudally bound to follow his suzerain, requires the order of his immediate chief, and the latter, when most wanted, is uncommonly likely to rat or to revolt. The mercenaries of Zanzibar nominally receive $2 to $3 per mensem, with rations : practically, the money finds its way more or less into the pocket of the Jemadar or C. O- The fort is here garrisoned by some 80 of these men and their negro slaves : the former are equal to double the number of Arabs in the field, and behind walls they are a match for a nation of savages. Police by day and night patrols are much wanted at Zanzibar, where every man must be his own 'Robert.' The slaves are unruly subjects; even those of the fort will commit an occasional murder, and the suburbs are still far from safe during the dark

---

[1] It is hardly necessary to correct in these days the error of Carsten Niebuhr, who made the 'Belludges' (Baloch) a tribe of Arabs. The Baloch mercenaries will be found further noticed in Part II. chap. vi.

WASIN TOWN.

hours. The garrison is securely locked up, aud in case of most urgent need no aid is procurable before morning.

I may now offer a catalogue raisonne of the late Sayyid's fleet, which was intended to keep up the maritime prestige of his predecessors, the Yu'rabi Imams. The Shah Alam, a double-banked frigate of 1100 tons, carrying 50 guns (45, says M. Guillain, i. 584), was built at Mazagon in 1820, and now acts guardship, moored off Mto-ni. The 'Caroline' (40 guns), the best of the squadron, and built at Bombay, was degraded to be a merchantman, in which category she visited Marseille (1849): she has, however, again opened her ports after returning from Maskat. The strong and handsome 'Sultana' was wrecked near Wasin when returning from India. The 'Salihi' was lost in the Persian Gulf; the 'Sulayman Shah' and the 'Humayun Shah,' in the Gulf of Bengal. The 'Piedmontese,' 36 guns, built at Cochin in 1836, might be repaired at an expense of £10,000. The "Victoria" frigate (40), teak-built in the Mazagon dockyard, is still sea-worthy. The 'Bahmani' corvette (24 guns), is a fast-sailing craft with great breadth of beam, hailing from Cochin: she was lately fitted out for a recruiting vessel to Hazramaut. The 'Artemise' corvette, formerly of 18 guns, now a jackass frigate with 10 guns *en barbette,* was built at Bombay of fine Daman teak, and was lately repaired there, at an expense of 22,000 Co.'s Bs. Called Colonel Hamerton's yacht, because always placed at his disposal by the late Sayyid, she will carry him on his last voyage, accompanying us to Bagamoyo upon the mainland. She is commanded by the sailing-master of the fleet, Mohammed bin Khamis, who has studied navigation and modern languages in London—of him more anon. The lighter craft are the 'Salihi' barque (300 tons), built in America about 1840, condemned and repaired in Bombay; and the 'Taj' brig (125 tons), launched at Cochin in 1829, and originally intended for a yacht. Besides there is a mosquito squadron composed of some 20 'batelas,' each armed with 2 to 6 guns, which serve equally for cabotage and for campaigning.

The useless, tawdry 'Prince Begent,' presented by H. B. Majesty's Government to the late Sayyid, was by him passed over, in 1840 to the Governor-General of India. It was sold at Calcutta, and for many years it was, as a transport, the terror of the eastern soldier. The Sayyid could not pray amongst the 'idols' of gilding and carving; he saw pollution in every picture, and his Arabs supposed the royal berth to he the Tabiit Hazrat Isa—Our Lord's coffin. Instead of this article he wished to receive the present of a steamer, hut political and other objections prevented.' Eastern rulers also will not pay high and regular salaries; and without European engineers every trip would have cost a boiler. Repairs were impossible at Zanzibar; and, as actually happened to Mohammed Ali's expensive machinery in Egypt, the finest work would have been destroyed by mere neglect. A beautiful model of a steam-engine was once sent out from England: it was allowed to rust unopened in the Sayyid's 'godowns.' Still the main want of the Island was rapid communication. Sometimes nine months elapsed before an answer came from Bombay: letters and parcels —including my manuscript—were often lost; and occasionally, after a long cruise, they returned to their starting-point, much damaged by time and hard usage. The Bombay Post-office clerks thinking, I presume, that Zanzibar is in Arabia, shipped their bags to Bushire and Mas-

---

[1] Wellsted's Travels in Arabia, vol. ii. p. 403. This author exposes, without seeming to know that he was doing so, the selfish and short-sighted policy of the H. E. I. Company which wanted a squadron subsidiary to its own.

kat, some thousand miles NWest instead of S.West of Bombay, and via Halifax—half round the world—was often the speediest way of communication with London. No wonder that letters were delayed from 7 to 9 months, causing great loss to the trade, and inconvenience to the authorities. Her Majesty's proclamation was published in India on November 1, 1858; the Prince of Zanzibar was obliged with a copy only in March, 1859. A line of steamers from the Cape and other places was much talked of; it would certainly obviate many difficulties, but the Zanzibar merchants who had a snug monopoly were dead against free-trade and similar appliances of modern civilization. The Trench Company then running vessels from Mauritius to Aden, proposed to touch at Zanzibar if permitted to engage on their own terms £ ouvriers libres.' The liberal olfer was declined with thanks.

The B-oyal Treasury is managed with an extreme simplicity. When the Prince wants goods or cash he writes an order upon his collector of customs; the draft is kept as an authority, and the paper is produced at the general balancing of accounts, which takes place every third or fourth year. I found it impossible to obtain certain information concerning the gross amount of customs, and inquiry seemed only to lead further from the truth. The ruler, the officers under him, and the traders all have several interests in keeping the secret.

The Custom House is in an inchoate condition; it makes no returns,, and exports being free, it requires neither manifest nor port clearings from ships about to sail. The customs are farmed out by the Sayyid, and 10 years ago their value was $112,000, or 38 per cent, less than is now paid. The last contractor was a Cutch Banyan named Jayaram Sewji. The 'ijareh' or lease was generally for five years, and the annual amount was variously stated at $70,000 to $150,000, in 1859 it had risen to $196,000 to $220,000.[1] He had left the Island before Sayyid Said's death, and though summoned by the Prince Majid, there was little chance of his committing the folly of obedience. His successor was one Ladha Damha, also a Bhattia Hindu, and a man of the highest respectability. These renters declared that they did not collect the amount which they paid for the privilege : on the other hand, they could privately direct their caste fel-

[1] The consular report of 1860 gives an aggregate value of the port trade at £1,667,577, viz. : imports £908,911, and exports (information furnished by the mercantile community, and evidently much understated) £758,666.

lows, do what they pleased with all unprotected by treaty, and having a monopoly as tradesmen between the wholesale white merchants and the petty dealers of the coast, they soon became wealthy.

Land cess and port dues were unknown at Zanzibar. The principal source of revenue was the Custom House, where American and European goods, bullion excepted, paid the 5 per cent, ad valorem provided by commercial treaties. Cargo from India paid 5·25, the fractions serving to salary Custom House officials. The import was levied on all articles transshipped in any ports of the Zanzibar dominions, unless the cargo was landed only till the vessel could be repaired. Of course the tariff was complicated in the extreme, ᵉ custom ' amongst orientals being the 'rule of thumb ' further west. The farmers appointed all subordinate officials, and as these received insufficient salaries, smuggling, especially in the matters of ivory and slaves, came to their assistance. The Wasawahili Makhadim, or serviles, contributed an annual poll-tax of $1 per head, and this may have amounted to 10,000 to 14,000 crowns per annum. The maximum total of the late Sayyid's revenue was generally stated as follows—

Maskat (customs) German crowns	...	$180,000
Mattra (Matrah) „ „	...	60,000
Maskat and Mattra (octroi from the interior)		20,000
Average receipts from otter parts of Africa ? and Arabia	> C	",", 20,000
Zanzibar (customs and poll-tax) ...	...	160,000
Total in German crowns	...	$440,000

In 1811 Captain Smee computes the revenue of Zanzibar at $60,000 per annum, adding, however, that he considers it to he much more. In 1846 M. Guillain gives the revenue arising from customs on coffee and cloves, Indian rice and melted butter, and divers taxes on shops, indigo, dyes, thread-makers, silk-spinners, and so forth, as follows—

Total of Oman ...	$136,600
„ African dominions	349,000

Grand total $485,600 = 2,500,000 francs.

The author, who appears to have been ably assisted in his inquiries by M. Loarer, also *states* that in the days of Sayyid Said's father the farmingof the customs at Zanzibar represented $25,000, from which it gradually rose to $50,000; $60,000; $80,000 ; $100,000 ; $105,000 ; $120,000 ; $147,000; $157,000; and $175,000 in 1846. We may safely fix the revenue in 1857 at a maximum of £90,000 per annum. The expenses of navy, army, and 'civil service,' and the personal expenditure of the Prince were easily defrayed out of this sum, whilst the surplus must have been considerable. The income might easily have been increased, and the outlay have been diminished by improving the administration; but the Sayyid had 'some time before his death reached that epoch of life when age and weariness determine men to consider the status quo as the supreme wisdom.'

Under the new regime affairs did not improve. An Indian firm farmed the customs throughout the Zanzibar dominions for the annual sum of $190,000, and the following is the official statement of the revenues derived by 'His Highness the Sultan,'[1] in 1863-4.

Customs dues	... $190,000
Pemba dues	... 6,000
Poll-tax of Makhadim	... 10,000
Private clove plantations ...	... 15,000
	Total $221,000
Deduct subsidy paid to Maskat	... 40,000
Balance	$181,000

The income, thus sadly fallen off, was hardly enough for the necessaries of the ruler, and left

[1] Commercial Reports, received at the Foreign Office from H. M.'s Consuls, between July 1, 1863, aud June 30, 1864. London, Harrison and Co. In 1862 the revenue of Maskat was computed to reach the very respectable cipher of £1,065,640 per annum.

no margin available for improvements or public works. At last tbe government, which by treaty is unjustly debarred from imposing export or harbour dues, or even from increasing the import duties, devised a modified system of land-tax, charging 5 per cent, per annum on cloves, and 2 pice (— fcl.) on mature cocoa-trees whose estimated average value is $1. This, if levied, would produce about $40,000 per annum.

Since that time prosperity has returned to the Island. The return of imports by the Custom House rose from £245,981 in 1861-2 to £483,693 in 1867-8.[1] One half of the trade was in the hands of English subjects, and the Committee remarks that Zanzibar is the chief market of the world for ivory and copal; that the trade in hides, oils, seeds, and dyes is on the increase, whilst cotton, sugar, and indigo, to which may be added cocoa, loom in the distance.

[1] **Eeport of Select Committee appointed to inquire into the whole question of the slave trade on the East coast of Africa.**

CHAPTER VII.

A CHRONICLE OB ZANZIBAR. THE CAREER OR THE LATE 'IMAM,' SAYVID SAID.

'Mais, comme le livre n'est point une œuvre de fantaisie, comme il traite de questions sérieuses, et qu'il s'addresse à des intérêts durables, je me résigne, pour lui, à l'inattention du moment, et j'attendrai patiemment pour que l'avenir *lui* ramène son heure, lui refasse, pour ainsi dire, une nouvelle opportunité.'—M. Guillain.

THERE is little of interest in the annals of Oman and of her colonies. Fond of genealogy, the modern Arabs are perhaps the most incurious of Orientals in the matter of history: they ignore the past, they disregard the present, and they have a superstitions aversion to speak of the future. Lawless and fanatical, treacherous, blood-thirsty and eternally restless, the Omani races, whose hand is still against every man, have converted their chronicles into a kind of Newgate Calendar, whilst the multitude of personages that appear upon the scene, and the perpetual rising and falling *of* Imams, princes, and grandees, offer to the reader a mere string of proper names. Ample details concerning Maskat will he found in the pages of Capt. Hamilton, Carsten Niebuhr, "Wellsted, and Salil ibn Bazik,[1] to mention no others. Zanzibar has ever been, since historic times, connected with Oman, whose fortunes she has reflected; the account of the distant dependency given by travellers is, therefore, as might be expected, scanty and obscure.

At an early period the merchants and traders of Yemen frequented the Island, and exchanged, as we read in the Periplus and Ptolemy, their homes of barren rock and sand for the luxuriant wastes of Eastern Africa. If tradition be credible, their primitive settlements were Patta (Bette), Lamu, and the Mrima fronting these islets; and here to the present day the dialect of their descendants has remained the purest. Themselves pagans, they lived amongst the heathenry, borrowed their language, as the

[1] **History of the Imams and Sayyids of Oman, from** A.D. **661 to 1856, by Salil'ibn Bazik. Translated, &c., by the Bev. Gr. P. Badger. Printed for the Hakluyt Society.**

Arabs and the Baloch still do, intermarried with them, and begot the half-caste Wasawahili, or coast population. In proof that these were the lords of the land, the late Sultan Ahmad, chief of the Shirazi, or free tribe of the mulattoes, received annual presents from the Arab Sayyid of Zanzibar. When the former died Muigni Mku, his wazir, or brother—here all fellow-countrymen are brothers—succeeded, in default of other heirs, to the position of monarch retired from business. He is a common-looking negroid, who lives upon the proceeds of a plantation and periodical presents : he is not permitted to appear as an equal at the Sayyid's Darbar, and it is highly improbable that he will ever come to his own again.

The Sawahil or Azania continued to acknowledge Arab and Persian supremacy till the appearance of the Portuguese upon the coast. D. Vasco da Gama passed Zanzibar Island without sighting it when first bound Indiawards, and authors differ upon the subject of his return voyage. The historian Toao de Barros (i. 4, 11) relates that the expedition made its land-fall from India below Magadoxo (Makdishu or Maka'ad el Shaat, [4] the sitting-place of the sheep'),[1] beat off a boat attack from 'Path '

[1] So called from some silly vision of an illuminated sheep

(Patta), visited Melinde, Mozambique, and the Aguada de S. Braz, and doubled tbe Cape of Storms on March 20, 1499. Goes[1] declares that da Gama, after touching at Makdishu and Melinde, arrived at Zanzibar on February 28, and was supplied by its ruler with provisions, presents, and specimens of country produce. The island is described as large and fertile, with groves of fine trees, producing good fruit, two others, 'Pomba ' (Pemba) and 'Mofia ' (our Monfia and the Arab Mafiyah), lying in its vicinity. These settlements were governed by Moorish princes ᶜof the same caste as the King of Melinde' —doubtless hereditary Moslem Shaykhs and Sayyids. The population is represented as being in ᶜ no great force, but carrying on a good trade with Mombassa for Guzerat calicoes and with Sofala for gold.' The 'King of Melinde ' made a name in Europe. Kabelais commemorates Hans Carvel, the King of Melinda's jeweller, and (in Book I. chap. v.) we read, 'thus did Bacchus

appearing to one of the Shaykhs. The city is supposed to have been founded in A.n. 295, about 70 years before Kilwa.

The three voyages of Vasco da G-araa, &c., as from the Lendas da India of G-aspar Correa, translated by the Hon. Henry C. J. Stanley, London, Hakluyt Society, 1S69, chap. xxi., note to page 261. M. Guiilain (i. 319) makes the expedition reach Zanzibar on April 29, 1499.

conquer Ind; thus philosophy, Melinde,'—meaning that the Portuguese taught their African friends more drinking than wisdom. *Joao de Barros* (ii. 4. 2) informs us that the Chief of Zanzibar was 'da linhagem dos Beys de Mombaca, nossos imigos.' The inhabitants were 'white Moors ' (Arabs from Arabia) and black Moors or Wasawahili; the former are portrayed as a slight people, scantily armed, but clothed in fine cottons bought at Mombasah from merchants of Cambaya. Their women *were adorned* with jewels, with Sofalan gold, and with silver obtained in exchange for provisions, from the people of St Lawrence's Island (Madagascar). And here we may remark that the Arab settlements in East Africa, visited by the Portuguese at the end of the 15th century, showed generally a civilization and a refinement fully equal to, if not higher than, the social state of the European voyagers. The latter, expecting to find savages like the naked Kafirs of the South, must not have been a little surprised to receive visits from the chiefs of Mozambique and Melinde, men clad in gold, embroidered silks, velvets, and 'crimson damask, lined with green satin; ' armed with rich daggers and swords sheathed in silver scabbards, seated on arm-chairs, and attended by a suite *of some* 20 richly-dressed Arabs. Tbe modest presents offered by tbe Europeans to these wealthy princelets, whose women adorned themselves with pearls and other precious stones, must have given a mean idea of Portuguese civilization. And even in the present day the dominions of the 'barbarous Arab ' are superior in every way to the miserable colonies on the West African coast, which represent Christian and civilized Europe.

Pour years afterwards (1503) Euy Louren§o Eavasco, a Cavalleiro da Casa d' El Eey, sailing with D. Antonio de Saldanha, cruized off 'Zemzibar,' as his countrymen called Zanzibar, and in two months captured twenty rich ships, laden with ambergris, ivory, tortoisesheE, wax, honey, rice, coir, and silk and cotton stuffs. This captain appears, like most of his fellows, to have been a manner of pirate : he did not restore them till ransom was paid. 'El Eey,' still friendly to the Portuguese, sent a spirited remonstrance, when the insolence of the reply forced him to take hostile measures. The Arabs manned their canoes with some 4000 men; but two launches, well-armed with cannon, killed at the first discharge 34 men and put the rest to flight. Thus the Malik or Eegulus was compelled by Eavasco to pay an annual tribute of 100 gold miskals in token of submission to the greedy and unprincipled Dorn Manuel. 'The conquered pays the conquest! ' exclaims with Christian emphasis the venerable Osorio. Portugal now began to gather gold from Sofala to Makdislru; 'Wagerage,' the chief of Melinde, contributed every year 1500 wedges (ingots) of the precious metal, and the insolence of the victors must have made the good old man deeply regret the welcome and the Godspeed which he had bestowed upon the exploratory expedition.

The Portuguese having wrested Kilwa and Mombasah from its Arab chiefs, D. Duarte de Lemos, appointed (A.D. 1508) by the King Governor of the 'Provinces of ^Ethiopia and Arabia,' attacked successively Mafiyah, Zanzibar, and Pemba, for failing in the paramount duty of paying tribute. Mafiyah submitted, the people of Pemba escaped to Mombasah, leaving nothing in their houses, and Zanzibar resisted, but the town was taken and plundered. The Shaykh retired northwards, and his subjects fled to the bush, £ depois de bem esfarrapados na carne con a ponta da langa, e espada dos nossos ' —after being, well pierced in the flesh by the lance-points and the sword-blades of our men—

says the chronicler. Prom this time probably we may date the pointed arches that still remain upon the Island, and the foundation of the fort, which is popularly attributed to the 'Paranj.' Mombasah and Pemba were presently occupied by the Portuguese; and the ruins of their extensive barracoons, citadels, and churches still argue ancient splendour. In other places upon the seaboard I found deep and carefully sunk wells, stone enclosures, and coralline temples, whilst vestiges of European buildings may be traced, it is said, contrary to popular opinion, many days' journey inland.

We read little about Lusitanianized Zanzibar, where the insalubrity of the climate must have defended the interior, and even parts of the coast, from the spoiler. In A.D. 1519 the Moors massacred certain shipwrecked sailors belonging to the expedition of P. Jorje de Albuquerque. Three years afterwards the Shaykh, or, as he styled himself, the Sultan[1] of Zanzibar, who, after submitting to itavasco, had acknowledged himself a vassal of D. Manuel, fitted out, with the aid of the factors Joao de Mata and Pedro

---

[1] The only Shaykhs who took the name of Sultan'were those of Kilwa and Zanzibar: he of Mombasah was tributary to the latter.

de Castro, a small expedition against the Quirimba islandry, who had allied themselves with the hostile tribes about Mombasah. The attack was successful, the chief town was pillaged and burnt, and terror of the invader brought all the neighbouring islets to terms. In 1528-9 the Viceroy of India, Nuno da Cunha, being about to attack Mombasah, was supplied with provisions by the Chief, and the Portuguese presently reduced the coast to a single rule whose centres were successively Kilwa, Sofala, and Mozambique. East Africa then became one of the four great governments depending upon the viceroyalty of India; the three others being Malacca, Hormuz, and Ceylon.

In this state Zanzibar remained till the close of the next century. When, however, Pedro Barrato de Bezende, Secretary to the Viceroy, Count of Linhares, wrote his 'Breve Tratado ' on the Portuguese colonies of India and East Africa (1635), the Island had ceased to be vassal and tributary, but the Sultan remained friendly to Europeans. Many of the latter occupied with their families rich plantations ; Catholic worship was protected, and there was a church in which officiated a brother of the order of St Austin. There was the usual massacre of the Portuguese, and expulsion of the survivors in imitation of Mombasah, about 1660 ; and the Islanders, doubting their power to procure independence, applied for assistance to the Arabs.

The reign of the Yu'rabi of Oman, a clan of the great Ghafiri tribe, began as follows. The Imam, Sultan bin Sayf bin Malik el Yu'rabi, the second of the family, having recovered Maskat (April 23, 1659), and Matrah, created a navy which added Kang, Khishm, Hormuz, Balirayn, and Mombasah (1660) to the Arabian possessions left by his ancestors. After investing Bombay this doughty chief died in A.D. 1668 or in 1669. His son, Sayf bin Sultan, after defeating an elder brother, Belarab, became the third Imam of the house of Yu'rabi, and summoned to submission the petty chiefs on the eastern mainland of Africa. Between A.D. 1680 and 1698, the powerful squadron of the warlike Moor[1] drove the Portuguese from Zanzibar, Kilwa, Pemba, and Mombasah, where he established as Governor Nasir bin Abdillah el Mazru'i, the first of the great family of that name. He failed only at Mozambique. Arabs still relate the legend how having closely invested the fort they were undermining the wall, when a Banyan gave traitorous warning to the besieged. Pans of water ranged upon the ground showed by the trembling fluid the direction of the tunnel; a countermine was sprung with fatal effect, and the assailants, retreating in confusion to their shipping, raised the siege.[1] The squadron, however, pursued its course as far south as the Comoros and Bukini (Madagascar, or rather the northern portion of the Island), whence, hearing of the ruler's death, it returned home. When the Island became Arab property the Wasawahili fled to the 'bush': they presently consented to render personal service, or to purchase exemption by annually paying $2 per head.

Sayf bin Sultan was succeeded, in A.D. 1711, by his eldest son, Sultan bin Sayf, who defeated with his fleet of 24 to 28 ships, carrying 80 guns, the soldiers of Abbas III. and of Nadir Shah. After his decease the chieftainship of Oman was seized by a distant relative, Mohammed bin Nasir, Lord of Jabrin, who according to some, first assumed, according to others, resumed, the title of ʽ Imam,' making himself priest as well as prince, like him of Sana'a in Yemen. It has ever been a Khdriji, and especially a Bayazi tenet, that any pious man, not only those belonging to the Kuraysh or the Pro-

---

[1] M. G-uiHain (i. 522) had vaguely heard of this tradition.

phet's tribe, might rise to the rank of Pontiff. In A.D. 751 they were powerful enough to elect Julandah hen Mas'ud, but the succeeding dynasty rejected the term. The usurped rule was recovered after his decease (A.D. 1728) by Sayf el Asdi, a younger son of Sultan bin Sayf: this indolent debauchee being shut up in Maskat by a cousin, Sultan bin Murshid—some corrupt his father's name to Khurshid—applied for assistance to that Nadir Shah, whom his more patriotic father had successfully resisted. In 1716 the Persians, aided by intestine Arab divisions, soon conquered Oman: Sultan bin Murshid slew himself in despair, and Sayf el Asdi, duped by his allies, died of grief in his dungeon at Rustak. The latter city was in those days the ordinary residence of the Imams; in fact, a kind of cathedral town as well as capital.

The power now fell from the hands of the Yu'rabis (Ghafiris) into the grasp of their rivals, the Bu Saidi (Hinawis). These ancient lords of Oman claim direct descent from Kahtan (Joctan), great-grandfather of Himyar, founder of the Southern Arabs, and brother to Saba, who built in Yemen the city that hore his name: the stock is held to be noble as any in the Peninsula. Oman remained under foreign dominion, paying tribute to, and owning tbe rule of, Nadir Sbab, till the Chief of Sohar, Said bin Ahmad el Bu Saidi, struck the blow for freedom. Eive years afterwards (A.D. 1744) his son, Ahmad bin Said, artfully recovering Maskat from Mirza Taky Khan, the Governor of Kars, who had revolted against Nadir Shah, expelled the Persians from Oman. When laying the foundation of the present dynasty he assumed the title of 'Sayyid' (temporal ruler) ; persuaded the Mufti to elect Mm 'Imam' (prince-priest), and was confirmed in his dignities by the Sherif of Meccah. Colonel Pelly (p. 184, Journal Boyal Geographical Society, 1865) gives a somewhat different account — 'It appears that the family of the Imams of Muskat were originally Sayeds of a village, named Bowthek, in the Sedair immediately below the Towaij hills. The founder of the family was Saeed. His son's name was Ahmed. They came to Oman, and took service under the dominant tribe called Yarebek. Subsequently they obtained possession of the strong hill-fort called Hazm, in the neighbourhood of Bostak. Eventually they became the rulers of Oman, and changed their sect from that of Sunnee to Beyathee.' Ahmad allied himself with the ex-royal Yu'rabis, by marrying a daughter of

Sayf el Asdi. After crushing sundry rebellions, he plundered Diu (A.D. 1760), and massacred the population, a disaster from which the great port and fort never recovered. He then sent an army of 12,000 men against the Ghafiri of Pa'as el Khaymah, who had assisted the Persians to attack the Kawasim, and against the Nuaymi, a powerful clan dwelling south of Sharjah on the Pirate Coast. His success was complete; Khurfakan, Khasab, Pamsah, Pa'as el Khaymah, Jezirat el Hamrah, Sharjah, and Pasht, all in turn submitted to him. In A.D. 1785 he personally visited Mombasah, and by his lion-like demeanour he secured its submission.

Dying shortly afterwards, Alimad bin Said left the government to his son, Said bin Ahmad, who was declared Imam, but was confined till the date of his death, in 1802, to Pustalc and its territory by his younger brother, the ambitious and warlike Sultan bin Ahmad. This prince occupied the islands of Kliishm, Hormuz, and Balirayn; he attempted to protect his commerce from the pirates of Julfar and Pm'as el Khaymah, especially the Kawasim, in our books called Jowasmee:[1] these Algerines of the East had now

---

[1] The "Western as veil as the Eastern Arabs turn the hard Kaf into a Jim, e. g. Jibleh for Kibleh. The Kawasim derive

become Wahhabis, and were backed by all the influence of Sadd, Lord of Daraiyyah. After vainly attempting to obtain aid from the Pasha of Baghdad, Sultan bin Ahmad was attacked whilst sailing to Bandar Abbas by five ships of the Kawasim, and was shot in the melee on Nov. 18,1801.

This decease brought to power the late Sayyid Said,[1] the second son born to Sayyid Sultan bin Ahmad in A.D. 1790. His maternal uncle, Sayyid Bedr bin Sayf, and the Wahhabi Chief, Saud, enabled him to defeat Sultan Kays bin Ahmad of Sohar, another uncle who aimed at usurpation; but the danger was shifted, not destroyed. At length, in A.n. 1806, Sayyid Said's aunt, the Bibi Mauza, daughter of the Imam Ahmad, and popularly known as the Bint el Imam, determined that Sayyid Bedr must be slain at a Darbar. Sayyid Said, a youth of 16, was unwilling, but the strong-minded woman— in every noble Arab family there is at least one —prevailed, and on July 31 the dangerous pro-

their name from a local "Wali, or Santon, the Shaykh Kasim.

[1] A detailed account of this Prince's early life is given in the 'History of Syed Said, Sultan of Muscat' . . . translated from the Italian. London, 1819 (written by his physiciau, Shaykh Mansur, alias Yincenzo). Buckingham, Praser, and Sir John Malcolm have also supplied notices of his eventful career.

tector whilst descending tlie stairs, was struck in the hack by his nephew's dagger. Sayyid Bedr sprang from the window, and mounted a stirrupless horse which stood below, when he was wounded with a spear; the £ Imam's daughter,' with a blood-thirstiness truly feminine, cheering on the assassins, till after riding half a mile on the highway from Birkat to Sohar, he fell from his animal and was speedily despatched. The young prince was, they say, so strongly affected by the scene, that through life he could hardly be persuaded to order a death.[1]

Thus Said became, with the consent of his elder brother, Sayyid Salim, an independent ruler, and the fourth of his dynasty, the Bu Saidi. His proper title was 'Sayyid,' which in Oman and amongst the Eastern Arabs means a chief or temporal ruler, whereas 'Slierif ' is a descendant of the Prophet. Many Anglo-Indian writers ignore this distinction. 'Imam ' is an ecclesiastical title, signifying properly the man who takes the lead in public prayer, and it demands both study and confirmation : in sectarian theology it is the hereditary head of El

[1] I give this account as it was told to me by Lieut.-Col. Hamerton. M. Gruillain (part II. chap. iii.) may be consulted for another and a more diplomatic version.

Islam. The 'Imam of Mascat,'[1] therefore, never followed the practice of his predecessors. His acclamation took place on Sept. II, 1806. He was immediately involved in troubles with Mombasak, Makdishu, and the unruly Arab settlements of the East African Coast. His possessions in Oman also were invaded and overrun by the Wahhabis, under Saud who died in 1814, and afterwards under his son Abdullah: these energetic Puritans converted, by much fighting and more intrigue, several tribes to 'Unitarianism'; the land was at once fettered with a five per cent. Zakat (annual tribute), of which Maskat paid 12,000 German crowns, and Sohar $8000. Yet his valour and conduct gradually raised Sayyid Said to wealth and importance, and the warlike operations of Mohammed Ali Pasha against the Wahhabis gave him power to throw off the yoke. His personal gallantry in the disastrous affair with the Benu Bu 'Ali (1820—21), won him the praise of India, and the gift of a sword of honour from the Governor-General. His tolerance, so unusual in Arabia, the patriarchal character of his rule, and his

[1] I cannot tut express my astonishment to see a geographer like hitter, and a veteran from tbe East *like* Colonel *Sykes* (loco cit.), confound 'Imam' with 'Imaun' (Iman), which signifies faith or creed.

love of progress, as shown by his concessions to European and Hindu traders, and by a squadron of three frigates, four corvettes, two sloops, seven brigs, and twenty armed merchant vessels, entitled him to a place amongst civilized powers. With England he became an especial favourite, after he had entered into the Palmerstonian views upon the subject of slave exportation. He began by sacrificing, it is said, 100,000 crowns annually, and he declined the various equivalents, £2000 for three years, and other paltry sums offered in A.D. 1822, as a compensation by Captain Moresby, R.N. His friendship with us, indeed, cost him dear : more than once he threatened that if other concessions were demanded by the unconscionable abolitionist he would escape the incessant worry by abdicating and retiring to Meccah.

Sayyid Said first left Maskat for Zanzibar in 1828, and finally in 1832, justly offended by our refusing to assist him, according to treaty, against Sayyid Hamud bin Azran bin Kays, the rebel chief of Sohar. Our policy on this occasion is generally supposed to have been prompted by Captain, afterwards Colonel, Sam. Hennell, British Resident at Bushire. This official, acting doubtless under orders, and living in constant dread of 'breaking the peace of the Gulf,' preserved it hy yielding every point to every man ; and the ignoble attitude which, amongst a warlike race, provoked only contempt, laid the foundation of the last Persian war. It was on a par with the orders which, under pain of dismissal, hound the officers commanding the Honourable East India Company's cruisers in the Persian Gulf not to open fire upon a squadron of pirates unless they began the cannonade; and which caused the capture by boarding of more than one man-of-war.

Zanzibar had, since its conquest by Oman, been governed by an officer appointed from Arabia. Sayyid Said found the town a line of cajan huts, with the fort commanding the harbour, which served only for an occasional pirate or slaver. Till A. D. 1822 some 15 or 16 Spaniards and Portuguese ranged these seas, committing every kind of atrocity: they were dangerous outside the port, and when at anchor they were guilty of every crime ; as many as three and four have been killed in a single night, and a priest was kept for the purpose of shriving the stabbed and burying the slain. These, however, were the days of large profits. The share of one Arab merchant in a single adventure was worth $218,000—he now (1857) begs his breach Sayyid Said at once began to encourage foreign residents. With a remarkable liberality he at once broke up the monopoly of trade which the Wasawahili had preserved for eight centuries, including the 200 years when it was perpetuated by the avidity and the fanaticism of the Portuguese. The United States, who being first in the market for ivory, copal, and hides, had dispersed their cottons and hardwares throughout Eastern Africa, concluded with him, in Sept. 1835, an advantageous treaty, and established, about the end of 1837, a trading consulate at his court. Pour years afterwards (December, 1811) Lieut.-Colonel Hamerton was directed to make Zanzibar his head-quarters as 'H. B. Majesty's Consul, and H. E. I. Company's Agent in the dominions of H. H. the Imaum.' Captain Domain Desfosses, the Mentor of the Prince de Joinville, and commanding the naval division of Bourbon and Madagascar, escorted by a squadron, signed a treaty on November, 1S44. He was accompanied by a consul without a chancellier, and the former at once receiving his exequatur, began residence.

The Sayyid was unfortunate in sundry attempts to subjugate the Zanzibar Coast: his conduct of war argued scant skill as a general, but he never forfeited his well-earned favour for personal gallantry. "With the true Arab mania for territorial conquest, he eventually succeeded in flying his flag at all the ports that belonged to the Yu'rabi Imams, and which had descended, hv the irregular right of succession, to his ancestor, Ahmad bin Said the Hinawi. The Mazara' (Mazrui) clan, alias the Arabo-Mombasah princes, a turbulent and hot-tempered feudality, who, after the massacre of the Portuguese, had heen allowed, by Sayf bin Sultan, to retain the city on condition of sending occasional presents and of doing certain baronial services, refused (A. D. 1822) allegiance to the Ayyal Bu Said. Captain Yidal, P,.N., finding this important place threatenedby Zanzibar, accepted an application from the citizens, who had hoisted the British flag; advised that they should be received as prot^g^s, and persuaded the claimant to withdraw. The Sayyid remonstrated against these measures with the Bombay Government; and the ministers of the Crown to whom the question was referred, eventually removed our establishment.

Sayyid Said, early in 1828, sailed with a squadron carrying 1200 men, to attack the town, but after taking and garrisoning the fort, he was compelled to make Zanzibar, and eventually Maskat. The retreat was in consequence of the troubles excited by Saud bin Ali bin Sayf, the nephew of Sayyid Bedr, supported by the sister of Sayyid Hilal, chief of Suwayk, who had been treacherously imprisoned. 3e was enabled, by the aid of Isa bin Tarif and his dependents, to invest, with a squadron carrying a force of 4000 to 5000 men, about the end of December, 1829, Mombasah Port, from which his garrison had been repulsed. The Mazru'is, numbering a total of some 1500, gallantly held their ground : the Sayyid's soldiers, suffering severely from fever, refused to fight: briefly two campaigns had little effect upon-the besieged, and the Sayyid was obliged to accept the semblance of submission, in order to return triumphant to Zanzibar. After visiting Maskat, and putting down Hamud bin Azran, who had taken Rustak, and was threatening the capital, he broke the treaty with Mombasah, and blockaded it throughout the N. East monsoon from November, 1831, to April, 1832. During the next year he attacked the jdace for the third time; but, after a week's campaign, he returned once more with Oriental triumph to Zanzibar in Eebruary, 1833. Then treachery was called in to do the perfect work. Rashid bin Salim bin

Ahmad, the Mazru'i Wali or governor, and twenty-six of his kinsmen, enticed by the most solemn oaths, which were accompanied by a sealed Koran—it is wonderful how liar trusts liar!—embarked on one of the Sayyid's ships, which carried his son Sayyid Khalid and Sulayman bin Ahmad. The vessel instantly weighed anchor, stood for Zanzibar, and consigned its cargo to life-long banishment and prison, at Mina and Bandar Abbas. The Mazara' at once sank into utter obscurity.

Sayyid Said was persuaded (Jan. 6, 1843) to attack that notorious plunderer, Bana M'takha, chief of Sewi, a small territory near Lamu, who had persuaded one Mfumo Bakkari, and afterwards his brother Mohammed bin Shaykh, to declare himself Lord of Patta, and independent of the Arab prince. The ruler of Zanzibar here failed to repeat his success at Mombasah, the wily African shutting his ear to the charmer's voice. The second son, Sayyid Khalid, then disembarked his 1200 to 1300 troops, Maskatis and Wasawahili, 'cowardly as Maskatis,' who with the Suri are the proverbial dastards of the race. He served out with Semitic economy five cartridges per head, and he marched them inland without a day's rest, after a ͨ buggalow '-voyage from Arabia. Short of ammunition, and worn out by fatigue, they soon yielded to the violent onslaught of the enemy. The Wdgunya, or as some write the word Bajunf, warriors, described to be a fierce race of savages, descended from the Wasawahili, the Somal, and the Arab colonists, charged in firm line, brandishing spear-heads like those of the Wamasai, a cubit long, and shouting as they waved their standards, wooden hoops hung round with the dried and stuffed spoils of men.[1] The Arabs fled with such precipitation, that some 300 were drowned, an indiscriminate massacre and mutilation took place, the 'England ' and the 'Prince of Wales ' opened an effectual fire upon their own. boats and friends; the guns which had been landed were all captured, and the Sayyid Khalid saved himself only by the speed of his horse. The operation was repeated with equal unsuccess next year, Sayyid Said himself embarking on board the 'Victoria: ' the general, Hammad bin Ahmad, fell into an ambuscade, and again the artillery was lost. After a blockade of the Coast, which lasted till the end of 1866, the Elazi of Zanzibar, Muhiyy el Din of Lamu, landing upon his

[1] **The trophies are drawn out with a lanyard, and cut off when the patient is still alive—after death they are not so much valued'; finally they are dried so as to resemble isinglass.**

native island, talked over the insurgents. Bana M'takha afterwards sent back the Arab cannon, saying that he could not afford to keep weapons which, ate such vast meals of powder, and acknowledged for a consideration the supremacy of Zanzibar, retaining his power, and promising but never intending to pay an annual tribute of $5000. Hence the Baloch mercenaries speak of their late employer as a king who bought and sold, and who was more distinguished for the arts of peace than for the nice conduct of war. Even his own subjects complained on this occasion of his folly in commencing, and of his want of energy in carrying on, the campaign.

The Sayyid's matrimonial engagements were numerous. In 1827 he married the daughter of the Parman-farma (Governor) of Ears, and a grand-daughter of Path 'Ali Shah, under an agreement in the marriage contract that the bride might spend every summer with her own family at Bandar Abbas or Shiraz. Disgusted with Arab homeliness, and with six years of monotonously hot life at Maskat, she obtained leave, and once in a place of safety she wrote hack a strong epistle. It began, 'Ya Dayyus ! ya Mal'un, alluding to the report that Sayyid Khalid had violated the harem of his father, as the latter was also said to have done in his younger days. The Arab prince had lowered himself in the eyes of his subjects by representing himself to be a Shiah. She called him a dog-Stinni, and upon this ground she demanded instant divorce. The Sayyid despatched two confidential elders with orders to represent that his spouse could not legally claim such indulgence : a singular bastinado upon the soles of their feet soon made the venerable learned discover that divine right was upon the lady's side. Her next exploit was to bowstring, in jealousy, a Katirchi (muleteer) with whom she had intrigued; and, driven from. Shiraz by the fame of this exploit, she died at Kazimayn, in child-bed, her lover being this time a Hammamchi, or bath-servant.

In A.D. 1833, four years after the death of Radama I., the Sayyid formed matrimonial designs upon the person of Ranavola Manjaka, Queen of the Hovas, and a personage somewhat more redoubtable than our good Queen Bess. Amongst his envoys on this occasion was one Khamisi wa Tani, who, under the Arabized name Kkarnis bin Osman, presently played some notable tricks upon the credulous 'comparative geographer,' Mr W. D. Cooley. The envoys were kept upon the frontier till the 'Tangi-man' arrived, bringing the Tangina. This nut, scraped in water, is administered as an ordeal, like the hitter water of the ancient Israelites and the poison nut of modern Calabar. The patient is ordered to walk about; after some 20 minutes he feels atrocious bowel-pains, prolapsus takes place, and he dies; if wealthy enough to pay the priest, another kind of nut is at once administered, and it may cure by emesis. As soon as this potion, which always destroys traitors with frightful torments, in fact, with the worst symptoms of Asiatic cholera, was proposed to the ambassadors, in order to., prove the purity of their intentions, and their affection for the royal family, all fled precipitately, as may be imagined, *from* the 'Great Britain' of Africa. Sayyid Said was also unlucky in the choice of another Persian bride, the daughter of Irich Mirza, a supposititious son of Mohammed Shah, and hardly a second-class noble. She came to Zanzibar in A.D. 1819, accompanied by a train of attendants, including her Barrashas (carpet-spreaders), her Jilaudar (groom), and her private Jellad (executioner) . She astonished the Arabs hy her free use of the dagger, whilst her intense relish of seeing her people ride men down in the bazar, and of superintending bastinadoes administered with Persian apparatus, made tbe Banyans crouch in their shops with veiled faces, and the Arabs thank Allah that their women were not like those of the A'ajam. In a short time the lady made herself so disagreeable, that her husband sent her back divorced to her own country.

The Sayyid kept a company of 60 or 70 concubines, and he always avoided those that bore him children. Though a man of strong frame and vigorous constitution, he exhausted his powers by excesses in the harem, he suffered from Sarcocele (sinistral) during later life, and an alarming emaciation argued consumption. The heat of Maskat, which he last visited when hostilities between England and Persia were reported, brought him to his grave. In October, 1856, he died at sea off the Seychelles Islands, on board his own frigate, the 'Victoria.' Aged 67, the 'Second Omar,' as his subjects were fond of calling him before his face, seems to have had a presentiment of death; before embarking he prepared, contrary to Arab custom, a 'Sanduk el Mayyit,' or coffin, and when dying he gave orders tbat his remains should be thrown overboard. The corpse, however, was carried to Zanzibar and interred in the city.

Sayyid. Said was probably as shrewd, liberal, and enlightened a prince as Arabia ever produced, yet Europe overrated his powers. Like Orientals generally, he was ever surrounded by an odious entourage, whom he consulted, trusted, and apparently preferred to his friends and well-wishers. He firmly believed in the African Eetish and in the Arab Sahir's power of metamorphosis ;[1] he would never flog a Mganga

[1] I have alluded to this subject in my exploration of Harar (chap. ii.), and a few more details may not be uninteresting. Strong-headed Pliny (viii. 32) believes metamorphosis to be a ' fabulous opinion,' and remarks, 'there is no falsehood, however impudent, that wants its testimony among them' (the Greeks), yet at Tusdrita he saw L. Coisilius, who had been changed from a woman into a man. Curious to say, the learned Anatomist of Melancholy (Part I. sect. 1) charges him with believing in the versipellis, and explains the belief by lycanthropy, cucubuth or Lupina Insania. Petronius gives an account of the 'fact.' Pomponius Mela accuses the Druidesses of assuming bestial shapes. Suidas mentions a city where men changed their forms. Simon Magus could produce a double of himself. Saxo Grammaticus declared that the priests of Odin took various appearances. John of Salisbury asserts that Mercury taught mankind the damnable art of fascinating the eyes. Joseph Acosta instances fellow-countrymen in the West Indies who were shot during transformation. Our ancestry had their were-wolf (homo-lupus), and the Britons their Biselavaret. Coffin, the Abyssinian traveller, all but saw his Buda change himself into a hyena. Mr Mansfield Parkyns heard of a human horse. In Shoa and Bornou men become leopards ; in Persia, bears; in Somali-land Cyn-hyenas; in West African Kru-land elephants and sharks; in Namaqualand, according to the late Mr Andersson, lions. At Maskat

(medicine-man), nor cut down a ᶜ devil's tree.' He sent for a Shaykh whose characts were famous, and with a silver nail he attached 'the

transformation is fearfully frequent; and illiterate Shiahs believe the good Caliph Abubekr, whom they call Pir i Kaftar (old hyena), to be trotting about the deserts of Oman in the semblance of a she-hyena, pursued by many amorous males. At Bushire the strange tale of Haji Ismail, popularly called 'Shuturi,' the ¹ Camel'd,' is believed by every one, and was attested with oaths by his friends and relations: this respectable merchant whilst engaged in pilgrimage was transformed by an Arab into a she-camel, and became the mother of several foals, till restored to human shape by another enchanter. Even in Europe, after an age of scepticism, the old natural superstition is returning, despite the pitch-fork, under another shape. The learned authoress of the Night-side of Nature objects to 'illusionists,' argues lyeanthropy to be the effect of magico-magnetic influence, and instances certain hysterical and nervous phenomena of eyes paralyzed by their own weakness.

For many years I have carefully sifted .every case reported to me in Asia and Africa, and I have come to the conclusion with which most men commence. No amount of evidence can justify belief in impossibilities, in bona fide miracles. Moreover, such, evidence mostly comes from the duperandthe dupe. Finally, all objective marvels diminish in inverse ratio to the increase of knowledge, whilst preternaturalisms and supernaturalisms gradually dwindle down to the natural badly understood.

Of course this disclaimer of belief in the vulgar miracle does not imply that human nature has no mysterious powers which, if highly developed and displayed in a dark age, would be treated as a miracle or as an act of magic. It has lately been proved that the will exercises positive and measurable force upon inert matter; such 'glimpses of natural actions, not yet reduced to law,'—as Mr Faraday said—open up a wonderful vista in the days to come.

paper to the doorway of Lieut.-Colonel Hamerton's sick-room, thereby excluding evil spirits and the ghost of Mr Napier, who had died at the Consulate. He refused to sit for his portrait—even Colonel Smyth's History of Knight-errantry and Chivalrous Characters failed to tempt him, for the European peasants' reason, —it would take away part of his life. When ' chivalry ' was explained to him, he pithily remarked that only the 'Siflah ' (low fellows) interfere between man and wife, master and man. His pet axiom—a fair test of mental bias—was 'Mullahs, women, and horses never can be called good till death,' in this resembling Pulci—

> Cascan le rose, e restan poi le spine ;
> Non giudicate nulla innanzi al fine.

The Societd Itoyale des Antiquaires du Nord sent him their diploma: he declared that he would not belong to a body of grave-robbers and corpse-snatchers. The census of Zanzibar having been proposed to hpn, unlike King David, he took refuge with Allah from the sin of numbering his people. When tide-gauges were supplied by the Geographical Society of Bombay, he observed that the Creator had bidden the ocean to ebb and to flow—'what else did man want to know about it ?' Such was his incapacity for understanding

European affairs, that until death's-day he believed Louis Philippe to have carried into exile, as he himself would have done, all the fleet and the public treasure of the realm. And he never could comprehend a Republic—'who administers the stick?'

Of this enterprising man, the Mohammed Ali Pasha of the further East, I may say, Extinctus amabitur idem. Shrewd and sensible, highly religious though untainted by fanaticism; affable and courteous, he was as dignified in sentiments as distinguished in presence and demeanour. He is accused of grasping covetousness and treachery—but what Arab ruler is not covetous and treacherous?. He was a prince after the heart of his subjects; prouder of his lineage than fond of ostentation or display, an amateur conqueror on a small scale, mild in punishment, and principally remarkable as the chief merchant, cultivator, and ship-builder in his dominions. An epitaph may be borrowed for him from a man of very different character—first in war, first in peace, and first in the hearts of his fellow-countrymen. Peace be to his manes!

Sayyid Said's territory at the time of his death extended in Oman from the Ra'as el Jebel (Gape Musseldom) to Sohar. In Mekran the seaboard between Ra'as .Task and Guadel belonged to him: in the Persian Gulf he had Khishm, Larak, and Hormuz, and he farmed from the Shah, Bandar Abbas and its dependency, Mina. His African possessions were far the most extensive and important. He ruled, to speak roughly, the whole Eastern Coast from *N.* lat. 5°, and even from Cape Guardafui, where the maritime Somal were to a certain extent his dependents, to Cape Delgado (S. lat. 11°), where the Arab met the Portuguese rule—an extent of 16° = 960 geographical miles. The small republics of Makdishu (Magadoxo, in N. lat. 2° 1' *4s"),* of Brava *(N.* lat. 1° 6' 48"), of Patta *or* Bette (S. lat. 2° 9' 12"), and of Lamu (S. lat. 2° 15' 42"), owned his protectorate, and in April, 1865, Marka received from him a garrison. The whole Zanzibarian Archipelago was his, and he claimed Bahrayn, Zayla, Aden, and Berberah, the first-mentioned with, the last three without, a shadow of right. His Arab subjects declared that they, and not the Portuguese, ceded Bombay to the British: the foundation of the story is a mosque built in ancient times by the Omanis, somewhat near the present Boree Bandar.

Sayyid Said left a single widow, the lady

Azza bint Musa, of the Bu Kharibdn, a granddaughter of tbe Imam Abmad, and consequently a cousin. Sbe is now (1857) in years, but ber ancient lineage and ber noble manners retain for ber tbe public respect. Sbe bad but one cbild, wbicb died young: all the male issue of tbe Prince are by slave-girls, a degradation in tbe eyes of free-born Omani Arabs. As usual amongst tbe wealthy and noble of tbe polygamous East, tbe daughters are tbe more numerous,[1] and many are old maids, the pride of birth not allowing them, like tbe Sherifehs of the Hejaz, to wed with any but equals. The eldest of tbe fourteen sons, Sayyid Hilal, who, in 1815, had visited England, it is said, after an escapade, died at Aden en route to Meccah in 1851. He was followed, after an interval of a few months, by bis next brother, Sayyid Khalid, called tbe Banyan. Tbe eldest surviving

---

[1] In the Journal of Anthropology (No. ii. Oct. 1870, Art. ix.), James Campbell, Surgeon, R.N., produces a paper upon 'Polygamy; its influence on Sex and Population,' showing, by 17 cases drawn from Siam, exceptions to tbe common theory that in the patriarchal family more female than male children are born. But the evidence is too superficial to shake the belief of men who have passed their lives in polygamous countries; moreover, in the families cited the male-producing powers may either have been unusual, or they may have been peculiarly stimulated.

heir (Sayyid Suwayni), the son of a Georgian or Circassian slave, born about 1822, became by his father's will, successor to and lord of the northern provinces. To Sayyid Majid, the fourth son, now (1857) aged 22, a prince of mild disposition and amiahle manners, contrasting strongly with the vigorous ruffianism of his elder brother, was left the Government of Zanzibar and of the East African Coast. There is, as usual amongst Arabs, a turbulent tribe of cousins : of these the most influential is Sayyid Mohammed, a son of Sayyid Salim bin Sultan, younger brother to the late Prince, who some years ago died of consumption. Hitherto he has used his powers loyally—ruling, but not openly ruling. Sayyid Said's valuable property, including his plantations, was sold, as his will directed, and the money was divided according to a fixed scale, even the youngest princes claiming shares. No better inducement to permanent dissension could have been devised. But Eastern monarch s apparently desire that their dynasties should die with them. Eath Ali Shah of Persia, when asked upon his death-bed to name a successor, drew a sword and showed what made and unmade monarchs : scarcely had the breath left his body than the chamber was dyed with the blood of Ms sons, each, hastening to stab some hated rival brother.

These lines were penned in 1857. Since 1859 the hapless and turbulent family has been in a state of fratricidal strife, and the province of Oman has reverted to its normal state of intrigue, treachery, and assassination. Sayyid Suwayni, a negligent and wasteful though not an unpopular man, to whom the English were especially obnoxious, threatened in 1859 an attack upon Sayyid Majid, and was prevented by British cruisers; in due time he was murdered by his son, Sayyid Salim, who usurped the Government. This Sayyid Salim was dethroned by his uncle, Sayyid Turki, who surprised Maskat, and made himself master of the situation. The European would • imagine that the stakes were hardly worth such reckless play : Arabs, however, judge otherwise.

CHAPTER VIII.

ETHNOLOGY OF ZANZIBAR. THE FOREIGN RESIDENTS.

> 'Quiconque ne voit guere
> N'a guere a dire aussi. Mon voyage depeint
> Vous sera d'un plaisir extreme.
> Je dirai; jYtais la; telle chose m'avint,
> Vous y croirez etre vous-meme.'—LA FONTAINE.

THE 300,000 souls[1] now (1857-9) composing the residents on, and the population of, the Zanzibar Island, are a heterogeneous body. The former consist of Americans and Europeans,

[1] The extremes mentioned to me were 100,000 and 1,000,000. Captain Smee (1811) gave 200,000. Dr Kuschenberger (1S35) made the population of the Island 150,000 souls, of whom 17,000 were free negroes. M. G-uillain (1846) places the extremes mentioned to him at 60,000 to 200,000: when he asked the Sayyid, the latter replied like a veritable Arab, 'How can I know when I cannot tell you how many there are in my own house?'

about 14,000 Banyans (including tbose of the Coast), a few Parsees and Portuguese from Goa, and sundry castes of Hindustani Moslems, Khojahs, Mehmans, and Borahs, numbering some 1200. There are also trifling numbers of free blacks from the Comoro Islands, Madagascar, TJnyamwezi, and the Somali country. To this accidental division I will devote the present chapter.

The Consular corps is represented by three members, who, as usual in these remote Oriental spots, assume, and are allowed to assume, the position of plenipos. The first American official was Mr Bichard Palmer, who was succeeded by sundry acting men : the second was Mr "Waters, who left in 1844: then came Mr C. Ward, Mr Webb, and Mr Macmullan. Captain Mansfield now (1859) holding office, is agent to Messrs John Bertram and Co. of Salem. This gentleman, who took a great interest in the East African Expedition, has had a more extensive experience of the East than his predecessors; he has also the advantage of being respectable and respected.

On the part of the Erench Government the first Consul was M. Broquant: he died of fever and dysentery at Zanzibar, and was succeeded by

M. de Beligny, a Drench Creole from Santo Domingo, afterwards transferred to Manilla and to Charleston, South Carolina. M. Yignard, a young man of amiable manners, and distinguished in Algeria as an Arabic scholar, fell victim to a sunstroke when voyaging from Aden, where I met him en route for his post. The present Consul is M. Ladislas Cochet: the Chancellier and Dragoman is M. Jablonsld, Pole and poet.

Lieut.-Colonel Atkins Ilamerton is, and has been, I have said, H. B. Majesty's Consul, and II. E. I. Company's Agent at the Court of Pl. H. Sayyid Said, since December, 18P1, 'when we first established relations with Zanzibar. Attached to his establishment is a passed apothecary, an Eurasian, the only attempt at a medico on the Island. Lieut.-Colonel Ilamerton had been on terms of intimacy with Sayyid Said during a quarter of a century; and their friendship, as happens, began with a 'little aversion.' The Britisher proposed to travel in the interior from Maskat, in those days a favourite exploration with the more adventurous; and the Arab, suspicious as all Arabs, thinking it safest to put the intruder out of tbe way, imprudently wrote a letter to that effect. This missive fell into the hands of the person whom it most concerned : he boldly carried it to the Prince, and reproached him in no measured terms with his perfidy. Sayyid Said found himself overmatched, submitted to Kismat, and, admiring tlie traveller's spirit and openness, determined to win his attachment. The two became firm friends; tbe Consul was tbe influential adviser of the ruler, and the latter intrusted him with secrets jealously hidden from his own. The reason why the trade of Zanzibar was surprisingly developed under the primitive rule of an Arab Prince is not only the immense wealth of Eastern Africa, it results mainly from the wise measures of a man who for the greater part of his life devoted himself to the task. It was an unworthy feeling which made M. Guiilain write of my late friend (ii. 28), £ Bref, sa reputation est de placer fort bien, et a beaux benefices, l'argent que lui donnent la reine et le gouvernement de la compagnie '—his generosity to his family left little after his decease. Not the least of Sayyid Said's anxieties upon Ills deatli-bed was to reach Zanzibar alive, and even when half-unconscious he continually called for Colonel Hamerton. It is suspected that he wished to communicate the place of his concealed treasures, which, despite tlie most careful search, were never found. When hiding their hoards it is not unusual for Arabs to put to death the slaves who assist in the labour, and thus to prevent negro indiscretion. The family, I may here say, firmly believes that Colonel Hamerton knows where the hoards lay, and yet refuses to divulge the secret.

It will not be easy properly to fill this appointment. Without taking into consideration the climate, it is evident that few Englishmen are prepared to settle for long years at remote Zanzibar, and Arabs do not care to trust new men. Yet it would be the acme of short-sightedness to neglect this part of East Africa. Our Anglo-Indian subjects, numbering about 4000[1] in the dominions of Zanzibar, some of them wealthy men, are entitled to protection from the Arab, and more especially from the Christian merchants. Almost the whole foreign trade, or at least four-fifths of it, passes through their hands; they are the principal shopkeepers and artisans, and they extend as far South as Mozambique, Madagascar, and the Comoro Islands. During the last few years the number of Indian settlers has greatly increased, and they have

[1] The extremes of the guess-work census are 2600 and 5000.

obtained possession from tbe Arabs, by purchase or mortgage, of many landed estates in the Sayyid's dominions. The country can look forward only to a moderate development whilst it continue in the present hands, but the capabilities of the coast are great. Labour only is wanted ; and a European power establishing itself upon the mainland—-this object has frequently been proposed, and is steadily kept in view—could in a few years command a territory and a commerce which would rival Western India.

The other white residents are commercial, and it is with no little astonishment that the Englishman finds no direct trade with Great Britain, and meets none of his fellow-countrymen at Zanzibar.[1] Their absence results not from want of venture or dearth of business, but from supineness on the part of the authorities. No merchant can profitably settle where he cannot freely correspond, receive advices that ships have been despatched, and obtain orders for cargoes and consignments. Moreover, large sums have been wasted by respectable houses in settling here trustworthy agents and sober men. The few favourable exceptions found the climate either

[1] In 1862-3 a Bombay firm established a branch on the Island, but I have not heard of the results.

unendurable or fatal. Hitherto, however, Englishmen have done little, and, I write it unwillingly, Englishwomen have done less, for the honour of the national name at Zanzibar than in most parts of the East. Two girls came out to the Island, married to the usual 'black princes,' who mostly turn out to be barbers or domestic servants; this proceeding greatly scandalized the white residents, and the Desdemonas gave more trouble to the officials than the whole colony.

The principal American houses are those of Messrs Bertram & Co., represented by Captain Mansfield, Mr Ropes, and Mr Webb : Messrs Rufus Green & Co., also of Salem, have three agents, Messrs Winn, Spalding, and Wilkins. Lastly, there is Mr Samuel Masury, of Salem, a 'general merchant,' distinguished for probity and commercial sagacity: he left Zanzibar during our exploration of the interior, and he presently came to an untimely end.

The French houses began with a misconception, a certain chancellier having reported officially to his Government, that 232 ships annually visited and loaded at Zanzibar. The intelligence caused considerable excitement: it was believed that every vessel left these shores crammed with copal, ivory, and gold dust, and the French merchants resolved hy concurrence to drive the Americans out of the field. Messrs Yidal fibres of Marseille despatched accordingly to Zanzibar Messrs Bauzan, Wellesley, and Peronnet, and appointed M. Mass their second agent at Lamu. They were opposed by Messrs Rabaud freres, also of Marseilles, a house from whom we received especial kindness : their Zanzibar manager was M. Hannibal Berard, and M. Terassin was sent to the 'bone of contention,' Lamu. These firms choose their employes amongst their captains, who act supercargoes as well as commanders ; they are estimable men, sober and skilful, but painfully lax in dealing with 'les n&gres.' Their Consul publicly declared that it was his duty to curb the merchants, as well as to protect the commerce of France.

The specialty of the French houses is oil. They export the cocoa-nut in various forms, sesamum and other oleaginous grains, wdiich Provence converts with such energy and success into hxiile cl'olives. The sesamum is a comparatively new article of commerce, yet the Periplus (chap. xiv.) numbers Elreon Ses&minon (oil of sesamum) amongst the imports from India. How it is supplied chiefly hy Lamu. Yast quantities could be grown there, but the natives, though large advances have been offered to them, will not extend their cultivation for fear of lowering the price, which has lately doubled. French ships now visit the West Coast of India as far North as Kurrachee, in search of sesamum, and last year (1856) 27 vessels took cargo from Bombay.

At length the Marseille houses found out that Zanzibar is overstocked with buyers; that demand in these regions does not readily, at least, create supply; that it is far easier to dispose of than to collect a cargo ; that the African man will not work as long as he can remain idle, and that sure profits are commanded only by the Banyan system; briefly, the two French houses are eating up each other. The Messrs Vidal are named for a loss of $400,000, which it will be impossible to recoup. It is also reported that too sanguine M. le Chancellier was threatened with a proces-verbal; of his 232 ships 70 were whalers, many names had been twice registered, and only 32 (232 minus 200) took in cargo.

The houses from Hamburg, that 'Carthage of the Northern Seas,' conclude the list of Europeans. The brothers Horn and M. Quas, agents for Messrs Herz and Co., are the most successful copal cleaners; they find it more economical to keep a European cooper than to depend upon the bazar. Messrs William and Albert Oswald, British proteges, represent their father; they are assisted by M. Witt, an intelligent young man, who having graduated in Californian gold-fields, proposes to prospect the Coast. M. Koll acts for Messrs Hansing and Co., and, lastly, M. Iloicli, lately returned to the Island, is the representative of Messrs Muller and Co.

Europeans are, as a rule, courteously treated by the upper classes, and civilly by the Arabs at Zanzibar; this, however, is not always the case on the Coast. They are allowed to fly flags; every merchant has his staff upon his roof, and there is a display of bunting motley as in the Brazil. Even a Cutch boat will carry the Sayyid's plain red colours, with the Union Jack in the corner, and the Turkish crescent and star in the centre.

Composed of patch-work material, the Europeans do not unite, and their disputes, especially between compatriots, are exasperated by commercial rivalries, which have led to serious violations of faith. All is wearisome monotony: there is no society, no pleasure, no excitement; sporting is forbidden by the treacherous climate, and, as in West Africa and the Brazil, strangers soon lose the hahit of riding and walking. Moreover, the merchants, instead of establishing the business hours of Bombay, make themselves at home to their work throughout the day, this is the custom of the Bonny Biver, where supercargoes are treated like shopkeepers by the negroes. European women, I repeat, seldom survive the isolation and the solitary confinement to which not only the place but also the foul customs of the people condemn them.

The necessaries of life at Zanzibar are plentiful, if not good. Bread of imported wheat is usually 'cooked⁵ in the house, and the yeast of sour toddy renders it nauseous and unwholesome. There have been two bakers upon the Island: one served at the Consulate, the other, a Persian, was in the employment of the Prince. Meat is poor ; a good preserved article would here make cent, per cent. Poultry is abundant, tasteless and unnutritious; fish is also common, but it is hardly eatable, except at certain seasons. Cows' milk is generally to be bad, but tbe butter is white, and resembles grease; fruit must he bought at the different bazars early in the morning. All such articles as tea, wine, and spirits, cigars, tobacco, and sweetmeats, are ini-ported from America or from Europe,—the town supplies nothing so civilized. Retail dealing is wanted, and the nearest approach to a shop is the store of a Khojah, who will buy and sell everything, from a bead to a bale of cloth.

All articles but money are expensive at Zanzibar, where the dollar represents our shilling.[1] This is the result of the large sums accumulated by trade and of the necessity of importing provisions ; 'we see tbe same process at work throughout the tropical Brazil. Moreover, in all semi-barbarous lands a stranger living like a native, may live upon ! half-nothing; ' if he would, however, preserve the comforts of home, and especially if he would see society, he must consent to an immoderate expenditure. Einally, where the extremes of wealth and poverty meet, and where semi-civilization has not discovered that prudence is a virtue and improvidence a blunder, tbe more man spends tbe more lie is honoured.

[1] I have been much amused by the comments of the Dress upon the expenses of minor officials living abroad, as elicited from Ministers and Charges d'Affaires *by* the Diplomatic Committee of 1S70. There seems to be a deeply-rooted idea in the British brain that, because heavily taxed, our native island is the most expensive of residences. On the contrary, I have even found England the cheapest country, and London the cheapest capital in Europe. At Fernando Po my outlay was never less than £1800; at Santos (Brazil) it was £1500; at Damascus, from £1200 to £2000, and so forth.

The humblest dwelling at Zanzibar lets unfurnished for £80 to £100 per annum. Eurniture of all kinds, porcelain, china, plate, and linen, no matter how old, fetch more than prime cost, and $1 will be paid for a patched and rickety chair worth in London a shilling. Clothing must be brought from Europe : broad cloth is soon spoiled by sun and damp, and shoes must not be exposed to the air—it is well to have the latter one or two sizes larger than at home. The luxuries of life are of course enormously dear, when they are to be purchased. Luring the Sayyid's absence the women of his harem have, through the eunuchs, sold for a song the valuable presents sent from Europe; and after the return of the royal vessels from Bourbon and the Mauritius, watches and chronometers, sextants and spy-glasses, have been exceedingly cheap. In both cases the stranger-purchaser would have done well to remember that he was buying stolen goods.

Another cause of expense at Zanzibar is the present state of the currency. The rouble of Russia is the franc of Erance, and here the standard of value is the Maria Theresa or German crown, averaging 4s. 2*cl.* Bearing the die of 1780, and still coined at the mint of Yienna for the Arab and tbe E. African trade, it is perferred by the people simply because they know it. The popular names are Riyal (i.e. real, royal) or Girsh (groschen, 'broad ' pieces). Spanish dollars (bu tiikeh, 'father of window,' whence our 'patak'), elsewhere 8 per cent, more valuable, are here only equal to Maria Theresas. In 1846 a French Mission failed to fix the agio of the 5 franc piece at 10 per cent, below the Spanish dollar, which still remained 12.50 to 14 per cent, more valuable. The Company's rupee, better metal than both the above, being still a comparative stranger, loses nearly a quarter of its value. Other silver pieces are the 'Robo ' (Spanish quarter dollar) of 25 cents, and the pistoline (20 cents); these, however, are subject to heavy agio. Small change is always rare, another sure sign of thriftlessness, and it is strange how scarce is bullion in a land so wealthy : I can only account for the fact by the Oriental practice of burying treasure.[1]

Where men reside solely for gain and sorely against the grain, little can be expected from society. Every merchant hopes and expects to leave Zanzibar for ever, as soon as he can realize a certain sum ; every agent would persuade his em-

.[1] For otter details concerning the currency see the Appendix.

ployer to recall Mm. Of late years, also, foreigners complain of a falling off in ivory, copal, cloves, and other articles which the natives, it might he supposed, could most easily supply ; thus profits are curtailed, and a penny saved is a .penny gained. Most residents are contented with an Abyssinian or Somali girl, or perhaps an Msawahili; with a Portuguese cook, who consents to serve till he also can get away; and with a few hired slaves or free blacks, the dirtiest, the least honest, and the most disorderly of domestics. The British Consulate is the only establishment which employs Indian Moslems, perhaps the best of Eastern attendants. This luxury costs, however, at least £25 per mens., each man receiving from $10 to $12, about double the wages paid in India, and all are ever anxious to return home, the mal de pays making them discontented and unhappy. The bumboat-men and the beach-combers are Comoro rascals, who sometimes gain considerable sums; there are also some half-a-dozen negroes, speaking a little had Erench, and worse English, who offer themselves to every stranger, and who fleece him till turned away for making the quail squeak. Workmen are hired hy the day. Carpenters demand $0.50, three times the Indian wage, and the day's work is at most 5 hours; of these men 4 barely did in 43 what 2 ship-carpenters managed in 5 days. The blacksmith and tin-man receive from $0.50 to $1 per diem; the gold,smith is paid according to the value of what he takes in hand—so much per dollar-weight.

The merchants, par excellence of Zanzibar, are the enterprising Bhattias or (Dutch Banyans. The Periplus (chap. xiv.) mentions an extensive import trade for Ariake and Barugaze, the latter generally identified with Baroch.[1] Yasco da Gama found 'Indians,' especially Calicut men, at Mozambique, Kilwa, Mombasah, and Melinde, and by their information he reached their native city. Prom the beginning of tbe present century tbe monopoly fell into the hands of the Bhattia caste. At first they were obliged to make Zanzibar, vid Maskat, in a certain ship which sailed once a year : they were exposed to many hardships and perils : several of them were murdered, and when a Hindu died the Arabs, like tbe Turks of Masawab, claimed the droit d'aubaine. They rose in mercantile repute by commercial integrity, frugality, and perseverance, whilst tbe inability of the Moslem Sarraf to manage ac-

---

[1] Pliny, however (vi. 35), calls Baricazu a 'town of ^Ethiopia.'

counts or banking put great power into their hands. At Maskat and the neighbourhood they number nearly 500, and here about 400.[1] They extend southwards to Angosh (Angoxa) and Mozambique, where they make fortunes by the sale of Casimir noir, and where they are now as well treated as they were formerly tyrannized over by the Portuguese. Thus, though never leaving the seaboard, they command the inland trade, sending, where they themselves do not care to travel, Arabs and Wasawahili to conduct their caravans of savages and slaves. Por this reason they have ever been hostile to European exploration, and report affirms that they have shown no scruples in compassing their ends. They are equally powerful to forward the discoverer ; they can cash drafts upon Zanzibar, Mandavi, and Bombay; provide outfits, supply guards and procure the Pagnzi, or porters, who are mostly their employes. Ladha Mamha farms the customs at Zanzibar, at Pemba Island his nephew Pisu has the same charge: Mombasah is in the hands of Lalchmidas, and some 40 of his co-religionists; Pangani is directed by Trikandas and contains 20 Bhattias, including

[1] la 1844 there were 500 Banyans on the Coast and Island, —the number has now nearly trebled.

those of Mbwerii; even the pauper Sa'adani has its Banyan; Ramji, an active and intelligent trader, presides at Bagamoyo, and the customs of Kilwa are collected hy Kishindas. I need hardly say that almost all of them are connected hy hlood as well as hy trade.

The Bhattia at Zanzibar is a visitor, not a colonist; he begins life before his teens, and, after an expatriation of 9 to 12 years, he goes home to become a householder. The great change of life effected, he curtails the time of residence to half, and furloughs become more frequent as transport waxes easier. Not a Hindu woman is found upon the Island; all the Banyans leave their wives at home, and the consequences are certain peccadilloes, for which they must pay liberally. Arab women prefer them because they have light complexions; they are generous in giving jewels, and they do not indulge in four wives. Most of them, however, especially those settled on the Coast, keep handsome slave-girls, and, as might be expected where illegitimates cannot be acknowledged, they labour under the imputation of habitual infanticide. On the other hand, their widows may not remarry, and they inherit the husband's property if not embezzled by relatives and caste-fellows.

The Bhattias are forbidden by their Dkarma ('easte-duty') to sell animals, yet, with the usual contradiction of their creed, all are inveterate slave-dealers. They may not traffic in cowries, that cause the death of a mollusc; local usage, however, permits them to buy hippopotamus-tusks, rhinoceros-horn, and ivory, their staple of commerce. We cannot wonder if, through their longing to shorten a weary expatriation, they have sinned in the matter of hides. This, together with servile cohabitation, caused a scandal some years ago, when the MaMraj, their high priest, sent from Malwa a Chela, or disciple, to investigate their conduct. Covered with ashes and carrying an English umbrella, the holy man arrived iu a severe mood; he rejected all civilities, and he acknowledged every address with a peculiar bellowing grunt, made when 'Arti' is offered to the Dewta or deity. The result was a fine of $20,000 imposed upon the rich and wretched Jayaram. The sum was raised amidst the fiercest and most tumultuous of general subscriptions, and since that day the spoils of the cow have been farmed to a Khojah employe. All oppose with might and main the slaughter of cattle, especially iu public, and they attempt to quit the town during the Moslem sacrificial days.

The long limp black hair, the smooth yellow skin, and the regular features of the Bhattia, are conspicuous near the woolly mops, the grinning complexions, and the flat faces of the Wasawahili. His large-peaked Cutch turban, white cotton coat or shoulder cloth, and showy Indian dhoti around the .loins, contrasts favourably with the Arabs' unclean garb. The Janeo, or thread of the twice-born, passes over his shoulder, and, in memory of home, he encircles his neck with a string of dry Tulsi stalks (Ocimum canum, a species of herb Basil), which he now grows at Zanzibar. His manners as well as his outer man are rendered pleasant and courteous by comparison with the rest of the population, and he is a kind master to his serviles, who would love him if they possibly could love anything but themselves.

These Hindus lead a simple life, active only in pursuit of gain. On the Coast, where profits are immense—•Trikandas of Pangani, for instance, claims $26,000 of debt—they have substantial stone houses, large plantations, and goodly gangs of male and female slaves. Those resident at Zanzibar are less anxious to display their wealth: all, however, are now entitled by treaty to manage their own affairs without the interference of the local Government. These Banyans will buy up the entire cargoes of American and Hamburg ships: the ivory from the interior is consigned to them, and they purchase the copal from the native diggers. They rise at dawn to perform the semi-religious rite 'Snan ' (bathing), apply to business- during the cool of the day, and dine at noon. Avoiding Jowari, the Arabs' staff of life, they eat boiled rice, vegetables, and ghee, or wheaten bread and Mung, or other pulse, flavoured with assafoetida, turmeric, and 'warm spices.' They chew tobacco, though forbidden by caste rule to smoke it, and every meal concludes with betel-nut and pepper-leaf, whose heating qualities alone enable them, they say, to exist at Zanzibar. They work all day, rarely enjoying the siesta unless rich enough to afford such luxury : they bathe in the evening, sup at 9 P.M., chew betel once more, and retire to rest.

As the Island contains no local Dewta, the Bhattias are careful to keep a Vishnu in the house, and to travel about, if possible, with a cow: in places like Pangani, where the horned god cannot live, they supply its place by a Hanuman (a small monkey, like the Presbyter Entellus of India) trapped in the jungle.

Pagodas not being permitted, they meet for public devotions at a house in the southern quarter of the city, where most of them live, and lately they have been allowed to build a kind of fane at Mnazi Moyya. As usual with Banyans, the Bhattias have no daily prayers : on such festivals as the Pitri-paksha—the 'Manes-Portnight,' from the 13th to the 18th of the month Bhadrapad—they call in, and fee a Brahman to assist them. Their proper priests are the Pokarna, who, more scrupulous than others, refuse to cross the sea : the Sarsat Brahmans, so common in Sind and Cutch, are the only high-caste drones who to collect money will visit Zanzibar and Maskat. With a characteristic tenderness, these Banyans cook grain at the landing-places for the wild slaves, half-starved by the 'middle-passage,' and inclination as well as policy everywhere induces them to give alms largely. Apostasy is exceedingly rare: none Islamize, except those who have been perverted by Moslems in their youth, or who form connections with strange women. The Comoro men, here the only energetic proselytizers, have, however, sometimes succeeded: a short time ago two Bhattias became Mohammedans, an d their fellow caste-men declared that the Great Destruction was drawing nigh. Yet Vishnu slept, and still sleeps the sleep of the just.

When a Bhattia's affairs become hopelessly involved he generally 'levants ' : sometimes, however, he will go through the Diwali or bankruptcy, a far more troublesome process than the - Gazetted The unfortunate places in his storefront a lighted lamp, whence the name of the ceremony, and with head enveloped in a sheet, he silently occupies the furthest corner. Presently a crowd of jeering Moslems collects to see the furious creditors ranting, scolding, and beating the bankrupt, who weeps, wails, calls upon his god, and swears to he good for all future time. These degrading scenes, however, are now becoming rare. They remind us of the Tuscans and the Boeotians of old, [c] who brought their bankrupts into the market-place in a bier, with an empty purse carried before them, all the hoys following, where they sat all day, *circwmtante plebe,* to he infamous and ridiculous.'

All Hindus are careful when returning home from foreign travel to purge away its pollution hy performing a Tirth or Yatra to some holy spring, and hy large payments to Brahmans. Moslems declare that when the death-rattle is heard, one of those present 'eases off' the moribund by squeezing his throat. Banyan corpses are burnt at a place about two miles behind the town, and the procession is accompanied by a guard to keep off naughty boys. When a Bhattia dies without relatives on the Island, a committee of his fellow caste-men meets by the order of II. B. Majesty's Consul; takes cognizance of his capital, active and passive; and, after settling his liabilities, remits by bill the surplus to his relatives in India.

The following is a list of the other Hindu castes to be found at .Zanzibar :—

Brahman, of whom there are now six individuals, two Glujrati, and four llajgarh, both sub-castes of the Sdrsat. One of them, Prad-Mn Joshf, is a Shastri—learned in the Teda.

Khattri, four in number : of these one is a trader, and the rest are carpenters capable of doing a very little very rough work.

Wani (pure Banyan) one. There are also three or four of the Lohana sub-caste from Sind and Cutch.

Lohar, or blacksmith: of this Shudra sub-'caste there are five; one acts Sutdr (carpenter), and a second is a Sonar, or goldsmith—in Cutch the occupations are not separated by 'Dharma.'

A few Parsees from Bombay visited Zanzibar; two were carpenters, and tbe third was a watchmaker, dishonest as his craft usually is. To the general consternation of Europeans, two Parsee agents lately landed on the Island, sent by some Bombay house whose name they concealed. These will probably be followed by others, and if that most energetic of commercial races once makes good a footing at Zanzibar, it will pre-. sently change the condition of trade. They are viewed without prejudice by the Arabs and the Wasawahili. The late Sayyid was so anxious to attract Parsees, who might free him from the arrogance and the annoyance of 'white merchants,' that he would willingly have allowed them to build a 'Tower of Silence,' and to perform, uninterrupted, all the rites of their religion.

The Indian Moslems on the Island and the Coast were numbered in 1841 at 600 to 700. Besides a few Borahs and Mehmans, Zanzibar contains about 100 Khojahs, who are held to be a 'generation of vipers, even of Satan's own brood.' Here, as in Bombay, they are called Ismailiyyahs, heterodox Shiahs, who take a name from their seventh Imam Ismail, son of Ja'afar el Sadik, while orthodox Shiahs believe the seventh revealed Imam to have been Musa el

Ivazim, another son of Ja'afar el S&dik ; and the founder of the Sophy (Safawi) dynasty, in the tenth century of the Hijrah (A.D. 1501). They have derived from the Batinis and Karmatis certain mystic and subversive tenets ; and they are connected in history with Ilasan Sabah (or Sayyah, the travelling Darwaysh), our Vetulus de montanis, or Old Man (Shaykh, i.e. chief) of the Mountains, and with modern Freemasonry, which begins to appear when the Crusaders had settled in that home of heresies, Syria and Palestine. Hence the tradition that the First Grand Lodge was transferred to Lake Tiberias, after the destruction of Jerusalem. They practise the usual profound Takiyyah (concealment of tenets), call themselves Sunnis, or Shiahs, as the case may require, and assume Hindu as well as Moslem names. The Imam to whom they now pay annual tribute is one Agha Khan Mahallati, a Persian rebel, formerly Governor of Kirman, and afterwards notorious upon the Bombay turf. This incarnation of the Deity is not intrusted ■with any of the secrets of his sect. The Khojahs have at Matrah, near Maskat, an enclosed house, which the Arabs call Bayt el Luti: They declare that both sexes meet in it, and that when on a certain occasion it Avas broken open, a large calf of gilt silver was found to be the object of worship. Other incredible tales are also told about the sect: they remind us of the legends of the Libanus, which make the Druzes, apparently another offshoot of the Batini, worship El Ijl (the calf) when the figure is placed in their Khilwahs, or lodges, in memory of the detested Nishtakin Darazi, and in contra-distinction to El Akl, Hamzeh, their greater 'prophet.'[1] No Agapomenical establishments exist at Zanzibar: the chief of the heretic sect is one Haymah, who has, however, but little authority, and who commands even less respect. The Khojahs at times repair to a tumbledown mosque on the sea-shore south of the city, in the quarter called Mnazi Moyya.

By no means deficient in intelligence, though unscrupulous and one-idea'd in pursuit of gain, the Khojahs are the principal shop-keepers in Zanzibar. They arc popularly accused of using false weights and measures; they opposed the introduction of a metallic currency, and they have ever advocated, with the Prince, a return to the bad old state of barbarism. Many have applied

[1] Such is the general view. There may, however, he a section of the Druze creed that retains the calf-image in honour.

themselves to slave-dealing, and lately one was deported for selling poison to negroes ; they are receivers of stolen goods, and by the readiness with which they buy whatever is brought for sale, they encourage the pilfering propensities of the slaves. They travel far and wide; several of them have visited the Lake Legions, and we afterwards met, at Kazeh of Unyanyembe,[1] one of their best men, Musa Mzuri. At Zanzibar all not in trade are rude artisans, who can patch a lantern and tin a pot; one of them, who had learned to mend a watch, repaired the broken wheel of my pocket pedometer.

Of the free blacks who visit and who sometimes reside in Zanzibar, I have mentioned the Malagash: these Madagascar Islanders occupy the easternmost suburb of the town. In early ages the Arab and Wasawahili settlers on the western coast of the Great Island traded with the Mozambique, the Sawahil, and even Arabia, and since 1829 the persecutions of the Queen lianavol a-Manj aka, and the heavy yoke of the Hova conquerors, caused many to leave their homes. The rare Somal need hardly be no-

---

[1] 'Handsome Moses ' is mentioned in 'The Lake Legions of Central Africa' (i. 323, et passim). He and his 'brother,' Sayyan, entered the country about 1830.

ticed. During the season a few run down from Makdishu and Brava, to trade and barter hides a,nd cattle. There are almost 2000 men from Angazijeh (Great Comoro), Mayotta, Hinzuwan or Anjuan (Johanna), and Muhayli. The word Comoro is evidently corrupted Arabic, meaning Moon-Island. The natives of the Archipelago here preserve their own language, which seems to he a superstruction of Javanese and Bali, Arabic, and Sanskrit erected upon a primitive insular dialect, meagre and un-Aryan. Others have detected in it a resemblance to that of the Philippine Islands,[1] and hold the people to he of Malay origin. The blood was Persianized and Arabized in the 12th century, and the Sultan and chiefs have ever since retained the Semitic physiognomy ; but the extensive negro innervation has so tainted the blood that no difference can he perceived in the characteristic effluvium between them and the Wasawahili. It is curious to hear them, withal, boast of their Koraysli descent, and pride themselves upon the glories of the ancient race that produced the 'Rasul Ullah.' In A.D. 1771 they hospitably entertained the

[1] I state this upon the authority of Lieut.-Colonel Hamerton. Capt. Guillain (iii. 414) appears to think the language Zangian much mixed with Arabic.

crew of an East Incliaman wrecked whilst en route to Bombay. The Sultan of Johanna received in return a magnificent present from the H. E. I. Company, and the Comoro Islanders gained for themselves a permanent good name. A considerable emigration was caused in the early part of the present century by intestine divisions and by piratical attacks from Madagascar, whilst the slave emancipation by the French in 1847 set a large class free to travel. Of late they have displayed a savage and mutinous spirit, and two men were put to death for attempting with peculiar audacity the life of the young chief, Abdullah.

Amongst Eastern impostors the Comoro, especially the Johanna men, are facile prineipes: the singular scoundrels have completely mastered the knack of cajoling Europeans — no Syrian Dragoman can do it better. Once or twice a year they tell-off begging-parties, who. visit Mauritius and Aden, Bombay and Calcutta, and who invariably represent themselves as being on ͨ Church-bijness,' i.e. pilgrimage. Linguists, after the fashion of Egyptian donkey-boys, they also have the habit, like the petty Shaykhs and Emirs in the Libanus, of calling themselves 'princes.' More than one scion of Comoro loyalty, after obtaining a passage on board our cruisers, insisting upon the guard being turned out, and claiming from our gullible countrymen all the honours of kinghood, has proved to be a cook or abumboatman. Unscrupulous as bigoted, they have induced half-starved Europeans to apostatize by promises of making them chiefs and of marrying them to princesses; after circumcision, the wretches were left to starve. The Comoro men settled at Zanzibar are mostly servants in European houses, where they recommend themselves by exceeding impudence and by being handy at any fraud. Others are rude artisans, and the rest are Mercuries, beach-combers, and bumboat-men, who supply sailors with Venus and Bacchus, both execrably bad. "When expecting invasion, Sayyid Majid equipped about 130 of these fellows as a garde de corps: they had flint muskets, two spears apiece, and lozenge-shaped hats., whereas the common troops wore woollen night-caps. Einally, they are cowardly as they are dishonest: it was not without astonishment that I heard of Ur Livingstone engaging a party of them for exploration in the African interior, and the trick which they played <u>him</u> is now a matter of history.

The I)iwans or chiefs of the mainland ports

and. towns occasionally visit the Island on public and private business. • Twice a year, in our midsummer and midwinter, a crowd of the Wanyamwezi and other races of the inner intertropical regions flock, vih the Coast, into Zanzibar, where they engage themselves as porters, and undertake carrying packs for the native traders to *the* Lake Regions and other meeting-places of commerce. They are so wild, that they cannot be induced to enter a house; and the terror of one who was brought to the consular residence was described as grotesquely comical: even the more civilized look' upon a stone abode as a cavern or a dungeon. These half-naked miserables may be seen devouring, like birds of prey, carrion and putrid fish in the outskirts of the city; they have also a ᶜ Devil's tree,' whose trunk bristles with nails, and whose branches are robed in foul rags.

Some years ago one of the chiefs of the interior, I was told, was brought to Zanzibar a prisoner of war. He is described as a man of kingly presence, 6 feet 2 inches tall, handsome in face, and well-formed in head; his skin was covered with scar and tattoo in patterns, amongst which the crescent shape predominated.[1] When

[1] One of my informants suggested tliat from this peculiar tattoo, 'TTnyanrwezi,' the Land of the Moon, might have taken

struck by his Arab owner he spat upon him, and declared that if burnt alive he would not cry out. Being carried before the late Sayyid, he boldly told him that 'God exalts men and brings them low, that both were kings, and that the same misfortune which had made one a captive might also happen to the other.' As he walked through the streets all the slaves, wild and domestic, prostrated themselves, to he touched by the point of his staff; they served him with food upon their knees; they remained in that position while he ate, and all wailed when he was placed in the Eort. The same story is told of an old 'Congo king,' who is still remembered at Bio de Janeiro. The prisoner of Zanzibar invariably placed his foot upon presents, and when the Sayyid restored him to liberty he departed empty-handed. M. Broquin, the Trench Consul, and other Europeans made inquiries about this black Jugurtha: all they could discover was that his country lay somewhere about the great Central Lakes.

A few Wazegura, Wasegejo, and Wadigo, heathen from the mainland, visit Zanzibar to buy and sell, or to fly from foes and famine. The

the name which the Greeks after their fashion literally translated 'Mountain-range of the Moon.'

greater portion, settle permanently npon the Island, the savage for the most part unwillingly exchanges the comforts and pleasures of semi-civilization for the wildness and freedom of 'Nature,' so dear to the man of refinement. These Africans live hy fishing and work in tbe plantations: they easily obtain from the large landed proprietors bits of ground, paying as a yearly quit-rent half a dollar and upwards according to crop, manioc, bananas, and sweet potatoes.

CHAPTER IX.

HORSEFLESH AT ZANZIBAR.'—THE OUTSKIRTS OF THE CITY, AND THE CLOYE PLANTATIONS.

'Peregrination cliarms our senses with such unspeakable and sweet variety, that some count him unhappy that never travelled, and pit}ʳ his case, that from his cradle to his old age beholds the same still; still, still the same, the same.'—
' ANATOMY on MELANCHOLY,' **Part II. sect.** ii. **mem.** 3.

MOST Europeans at Zanzibar keep borses winch they seldom ride. The Sayyid, however, had, after hospitable Arab custom, placed a large stud at the disposal of Lieut.-Colonel Hamerton and his guests. I had heard much of the Oman blood, so before excursioning to the outskirts of Zanzibar City we proceeded to the Prince's stables.

The late ruler had rarely less than 200 mares, whose value ranged between $1500 and $2000:

at present, however, the number is greatly reduced. They require as much nursing as European dogs: in the morning they must he picketed in the courtyard to. 'smell the air '; during the day they must take shelter from the sun under a long cajan-roofed shed; they must at all times be defended from rain.and dew; and they must be fed with dry fodder—here, as in Paraguay, the belief is that the indigenous green meat becomes fatal to imported beasts. We found the treatment very rough. The animals were ungroomed, and mostly they had puffed legs, the result of being kept standing night and day upon a slope of hard boarding. Amongst them I was shown a curious Nejdi, which reminded me of Lady Hester Stanhope's pampered beasts; the coat was silver-white, the shoulders were pinkish, and the saddle-back amounted almost to a deformity. The favourite charger of the late Sayyid is a little bay with black points, standing about Id hands 2 inches : its straight fetlocks are well fitted for stony ground, it wears the mane almost upon the withers, and the shoulder is well thrown back, barely leaving room for the saddle. The hindquarter, that weak point in the Arab, is firmly and strongly made, and the tail is thin, switch-like, carried nearly straight, as usual with the best blood, and remarkably high. The beau-ideal of a Nejdi is an animal all shoulder and quarter, connected hy a hit of barrel; and to this pitch of excellence we are gradually breeding up our English horses. The charger in question is of the ancient Oman race, once celebrated for endurance : the late Sayyid, however, injured his stud by crossing foal and dam, brother and sister, till the animals fined down and dwindled to mere dwarfs. I remarked that, here as elsewhere, the Arabs have learned from Europeans to trace the genealogy of their horses through the sire, a practice unknown to the sons of the desert.

All the best horses in Zanzibar come from Oman: an inferior strain is exported by Brava (Barawa), and the Somali country. The latter sends good little beasts somewhat like those of the Pernambucan Province; but, worn out by long marches and scant feeding, they usually die during the first rains. Upon the mainland they will live for years. Here, however, the new importations at first fatten; then they get foul; the sweat becomes fetid; they lose breath and become unfit for work, till fatal disease manifests itself by foam from the mouth. As in

Malabar and Mauritius, where the field-officers have often been dismounted, it is next to impossible to keep horses in health and condition: they are also costly, $150 . to $200, German crowns, being asked for Kadishs or garrons.

The Government stables at Zanzibar also contain a few mules brought from the Persian Gulf. They become liable to inveterate drowsiness ; they start when approached, refuse food and drink, and soon succumb to the climate. The ass, on the contrary, here as in the East African interior, thrives even upon hard food, and consequently it is prized by the Arabs. There are many breeds. During the season fine animals are brought from Oman; iron-grey mares with white legs being preferred; Bahrayn and the Persian Gulf send a large light-coloured beast, resembling that of Baghdad; it is not, however, considered lasting. Asses imported from Brava and the Somali country are held fit only for carrying burdens, and the Unyamwezi breed, known by its lopped ears, though strong and serviceable, is always but half tamed, and is often vicious. The most useful and lasting are the Mutawallid or Muwallid, the progeny of Maskat beasts, Creoles born upon the Island— these we were advised to buy before leaving for tlie interior. I subsequently purchased thirty, and the last died within six months of landing : we then mounted Unyamwezi animals, and had nothing to complain of. Asses are ridden, as they always should be, upon the crupper; the 'hulus ' are rather pads than saddles, covered with thick cloths and black sheepskins ; no one uses stirrups, and the bridle is the rudest of contrivances. The price of donkeys ranges from $15 to $100 : I bought a tolerable riding animal f or $60, and I heard of one costing $-350. Finally, the Sayyid keeps for the use of his plantation-mills a few miserable mangy camels from Brava and Makdisliu: they may be worth $10 to $12 a-head.

Mounted on the Prince's best we passed through the town, where the long sharp poles projecting from the low house-eaves are not pleasant to those riding spirited nags. This is the labour hour, and all are not inactive. The weaver on his raised clay bench, and shaded by his dwarf verandah, is engaged upon a turban, whilst his neighbour converts copal, reddened by cinnabar, into ear-rings and other ornaments. The tinsmith and the Comoro blacksmith, with the usual African bellows, are also at work hammering at pots and pans, fashioning the normal weapons, arrow and spear lieads, and repairing old guns. The leather-worker is moulding a targe of rkinoceros-hide, apparently all umbo, and the vendors of oil and grain, spices and drugs, glass and 'potions,' are on the alert. By the way we walked into the partially-walled compound or court representing the slave-market, a bona fide affair, not like the caravanserai which used to he fitted up and furnished by the Cairene Dragoman for the inspection of curious tourists. In 1835 a wooden cage some 20 feet square often contained some 150 men, women, and children, who every day were [4] knocked down ' to the highest bidder in the public [e] place.' In those times the yearly importation was 6000 to 7000. The bazar was subsequently held in the Changani Quarter, near the Western Point; the late Sayyid, however, having forbidden, by way of sop to the British Cerberus, the sale of men in the streets of Zanzibar as of Maskat, it was shifted to a plantation called Kirungani. As this was found inconveniently distant, it migrated to its present site. Lines of negroes stood like beasts, the broker calling out 'bazar kliush I '—the least hideous of the black faces, some of which appeared hardly human, were surmounted by scarlet night-caps. All were horridly tliin, with ribs protruding like the circles of a cask, and not a few squatted sick on the ground. The most interesting were the small hoys, who grinned as if somewhat pleased hy the degrading and hardly decent inspection to which both sexes and all ages were subjected. The woman-show appeared poor and miserable; there was only one decent-looking girl, with carefully blacked eye-brows. She seemed modest, and had probably been exposed for sale in consequence of some inexcusable offence against decorum. As a rule, no one buys adult domestic slaves, male or female, for the sufficient reason, that the masters never part with them till they are found incorrigible. These, however, are mostly Bozals, or wild serviles newly driven from the interior, and they are not numerous, the transactions of the year being now concluded. The dealers smiled at us, and were in good humour.

It would be easy to adorn this subject with many a flower of description; the atrocities of the capture, the brutalities of the purchase, the terrors of the middle-passage, and the horrors to which the wretches are exposed when entering half-civilized lands. It was usual to throw the slaves overboard when the fatal symptom, eoprophagism, appeared amongst them. A single Dan (Dow) belonging to the late Prince Khali cl lost when running a course 500 slaves by sickness, and by the falling of the pont-hottant or flying-deck—many a desperate naval action could not show such a butcher's bill. A. certain Charles L- , a kiln-dried Mauritius man, crucified seven negroes in terrorem: two were fastened outside the ship, the others were nailed by the feet to the deck, and by the hands to capstan bars, lashed across the masts. With a lighted tar-barrel in an empty boat he nearly caused the loss of an English cruiser, and when she was well on the reef he let off rockets and saluted her. Another man, a Spaniard, finding his ventures likely to die of dysentery, sewed them up before he sent them to the bazar; this slaver made an act of contrition before he died, and severely blamed his bowie-knife. Sensational paragraphs, however, are not wanted by those to whom the subject is familiar, and they are likely to mislead the many who are not. I shall return to the subject of slavery in another chapter.

Thence we entered the Malagash Quarter, where the land belongs chiefly to Sayyid Sulayman bin Hamed, a former Governor of Zanzibar; he is said to be so wealthy that he ignores tlie extent of his means. Here is the Lai Bazar, the very centre of prostitution, an Agapemone of some twenty Cyprians : all are "Wasawahili—the Indian women, who appear almost European in complexion and features, having now left. Their faces like skinned apes, and lean legs encased in red silk tights, make their appearance revolting as their society is dangerous. . Some of them cool the orbits of the eyes by a kind of loup of perfumed turmeric, whose golden tint causes the outer darkness to gloom extra sooty; others apply curry-coloured dabs to the woolly hair. Sundry of these patches are frontlets or medicines applied to the temples: In former days we used, for instance, 'rose-water and vinegar, with a little woman's milk, and nutmegs grated upon a rose cake,' and the Jews are said to have smeared themselves with Christian blood.

The Malagash Quarter is at the far east of the city, leading to two tumble-down bridges which span a lagoon more deadly than that of British Accra. These ruins might easily be converted into dykes, and in process of time the mouth would be sanded or silted up; they are however, fated to make way for iron improvements. In my day the lagoon was connected by fresh, water with the sea, and became now a muddy pool at the ebb tides of the Syzygies, then a sheet of festering mud which nearly encircled the settlement, and which converted the site of Zanzibar city into a quasi-island. Every evening a pestilent sepulchral miasma arose from it, covering the skin with a clammy sweat, and exhaling a fetor which caused candles to burn dim, and which changed the sound of the human voice. Lazy skippers anchoring here for facility of watering, thus exposing their men to the breath of the fetid lagoon, have lost in a few days half the crew; and although the water appeared to be of the purest, it became so offensive that often the casks had to be started.

We then passed over a sandy flat, thinly powdered with black vegetable humus. To the left was a creek upon whose sandy beach vessels are hauled up, and where ships of 300 to dOO tons can be safely careened : in a few years there will here be a dock. A mile of neat footpath placed us at the late Sayyid's Summer Palace, Mto-ni, which is distant about three direct miles from the Consulate. After escaping the unpleasant attentions bestowed upon us by the tame ostriche_, who are apt to use beak and wing, we dismounted for inspection. The building is of coral rag, pierced with square windows, and the wings are nnited hy a verandah-terrace, supported hy wooden pillars, and facing Meccah, for convenience of prayer. A few feet above the centre is the peaked roof of the Kiosk, which makes the place remarkable to crews entering the harbour. In front floats from sunrise to sunset the red flag of the Sayyid : the rear is brought up by a small cemetery, sundry offices, and lowly cajan-thatched hovels tenanted by slaves. The work of man is mean enough, but it is surrounded by the noblest handiwork of Nature, cocoas and mangoes, whilst the borders of the little stream could be beautifully laid out.

Gum Oopal, formerly called in the trade Gum Anime, now Gum Elemi, is washed down by the rains, and is picked up by the slaves about the debouchure of this fiumara. On the Mto-ni road also we passed sundry .places where pits, never exceeding five feet deep, had been sunk in the sandy plain, thinly clothed with sedgy grass. TJpon the higher grounds, also, to judge by the eye, about 100 feet above sea-level, we found many deserted diggings. The soil is a dark vegetable mould, varying in thickness from a foot to 18 inches, and based upon the raised sea-beach of blue clay. This becomes fat and adhesive, clogging the hoe as it descends: the half-decayed blood-red fibre with which it is mixed throughout was recognized hy the negroes as cocoa-roots. Bits of scarlet-coloured earth also variegated the faint blue marl, and at a depth of feet water began to. exude from the greasy walls of the pit. These, places supply only the raw or unripe copal, locally called Chakazi,[1] and hy us corrupted to Jackass: the true vegetable fossil must' he brought from the coast. The tree was probably once common on the Island, but it has been cut down for masts and similar uses. Copal does not appear under that name in the list of exports from Zanzibar given hy Captain Smee in 1811: possibly that officer alludes to it when speaking of 'hammer.' In early days ᶜ gum-anime ' was held a precious medicine for rheums and heaviness of the head. It was imported via the Levant ᶜ from the place where incense is found, and that lande or soyle is called *Animitim*, and therefore the thing is called, Anime,' says Dr Monardes, treating of the ohj,ects that are brought from the West Indies. He adds that American Anime was whiter, brighter, and said to he a [4] spice of *Oharabe* or *Succino*, which is

[1] Tchakazi, espece de gomme-resine, dont j'ignore l'origine (M. Guiilain, Part II. p. 87).

called amber congealed.' In 1769 Portugal forbade tbe importation of true copal, in order to protect tbe Jataycica or gum of tbe Jatoba (bymenoea), of wbicb *14s* Arrobas bad been sent from Turiassu in tbe Brazil.

Leaving Mto-ni, after balf a mile of beach, we turned towards tbe interior, and ascended tbe gently rising ground, beautifully undulated, wbicb leads to tbe royal estates called Bauzah and Taif,. formerly Kizimba-ni or Sebbe. Por two or tbree miles a narrow patb, wbicb compelled us to ride in Indian file, wound through cocoa-groves and patches of bigbly-cultivated ground, witb bere and there a but buried under fruit-laden mangos. Tbe track, tben 254 feet above sea-level, widened into a broad avenue of dark conical clove-trees, varying in beigbt from 6 to 16 feet according to age; feathered almost to tbe ground, and extending, like tbe well-berried coffee-slirub, its brandies at rigbt angles to tbe trunk. All, however, bore tbe impress of neglect, where Dr Buschenberger found a 'picture of industry and of admirable neatness and beauty' that employed from 500 to 700 slaves.

We saw bttle to admire in tbe 'palace,' a single-storied lodge of coral rag, and ample porches looking upon sundry courts and yards, negro quarters and drying-grounds. There is here a well said to he 100 fathoms deep, which gives water only in the rainy seasons ; most of the upland plantations must draw the element from the little streams. The Arab care-takers, after refreshing us with cocoa-nut milk, led us out to inspect the grounds. These Semites, satiated with verdure, despise the idea of assisting nature, and yet at Maskat they will gaze delighted upon a dusty, ragged plot of sand-veiled rock, dotted with consumptive trees, and dignified hy the name of a garden. Some years ago Lieut.-Colonel Ilamerton taught the late Sayyid to plant rose-trees, which gave a crop as abundant as those of ancient Syria: during their' owners' absence the slaves uprooted the young growth in very wantonness. The nutmeg fared as badly. The Consul also succeeded in producing wall-flowers, lavender, and the apple-scented as well as the common geranium: imported from Europe with abundant trouble, they met the fate of all the roses. The Ravenala, or Travellers' tree, was brought from the Seychelles hy the Sayyid with the same unsuccess. Several kinds of jasmines were transported from Cutch to.Zanzibar: the Arabs objected to them, that the see; t depresses the male sex and unduly excites the feminine. Many flowers—for instance, the Narcissus and certain Acacias—labour under the same ill-fame.

Here, after admiring the delicious view of the tree-crowned uplands, the low grounds buried in the richest forest, the cocoa-fringed shore of purest white, and the sea blue as a slab of lapis lazuli, we had an opportunity of inspecting the celebrated clove plantations of Zanzibar. According to Castanheda, when Vasco da Gama first touched at Mombasah and Melinde, their Iteguli sent him, amongst other presents, cloves, and declared, that their countries grew the spice. Other travellers mention, the clove being found at various parts of East Africa, and Andrea Corsali in Eamusio describes the produce as e not like those of India, hut shaped more like our acorns.' The Hutch, however, since their conquest of the Moluccas or Spice Islands in 1607, monopolized the clove like the nutmeg; and hy destroying the former and enslaving the cultivators, they confined it, lest the price should fall, to the single Island of Amboyna. The naturalist traveller, M. Poivre, when governor of the Isle of Erance, brought from the least frequented of the Moluccas, in June 27, 1770, some 450 nutmeg stalks and 10,000 nutmegs in blossom or about to blossom, together with 70 clove trees and a box of plants, many of them well above tbe earth. In 1712 a further supply was procured; the greater part was kept in the[5] Isle of Prance, the rest were dispersed amongst the Seychelles, Bourbon, and Cayenne. All the specimens given to private individuals died: skilful botanists, however, succeeded in preserving 58 nutmegs and 88 clove trees. Of the latter two bore blossoms in 1775, and. the fruit was gathered in the following year; the produce, however, was small, light, and dry, and all deemed that the Butch had been unnecessarily alarmed.[1] The project, however, proved completely successful.

In 1818 the clove-tree (Caryophyllus aromaticus) was introduced from Mauritius and Bourbon into Zanzibar; requiring little care, it speedily became a favourite, and in 1885 the aristocratic foreigner almost supplanted the vulgar valuable cocoa-nut, and the homely rice necessary for local consumption. The Banyans, Americans, and Europeans shared amongst them the principal profits of other commerce, and the cloves enriched the squirearchy, the landed proprietors. Yet it was early predicted that this prosperity would end in ruin; and presently the man who first introduced the spice became a

[1] Establicimientos TJltramarinos, vol. iii. Madrid, 1768.

beggar. After a few years extensive plantations, some containing 15,000 to 20,000 feet, were laid out in the richest parts of the Island. The trees, however, set at intervals of 11 to 10, and now 20 feet, occupied large tracts of ground, and they were so rarely trimmed, that degeneracy soon ensued. Similarly the Brazilian planter, though well aware of his loss, cannot prune his coffee shrub : his hands are all negroes, and if allowed to use cutting instruments, they would hack even the stem. Now the Zanzibar article cannot compete with the produce of Bourbon; and the Butch having thrown into the market the valuable and long-withheld produce of the Moluccas, it threatens to become a drug. The people would do well to follow the example of Mauritius, whence the clove has long departed in favour of sugar. Bor the latter Zanzibar is admirably adapted: when factories shall everywhere be established, the Island will have then found her proper profession, and will soon attain the height of her prosperity.

The clove (Karanful), planted in picturesque bands, streaking the red argillaceous hills, is allowed to run to wood, and to die, withered at the top, in the shape of a bushy thick-foliaged tree 35 feet tall, and somewhat resembling a laurel. Grown from, seed, it bears in the fifth year, and the fruit, the unexpanded flower-bud, is usually ripe in October. In rainy years the harvest beginning with early September is continued uninterruptedly : when the season, however, is dry the picking ceases in November and December, to be resumed in January. Hence the tales of two yields per annum. The crop, which lasts even till March, and which appears to be very uncertain, is hand-picked by Wasawahili and slaves—gathered, in fact, like coffee, except that, requiring ladders and more labour, it is a very slow process. Under favourable circumstances the tree should produce a maximum of 6 lbs; here,' however, the ground is neither cleared nor manured, and the consequence is, that 30 trees rarely yield more than 35 lbs per annum. The fruit is sun-dried upon matting for three days: the workmen forget to turn it, and allow it to be broken and injured; moreover, they will not smoke it, and thus prevent over-shrinking and wrinkling. Some years ago Mr Wilson, an English engineer who died at Zanzibar, produced, by attending to the tree, and by properly desiccating his cloves upon iron hurdles, a superior article, with red shanks and large full heads. M. Sausse, a Creole from Bourbon or Mauritius, also succeeded iu extracting an excellent * oil, tlie clove oil of commerce being generally made by distilling cinnamon leaves. Tbis novelty became a universal favourite with tbe Zanzibar public, who held it to be highly medicinal, and use'd it especially for *inflammations*. Locally the spice is employed as a condiment and infused as a medicine and a tonic : women of the poorer classes make necklaces and ear-rings of the corns they also pound them to a paste, and mould them into different shapes.

The Asdkif, or stalks pulled off when the fruit is dry, are exported to Europe under the name of 'clove stems,' and are used as a mordant for dyeing silks. An English house once provided tin canisters to preserve its purchases, whereas they are mostly sent home in bulk. Certain other merchants, £ born with the pencil behind their ears,' open the hatches, and to make the cargo 'weigh out' heave in sea-water, which, they say, does not much affect the flavour of pepper and cloves. The stems fetch from one-eighth to half of a German crown per Earsilah, or frail of 35 lbs. The price of cloves, originally $5 to $6 per Earsilah, has now fallen to $2 and even to $1. In 1856, the Island exported five millions of lbs ; the next year, however, was unfavourable—tbe trees bad been injured by drought; tbe over-supply bad sunk tbe price 70 per cent., and many Arab proprietors talked of returning to rice and cocoa-nuts. Yet, in ' 1859, tbe crop rose to some 200,000 Par&silah — 7,000,000 lbs, valued at about £85,000; whereas 10 years before tbe total produce of Zanzibar, including Pemba, was 120,000 to 150,000 Pardsilab, and in 1839-40 it barely numbered 9000. —

We returned via, tbe bush to tbe south of tbe city, passing through a luxuriant growth of tbe hardest woods. After a stiff ride over tbe worst of paths, a mere ᶜ picada,' as tbe Brazilians say, we skirted tbe fetid lagoon wbicb subtends tbe eastern city from north to south, and reached Mnazi Moyya, 'One Cocoa-nut Tree.' This bit of open ground is tbe Bois de Boulogne of Zanzibar, tbe single place for exercise, and we did not wonder tbat so many prefer to stay at home.

During tbe 'Id Saghb or Kuchuk Bayram, here called Siku-kku za Idf, 'One Cocoa-nut Tree' is a lively place. Whilst tbe boys sing and dance about tbe streets, and tbe garrison blacks, armed witb sabres, engage near. tbe fort in a Zumo or Pyrrhic, wildly waving their tremulous blades, and tbe Wabiao or Bozalsfrom about Kilwa execute tlieir saltations near the bridge, and tbe other slaves carouse and junket in their own quarter of the town, each clan from the mainland keeping itself distinct, the grandees, fingering their rosaries and supported hy long staves, proceed to Mnazi Moyya, where gallops, called races, form the attraction. About half-a-dozen garrons, rushing wildly about, represent the performers, and the performance is nothing new to the Anglo-Indian. The groups are motley if not picturesque. Here and there, surrounded by rings of sable admirers, are women boisterously singing and clapping hands, dancing and acting lionnes with all them might. Tremendous are the Yijelejele, the Kil, Zagharit, or trilling of the spectatresses. Men also stamp and wriggle in a rude 'improper ' style to the succedanenm for a drum, a hollow wooden cylinder one foot in diameter, with the open end applied to the breast, and the dried and stretched snake-skin patted upon with finger and palm. Most of these people, regardless of fever or cholera, are primed with fermented cocoa juice. The heavily-clad Shaykhs, bestriding their asses, are preceded by outrunners, who mercilessly push aside and 'bakur ' the crowd; and the latter turn viciously as bull-terriers. There is not much striking, but jostling and thrusting away are the rules. At Lanin and the wilder places swords and daggers are often hared on these occasions, and the Shaykhs have no little trouble to preserve the peace. Contrasting with the full-dressed crowd are the naked children, who seem all afflicted with umbilical hernia. This is the result of careless cutting, but the unsightly protuberance will wear away in after life, and a pot-belly is here, as elsewhere in Africa, looked upon as a good sign. The negro faces and bodies are marked with the tattoo in almost every possible fashion; some wear straight black lines, others curved; these have perpendicular, those horizontal marks, and not a few wear painted squares with' central spots, like the wafers upon the garment of the old country clown. At length the princes make their appearance, and are received with a file-firing of guns and pistols, whilst shouts and drums disturb the air; the races are formally run, and the crowd disperses through the unclean streets of the city.

There is still some exploration to be done on the west or landward front of Zanzibar Island. Colonel Hamerton, however, strongly advises us not to risk fever, and to reserve every atom of strength and energy for the Continent.

CHAPTER X.

COMPARATIVE ANTHROPOLOGY (ETHNOLOGY) OE ZANZIBAR. THE ARABS.

'Les Arabes ne sont maintenant, dans l'Afrique Orientale, que des parasites, comme l'est tout peuple exclusivement commerçant.'—M. OuiLtAiir. vol. ii. part ii. cbap. ii. p. 151.

The Arabs upon the Island may amount to a total of 5000,[1] all Omans; and they are divided, as in their fatherland, into two great Kahilah or tribes, the Hindwi and the Ghafiri.

When Malik bin Pakhm, of the Benu Hunayfah tribe, marched from his own country, Nejd, to recover Oman from the Persians under Bara, son of Bahman, son of Isfandiyar, an event popularly dated about the end of our 1st century, he was joined by some 100 Yemeni warriors who were

[1] In 1846 M. Guillain proposed 3000, including a floating population of 300 to 400. Documents, &c., part ii. p. 78.

called Benu Yemin, sons of the right hand, because they dwelt to the south or on the right hand of the Ka'abah. Their migration is attributed to the bursting of the dyke of Arim, near Mareb, the Mariaba of Ptolemy, which is the Babel-tower of Arabian history in the Days of Ignorance. The learned Dr Wetzstein (p. 104, Ileisebericht iiber Hauran, &c. Berlin, 1860) believes this event to have taken place about the beginning of our era; most authors, however, place it at the end of the 1st or the beginning of our 2nd century. It was probably the over-populating of the land which sent forth the two great Sabsean tribes of Azud and Hirnyar to Bahrayn and N. Eastern Arabia; they united, and were known as the Tanukh or Confederates. The former, also called from a chief 'Nasri,' settled upon the Euphrates, and founded the East Tanukh kingdom, whose capital was afterwards Hira. The Himyar or Kudai originated, in the Hauran and the Belka, the West Tanukh kingdom, also termed from a chief ʿ Salih.' These men, converted to Christianity, were probably the builders of the 'Giant cities ' of Bashan, mere provincial towns of the Greco-Homan Empire. Ta'alab (Thalaba), one of the sons of Malik bin Eakhm, is mentioned as the first ruler of East Tanukh. The extinct family of the Druze

Tanukhs claimed descent from the western kingdom. The Ya'rubah considered themselves to he of the Arah el Arihah (Joctanites), through their ancestor Yarub el Azud (j;31 bin Ealigh (Peleg, the brother of Kahtdn or Joctan),bin Abir (Eber), bin Salih, bin Arfakhshad, bin Sham (Shem), and to the present day their descendants boast of this ancient lineage. Malik bin Eakhm routed 40,000 horsemen supported by elephants, slew Mirzban (the Marz-ban or warden of the Marches) the Satrap-lieutenant of the King of Kings, whose head-quarters were at Sohar, and conquered the country from Sharjah to the Ea'as el Hadd (Easalgat),the eastern Land's-end of the Arabian shore. Eeinforced by fresh drafts of the Benu Yemin, he showed his gratitude by incorporating them with his own tribe. The word Hin&wi, meaning a patrician or 'one having a founder,' arose from Malik bin Eakhm, proposing himself as the Hanu (yj*) or originator of the emigrants: certain Arabs derive it from Hind, a fanciful ancestor, and even call themselves Benu Hind. According to some authorities, Oman took its name from a place in the neighbourhood of the dyke of Mareh; others derive it from a valley which, like the Wady el Arab, gave its name to the whole country; the Arah geographers make it the ancient term for Sohar, and the classical geographer holds that the Ommanum Emporium of Ptolemy was applied to Maskat.

When Malik bin Eakhm had been slain hy his son Selima, and another son, Zayd, ruled Oman in his stead, a thousand of the Benu Nezar came to him from the town of Char, and were settled upon a tract of low open ground whence they took the name of Ghdfiri. These immigrants were Arah el Musta'arahah, which, in Omanic usage, denotes the insititious or Ismailitic clans derived from Adnan, son of Ishmael; and the gift of land had made them clients of Zayd and of his trihe, the Hinawi. Intermarriage, however, soon amalgamated the races. When El Islam brought the sword to mankind, and when the rival prophet Musaylimah, generally known as the liar, paved the way for the Karmati (Carmathians) and for a copious crop of heresies, the Ghdfiri, cleaving to the faith of Meccah, were preferred hy the Caliph Abubekr to their former patrons, for the chieftainship of Oman. In his turn, the Caliph Ali restored precedence to the Hinawi who had espoused his cause. Hence an inveterate feud, a flame of wrath, which rivers of blood have not quenched. Throughout Oman the rival tribes still occupy separate quarters; they will not connect themselves hy marriage, and they seldom meet without a 'faction fight.' Even at Zanzibar, where the climate has softened them, they rarely preserve that decency of hate which is due hy Arahs of nohle strain to hereditary and natural enemies.

Here the principal clan of the Hinawi tribe is the Harisi (plural Hurs), under Abdullah bin Salim and Husayn bin Mahommed: once flourishing in Oman, it now barely numbers 15,000 sabres, and in the Island it may amount to 300, mostly merchants and wealthy planters. The other divisions are the Bu (or Ayydl) Sa'id; the ruling race which forms one large family—• that of the Sayyid. There are also about a dozen of the Benu Lanik, whose preponderance in Oman was broken down by the Yu'rabi Imams. The minor sections of the Hindwi are the Benu Yas of Sur; the Benu Menasir near Sharjah; the Benu Ali; the Benu Baktashi; the Benu TJhaybi; the Benu el Hijri; the Benu Kalban; the Benu el Abri; and the Benu bu Hasan, generally pronounced Bohsan. A few of the Benu Dafri or Dafil at times visit the Island: they are professional carriers, and therefore they have no blood feuds with other tribes. Besides, these are Amman, Adwani, Kuruni, Khuzuri, Sal all am eli, and Nayyavareh; most of them frequent Zanzibar during tbe trading season.

Tbe pure Gbafiri stock is still, they say, to be found in Nejd. Throughout Oman they are a wild unruly race, hostile to strangers, and inclined to Wahhabi-ism. They possess at several places little castles armed with guns which are mere robbers' dens; near Mina the Chief Musalim refused allegiance to Sayyid Said, and south of the Jebel el Akhzar, or 'Green Mountain,' they made themselves the terror' of the country-side about Buraymah. The worst of the Ghifiri are the Kawasim pirates (the Anglo-Arabic 'Jowasmees') of Pas el Khaymah and our old enemies the Benu bu Ali of Ba'as el Hadd. To them also belong the Shaksi or Benu Buwayhah, popularly called Ahl Rustak, from the settlement founded by the Persian Anushirawdn on the eastern slope of Jebel el Akhzar, the mountainous district of Oman. It is about 70 miles west of Maskat, which, now the capital, began life as its harbour. The present representative of the Rustak chiefs, Sayyid Kays bin Azan, receives an annual indemnification of $3000 from Sayyid Said, who had dispossessed him of Sohar and its dependencies. Siir also belongs to the Gkafiri, of whom' in these places, little good is spoken; they are said to he at once cruel and cowardly, to fear no shame, and to respect no oath. We shall soon he compelled to chastise these petty sea-thieves and kidnappers.

At Zanzibar the Ghafiri is represented chiefly hy the Masakirah or Maskari clan, which under its chief, Sayf hin Khalfan, may number 2000 sabres. The Mazru'i of Mombasah, so well known in Sawahil history, were also Ghafiri: they are now scattered about Gasi and other small Bandars, retaining nothing of their political consequence. The Tu'rahi clan, which gave to Oman its old patriotic Imams, is of scant account. The other sections, who are for the most part visitors during the commercial season, comprise the Jenabah, the Bimini, the Benu Katub, the Benu bu Ali, and the Benu Biyim of bTezwah in the Jebel el Akhzar.

The Arab holds, and, according to old Moslem travellers, has long held in these regions the position of an Qsmanli in Arabia; he is a 'superior person.' As the Omani chiefs, however, like the Sherifs of El Hejaz, did not disdain servile concubines, many of their issue are negroids: of these hybrids some are exceedingly fair, showing African pollution only by tufty and wiry hair, whilst others, 'falling upon their mothers,' as the native phrase is, have been refused inheritance at Maskat, and have narrowly escaped the slave-market. The grandsons of purest Arabs who have settled in Africa, though there has been no mixture of blood, already show important physical modifications worked by the 'mixture of air,' as the Portuguese phrase is. The skin is fair, but yelloAV-tinted by over-development of gall; whilst the nose is high, the lips are loose, everted, or otherwise ill-formed; and the beard, rarely of the amplest, shrinks, under the hot-house air, to four straggling tufts upon the rami of the jaws and the condyles of the chin. Whilst the extremities preserve the fineness of Arab blood, the body is weak and effeminate; and the degenerate aspect is accompanied by the no less degraded mind, morals, and manners of the coast-people. The nervous or nervoso-bilious temperament of the Sons of the Desert here runs into two extremes: many Arabs are bilious-lymphatic, like Banyans; a few, lapsing into the extreme of leanness, are fair specimens of the 'Living Skeleton.' This has been remarked even of Omanis born and bred upon the Island. Those who incline to the nervous diathesis have weakly drooping occiputs and narrow skull-bases, arguing a deficiency of physical force, and they exaggerate the flat-sided nnconstrnctiye Arah skull—here an Indian may almost always he recognized hy the comparative roundness of his calvaria. And as the Zanzibar Arah is mostly of burgher race in his own land, the forehead rarely displays that high development of the perceptive organs which characterizes the Bedawin.

The Arah noble is still, like those of Meccali in Mohammed's day, a merchant, and here wealth has done much to degenerate the breed, climate more, and slavery most. The 'Californian fever '—indolence—becomes endemic in the second generation, rendering the race hopeless, whilst industry is supplied hy the gross, transparent cunning of the Wasawahili and of the African generally. Honesty is all hut unknown; several European merchants will not have an Arab's name in their books. A Nakhoda (Captain, Maskat R.JNT.) in the Prince's service, commissioned to bring a watch or other valuables from Bombay, will delay to deliver it until threatened with the bakur, and the terrors of being blown from a gun do not defend the ruler from the most shallow and impudent frauds. Like their kinsmen of Oman, they despise truth, without versatility enough to employ it when required, and few rise to the height of

Bacon's model, 'who hath openness in fame and opinion, secrecy in hahit, dissimulation in reasonable use, and a power to feign, if there he no remedy.' Haughty in the highest degree, and boasting descent from the kings of Yemen, they hold themselves to he the salt of the earth. Man's nature everywhere objects to restraint, these people cannot endure it: nothing afflicts them so much as the necessity of regular occupation, as the recurrence of 'duty,' as the weight of any subject upon the mind. Constant only in procrastination, as they are hebetous in body so they are mentally torpid and apparently incapable of active exertion, especially of immediate action. Like their congeners of Maskat and Sur, they have distinguished themselves on all occasions when opposed to any hut Arabs, by excessive poltroonery. They seldom mix with strangers, for whom they have generally an aversion, and they Avill refuse a dollar to a wretch who has changed his faith to save his life. They are never worse than in youth, when excessive polygamy and debauchery have enslaved them: as with the Arabs of the Peninsula, a people of violent and unruly passions, and seldom ripe for use till their beards are grey, these Zanzabaris improve by age, and body and mind seem to grow "better, to a certain point, as they grow old.

To this sweeping evil account there are of course exceptions. I have rarely met with a more honest, trustworthy man than Said bin Salim, the half-caste Arah, who was sent with us as BA as Kafilah, or guide. Such hitherto has been his character ; but man varies in these regions: he may grievously disappoint me in the end.[1]

The poorer Arahs who flock to Zanzibar during the season are ITazramis, and they work and live hard as the Hammals of Stamboul. These men club and mess together in gangs under an Akidah (head man), who supplies them with rice, ghi, and scones, and who keeps the accounts so skilfully, that the labourer receives annually about $35, though he may gain four times that sum. Pauper Arabs settled upon the Island refuse 'nigger work,' the West Indian synonym for manual labour, and, as a rule, the Mashamba or plantations supply them, like Irish estates of old, with everything but money. At first many were ruined by the abolition of slave export: at present most of them confess that the measure has added materially to the development and the prosperity of the Island. There are now Arab merchants who own 80,000 clove-trees, $100,000

[1] I have the words as they were written early in 1857.

floating capital, a ship or two, and from 1000 to 2000 slaves.

The results of wealth and general aisance have been luxury and unbridled licentiousness. As usual in damp-hot climates, for instance, Sind, Egypt, the lowlands of Syria, Mazenderan, Malabar, and California, the sexual requirements of the passive exceed those of the active sex; and the usual result is a dissolute social state, contrasting with mountain countries, dry-cold or damp-cold, where the conditions are either equally balanced or are reversed. Arab women have been described as respectable in the Island, because, fearing scandal and its consequences, they deny themselves to Europeans. Yet many of them prefer Banyans to those of the True Eaith, whilst the warmest passions abandon themselves to African slaves:[1] these dark men are such pearls in beauteous ladies' eyes, and their fascinations at Zanzibar are so great, that a respectable Hindostani Moslem will not trust his daughter to live there, even in her husband's house. A corresponding perversion and brutality of taste make the men neglect their wives for negresses; the same has

[1] It is easy to explain, the preference of Arab women for slaves, and the predilection of the husbands for negro women : .the subject, however, is somewhat too physiological for the general reader.

"been remarked of our countrymen in Guiana and the West Indies, and it notably prevails in the Brazil, where the negress and the Mulatta are preferred to the Creole. Considering the effect of the African skin when excited hy joy, rage, fear, or other mental emotion, of course a cogent reason for the preference exists.

Public prostitutes are here few, and the profession ranks low where the classes upon which it depends can always afford to gratify their propensities in the slave-market. I have alluded to the Wasawahili women of the Madagascar Quarter; a few also live scattered about the town, hut all are equally undesirable—there is not a pretty face amongst them. The honorarium varies from $0.25 to $1, and the proceeds are expended upon gaudy dresses and paltry ornaments. Retired Corinthians who have not prospered, live hy fishing upon the sands, or make rude pottery at Changani Point: those who can afford it buy a slave or two, and give the rest of their days to farming. Girls who work for hire are always procurable, but such amours are likely to end badly : the same may be said of the prostitutes ; consequently most white residents keep Abyssinian or Galla concubines. The 'Liwat'[5] is here considered a mere peccadillo: the late Sayyid, however, denied Moslem burial to a nephew who built the British Consular residence. This 'Mat'ill' died in agony after the bungling performance of an operation which his debaucheries rendered necessary, and the body was cast naked into the sea.

Both sexes and all ages delight in drinking. The rich use bad but expensive Trench and American liqueurs, gin, brandy, and rum, from Marseille, India, and the Mauritius. Some eat opium, others prefer Bhang in its several forms : the material is imported from Bombay and Cutch. We found it near the continental seaboard, and therefore the Indian shrub is also probably grown upon the Island. A distillation, I have said, is made from the Cashew-nut and from palm-wine; this alcohol is called Zerambo. and a free-born Arab is disgraced by touching it; preserved in foul old pots, it has the effect of poison; a drunken sailor will fall down insensible, breathe with stertorous loudness, and gradually pass from insensibility to death. Tembo or toddy is of two kinds—Tamil, the sweet and unintoxicating, and Khali, sour or fermented. The liquor is drawn from the trees by the Wasawahili and the slaves insular and continental. The Pombe, like the Buzah of Egypt and Berberia, Adel, and

Abyssinia, is a simple hopless beer, made from maize or bolcus. Drunkenness amongst the poor is very properly punished only when it leads to crime. It is singular that the late Sayyid, who never touched an intoxicating drink, should have been so tender to an offence with which Moslems usually deal so barbarously.

The Arab's head-dress is a Kumrneh or Kofiyyab (red fez), a Surat calotte (Alfiyyah), or a white skull-cap worn under a turban (Kilemba) of Oman silk and cotton religiously mixed. Usually it is of fine blue and white cotton check, embroidered and fringed with a broad red border, with the ends hanging in unequal lengths over one shoulder. The coiffure is highly picturesque. The ruling family and grandees, however, have modified its vulgar folds, wearing it peaked in front, and somewhat resembling a tiara. The essential bodv-clothing and the succedaneum for trowsers is an Izar (Nguo ya ku chini), or loin-cloth tucked in at the waist, 6 to 7 feet long by 2 to 3 broad. The colours are brick-dust and white or blue and white, with a silk border striped red, black, and yellow. The very poor wear a dirty bit of cotton girdled by a Hakab or Kundavi, a rope of plaited thongs ; the rich prefer a fine embroidered stuff from Oman, supported at the waist hy a silver chain. None hut the western Arahs admit the innovation of drawers (Suruwali). The ʿJama',' or upper garment, is a collar-less coat of the best broadcloth, leek-green or some tender colour being preferred. It is secured over the left breast[1] hy a silken loop, and the straight wide sleeves are gaily lined. The Kizbdo is a kind of waistcoat, covering only the bust: some wear it with sleeves, others without. The Dishdasheh (in Kisawahili Khanzu), a narrow-sleeved shirt, buttoned at the throat and extending to mid-shin, is made of calico (baftah), American drill, and other stuffs called Doriyah, Tarabuzun, and Jamdani. Sailors are known hy Khuzerangi, a coarse cotton, stained dingy red-yellow with henna or pomegranate rind, and rank with Wars (bastard saffron) and sharks' oil. Respectable men guard the stomach with a ʿHizam,' generally a Cashmere or Bombay shawl; others wear sashes of the dust-coloured raw silk manufactured in Oman. The outer garment for chilly weather is the long, tight-sleeved Persian Jubbeh, Jokhah, or Caftan, of European broadcloth. The Na'alayn, Yiatu, or sandals of peculiar shape, made at Zanzibar, have already been described. Most men shave their heads, and the Sha-

[1] **In Moslem countries Christians prefer the right breast.**

f'eis trim or entirely remove the moustaches. The palms are reddened with henna, which is either brought from El Hejaz or gathered in the plantations. The only ring is a plain cornelian seal, and the sole other ornament is a talisman (Ilirz in Kisawahili Hirizi). The eyes are blackened with Kohl or antimony of El Sham—here not Syria, but the region about Meccah—and the mouth, crimsoned by betel, looks as if a tooth had just been knocked out.

None but women and slaves leave the house unarmed. The lowest Arab sticks an old dagger in his belt, handles a rusty spear, or shoulders a cheap firelock. Gulf men are generally known by their round targes (Tursi) made of carved and spangled rhinoceros or addax hide, toys with high central umbo, and at the utmost a foot in diameter; others have fish-skin shields, and the Baloch affect the Cutch 'Dhal,' or buckler. The sword is of three forms, of which the Sayf Earanji (Erankish sword, in Kisawahili Upanga) has long been the favourite. It is a straight, broad, two-edged, guardless, double-handed weapon, about 4 ft 3 in. long, sheathed in a scabbard of red morocco: the thin and well-worn blade vibrates in the grip, and by the side of its razor-like keenness our weapons resemble iron bars. The price varies from $10 to

$100, and, as at modern Damascus, cheap German imitations abound. The usual handle is wood hound with thread-like plaits of black leather and silver wire forming patterns; the pommel is an iron knob, and the general aspect of the article suggests that it is derived from the Crusading ages. The 'Kittareh' is a curved European sabre : the young princes and those about the coast carry in hand expensive specimens with ivory hilts and gold mountings. Thirdly, the 'Imani,' as they call it, is a short straight blade made in Europe, Oman, or Hazramaut. The Arab knows but two cuts,—one the 'Ivalam,' across the ankles, and the other our No. 7, directed at the head or preferably at the shoulder : the former is evaded by leaping or breaking ground, the latter is parried with the shield. Jambiyahs, Khanjars, or daggers, worn strapped and buckled round the waist, are curved till the point forms almost a right angle with the hilt. It is a silly construction; but anything will serve to stab the enemy's back above the shoulders. The dudgeon of black or white rhinoceros or buffalo horn is adorned with a profusion of filagree-work, and silver or gold knobs; the blade, sharp on both sides, is nearly three inches broad at the base. The sheath ('AM) is similarly ornamented upon a ground of leather, cloth, or hrocade, dark or scarlet, with the usual metal rings and 'fixings/ The Khanjar often costs $200, and a handsome dagger is a sign of rank.

Not having seen at home the higher classes of Arab women, who are said to he sometimes remarkably handsome, I can describe them only from hearsay. In the house they wear tight Mezar, Sarwal, or pantaloons of Oman silk or cotton fastened at the waist with rich tasselled ties brought from Maskat, the Hejaz, and Bandar Abbas : the body dress is a long chemise of Bengal or Surat stuff, worn oyer a Mkaja or loin-cloth. The hair is plaited into Masukd (pig-tails) or Nyule (curls), and here, as elsewhere, the back of the head being the most sacred part of the feminine person, adults bind round the forehead a kerchief (Ngfio ku jitanda) or dastmal of bright-coloured silk, which depends behind to the waist. Abroad they appear masqued with the hideous black 'Burka veil of Oman, whilst a Bida, Kitambi, or sheet of white calico or black silk, conceals even the dress from prying eyes. A Mavuli or umbrella shows dignity; some wear sandals (Yyatu), like the men, others Egyptian Papushes.

The favourite feminine ornaments are Banajireh, or Ehalkh&l, bracelets or bangles, gold, silver, or copper rings, solid or hollow, plain or embossed, with or without hinges. A Yelidani (single gem, or ᵉ union '), a cordiform or oval brooch and pendents of precious stones or stained glass, massively set in gold, hangs round the neck by a string of bullet-sized gold-foiled beads. The Matale (anklets) are of silver worth, that is to say weighing, from $10 to $20. A Kirt, Kupini, P'hete ya Pua, or flower-shaped ornament of gold, silver, or base metal, is worn in the wing of the left nostril. Earrings are of many varieties : the rim is pierced sometimes all round for silver Halkeh or rings, whose place is supplied amongst- the poor with leaden 'Kipini (in the plural 'Yipini '). The lobe is bored and trained to encircle a disk of silver or ivory; the slaves use a bright-coloured roll of palm leaf, and when that is not procurable, a betel-nut: the result is unnatural distension, and in age the ear, as among the Moplahs of Malabar, hangs down, a mere strip of skin, to the collar bone. They have also the ICengele, copper balls for the neck; the Mpogo, or ivory ring; the Kikomo, a copper or brass bracelet; the Mkhufu, or silver necklace chain; the Mchuhu, or coarse Cassolette, and a variety of Talismans or Grigris (Hirizi) round the wrists and ankles. These women, like most Easterns, prefer strong and heady perfumes of musk, ambergris, ottar of roses, and the large Indian jasmine; their cosmetics are oil, henna, Kohl, or Collyrium (Wdnjd), and saffron applied to the head and eyebrows; and they are cunning in the matter of fumigation, which might with benefit be introduced into Europe.

The Zanzibar Arab's day is regular, varied only by a journey, a family festival, a debauch, or the yearly Bamazan fast. He rises at dawn for ablution and prayer, eats 'Suwayk,' a kind of vermicelli, wheaten bread, or even a little meat, drinks a cup of coffee, and chewing betel, repairs to the bazar for business or calls upon his friends. Men shake hands when meeting, wish good-morning, and ask, 'How is thy state ?' to which the reply is, 'And how art thou?' They then sit down and renew queries, interspersed with many Marhabas, Sdmt-B'dnas and Na shikamaus, 'Allah preserve thee ! ' and £ Thanks be to Allah, we are well!' If one sneeze,-the others exclaim, 'May Allah have mercy upon thee ! ' which he acknowledges, with 'Allah guide you! ' —this is an old Arab superstition. Sneezing being an omen of impending evil to the patient, an ejaculation was made to the gods : 'Homer mentions the custom; Aristotle fruitlessly attempts to explain its existence; Apulelus refers to it; and Pliny lias a problem on it: " Onr sternutantes salutantur ; " ' Asia still practises it, and tbe older Brazilians have not forgotten it. Here tbe convulsion is considered unsonsy : many a deputation waiting upon the late Sayyid has been prematurely dismissed because tbe ill-omened sternutation happened. As in Turkey and the Moslem East generally, the visitor's place of honour is on the host's left hand. Where coffee is offered on ceremonious occasions, all rise and take the little Einjan or thimble-cup from the house-master, who does not allow the servant to hand it; they then sit down, and they drink, contrary to usual Arab custom, more than one cupful. The hospitality concludes with a glass of sherbet. Amongst the wealthier classes at Zanzibar and Mombasah, tea is becoming a favourite beverage; not only 'fashionable,' but held to be hygienic because less heating than coffee.

At 5 o'clock, our 11 A.M., the Arab, like the . Syrian, eats the ͨ Ghada ' of fish and meat, of wheaten bread and vegetables, and of rice boiled with the cream of rasped cocoa-nut, ending with half-a-dozen Einjans of coffee and with betel. Some then repair to the Mosque; most men pray the noon-day at home, and sleep like the citizens ' of Andine Mendoza till the Asr or after 3 P.M.

They again perform ablution and devotions, after ■wliicb they dress for out-of-door business and for home visits. The evening prayers are generally recited in public. Some eat tbe Isba-supper before sunset; usually it is deferred till after worship. Tbe climate effectively prevents those last pleasant rambles by moonlight and open air seances—the Makamat so much enjoyed in the hot-dry sub-tropical regions. Here the evening is spent sometimes in society, oftener in the harem, and all apply to sleep between 10 P.M. and midnight.

The yearly fast begins with the new moon of Ramazan; crowds assemble in the open places and upon the terrace roofs till the popping of pistols and matchlocks and salvos from the squadron warn the faithful that the crescent has appeared. In the days of Sayyid Said the strict Arab salute of three guns (our 21) was kept up ; five denoted a victory, and seven the decease of some eminent person. Arabs observe the dietetic law strictly; their women are expected to fast, and boys of 13 and 14 take a pride in imitating their parents. Many, especially those with weak digestion, cannot eat the dawn meal general throughout Egypt, Syria, and Persia. The Shafei ordeal ends when the sun has wholly sunk below the horizon ;

tlie Bavazi waits till daylight has almost faded from the *east*, and he prays before breaking bread. Most men begin hygienically with something easily digested, as dates and sonr milk,—a more substantial meal follows after an hour. The rich pass much of the fasting time *in sleep, and the* burden here, as elsewhere, falls far more heavily upon the poor. At Zanzibar, however, the infliction is lightened by the damp climate and by the equinoctial day, short compared with the terrible 16 hours which must sometimes be endured in s ubtropical latitudes. Tet the servants and slaves are useless during Ramazan: idle at all times, they then assert a right to do nothing : as I before observed, the fast is one-twelfth of the year thoroughly wasted. On the other hand, it may be remarked that El Islam has wisely limited its festivals to six days in the year, a great contrast to the profuse waste of time which still characterizes the faith of Southern Europe.

As at the beginning of the. month, crowds assemble to sight the new moon which ends the fast, and every fellow who has a matchlock wastes powder and ball, without much regarding where the latter flies. Here, as in the Brazil, nothing can be done without wasting gunpowder: at Zanzibar the matchlock is perforce preferred, in

Rio de Janeiro the rocket and the squib have taken its place. This year (1857) a storm of rain on the evening of May 24th concealed the crescent, and it was not till half-past five P.M. on the 25th, that a salute from the shipping announced, despite the thick drifting scud which hid every inch of sky, that the weary 'blessed month ' was no more. Then the men gathered about the palace, the women flocked to the house-tops, and the city, usually so sadly silent, rang with shouting, singing, the braying of trumpets, and irregular discharges of small arms. After sunset again all was still as the grave.

The 'Id el Saghir, or lesser festival, that concludes the Ramazan, began at dawn on May 26th; the usual public prayers were recited in the mosques, and at 8.30 A.M. the squadron, dressed with flags, fired whilst the townsmen followed suit. The servants and slaves gathered in their new clothing to kiss the master's hand and to wish him a happy festival. The Princes rode out in state. In the bazars an endnnanohe mob assembled despite the heavy rains, and before sunset they trooped through the miry lanes to witness the races at Mnazi Moyya, which take place only when the tide is out. These festivities —they have already been described—continued to a late hour, and. thus passed away the earliest and the noisiest day of the 'Id.

The second and the third days are diluted copies of the first; visits are exchanged between all acquaintances, and the Prince holds levees in full Darbar. Here the sons of Sayyid Said and their blood relations occupy one side of the long bare hall, opposite them are the high officials and interpreters, whilst the honoured guests sit by the ruler at the Sadr, or top of the room, and fronting them, near the door, stand the eunuchs and the slaves. On leaving, as on entering, the stranger shakes hands with the whole family according to seniority, and he is accompanied by the Prince either a few paces or to the doorway, the steps, in fact, being carefully proportioned to his rank.

There is little peculiarity in the religious ceremonies of the Zanzibar Arab. An Azan (call to prayer) is repeated in the ear of the new-born babe, and on the Arba'in (10th day) the mother and infant are bathed, and become pure—until then the husband will not sit by *his* wife's side. On this occasion the head of the male child is shaved, as usual amongst Moslems. Marriage is expensive, seldom costing the respectable man less than $500; all the food provided for he occasion must be eaten, even if guests be sought in the streets; this indeed is the rule of Arab feasts. Half the Mahr, or settlement-money, should be paid before the Eatihah is recited; the, remainder is claimed upon separation or after the husband's death. A woman cannot demand divorce except for the usual legal reasons, and the 'Iddeh,' or interval before re-marriage, is three months and ten days. After a Khitmah or perfection of the Koran, the relict, who has hitherto been confined to the house, is bathed by her feminine friends, in token of readiness for engagement. Many widows refuse to change their condition, and apply themselves to money-making by commerce, plantations, or slave-dealing. I heard of one jovial 'Armalah ' who invited Europeans to *petit soupers* and *parties fines,* in which merriment takes precedence of modesty. The Arab women of Zanzibar appear unusually spirited, especially when compared with their lords ; in every great house some energetic petticoat or rather browsers takes or forces her husband or her brother to take the lead—perhaps, as nearer home, they are the more courageous and venturous in braving danger because the risk and the brunt do not fall upon their heads. Men of pure family will not give their daughters to any but fellow-clansmen. They themselves do not object to Waswahili, andnegro-girls, bnt the single Arab wife—there is rarely more than one—rules the concubines with a rod of iron.

Men, women, and children weep at funerals, but it is not the custom to hire 'keehers.' The feminine mourning dress is black, and the period, as general among Moslems, lasts 40 days. Contrary to Arab custom, tbe graves are lined with boarding. The exterior is a wall of coralline rag and lime from a foot to a foot and a half high, with little raised steps at the head and feet; here a porcelain saucer or an encaustic tile is sometimes mortared in by way of ornament. Old cemeteries abound throughout the city and the suburbs, sometimes showing offensive sights. A simple slab sufficed for the late Sayyid's ancestors; on the spot, however, where he and his son Khalid lie, they are building a dwarf truncated pyramid of stone and cement, an unusual memorial to a Bayazi or a Wahhabi. Of late years the Arabs have begun to inter their slaves. Formerly the corpses were thrown to the beasts or tossed into the sea, and from the windows of ELM.'s Consulate I have seen more than one body bleached snow-white by sea-water, and stranded upon the beach where no one cared to bury it.

Daring the reign of the last rnler, El Islam at Zanzibar was tolerant by compulsion; the Shiahs were allowed an Imambara at which they bewailed the death of Hasan and Husayn—few Sunni countries would have tolerated the abomination. ' But as these ⁚ sectarians ' almost worship whilst others absolutely adore Ali and his descendants; and as the 'Khariji ' schism slew the former and well-nigh damns all the rest, they join issue and agree to differ. This indeed is a recognized rule in religions, where the most minute distinctions cause and perpetuate the deadliest feuds, and the family quarrel will not he reconciled, because love perverted becomes not indifference hut hate.

The Arabs are here all Shafei or Bayazi. As the latter schism is now rare under that name in the Moslem world, some notice of it may he considered advisable. I have seen the Bayazi confounded with the Mutazali (Motazilites who support Eree-will *versus* Predestination), hut there is an important difference: the latter hold Ali in high esteem and object only to the Caliph Muawiyah.

The Baydzi, also called Ab&zi,[1] Ibaz and

---

[1] Niebuhr terms them Beiasi and Abadhi (Travels in Arabia, chap. cxiv.). Salll ibn Razik makes Abdullah the son, not the grandson, of Abaz.

THE BAYAZI. 397

Ibaziyyeh derive their name from Abdullah bin Tahya bin Abaz (in our dictionaries 'Jbaz '). *Some* authors have corrupted this name to Beydan, that of a Persian sectarian; others translate it the 'Whites,' as opposed to the *green* of the Patimites, and the black of the Abbasides. This arch-heretic, according to the Jehan-Numa, began to preach under the reign of El Merwan, the last Ommiade Khalifeh, between A.H. 127—132 (A.D. 744 and 749), and was shortly afterwards conquered and put to death. His tenets spread far and wide amongst the Ithawdrij of Aezwah, extended to the littoral, and tilled the land with battle and murder.

The Bayazi, who through their Imams governed Oman for 163 years, beginning from A.n. 751, are thus one of the many Khariji (in the plural Khawarij) sects whose origin may be traced in the rival faiths of Sabeism and Kuraysh idolatry; in the contest of the 'Prophets ' Mohammed and Musaylimeh, and in the political interference of the first Caliphs between the turbulent tribes of Oman. Under the names of Shurah (ilpi); Haruriyah (< o ª ⁿ < 1 Muhakkimah these 'Seceders' were once numerous in northern Africa, Spain, and Arabia; in A.D. 1350 Ibn Batuta found them at Timbucktu.

They are now mostly confined to a few cities in Morocco, and to the parts about Maskat. Some theological writers derive these Kharijites fi'om the malcontents who declared that both Ali and Muawiyah had forfeited their right to the Caliphate by appealing from Allah's judgment to human decisions, and who carried out their objection by murdering Ali and by attempting the murder of Muawiyah and Amru. Their descendants are held to have formed 20 schools like the Shiahs (or Baw&fiz) and the Mutazali; whilst the Mai'jiyyeh number six; the Mujbirah or Sunnites four, and, together with the Batiniyah, the Hululiyah, and the Zaydi, make up the 73 divisions into which the first Moslem declared El Islam would split. The principal Kharijite schools (TJsul el Eirak) have, however, been reduced to the following five. The first four are now common only in books.

1. The Azarikah, or followers of Abu Itashid Nafi' ibn el Azrak. They permit, in religious warfare, the massacre of women and children; they do not lapidate adulterers, Koranic command being absent, and they severely punish the male, not the female, slanderer of the Eaithful.

2. The Kajd&t, disciples of Najdat bin Amir, formerly abounded in Mekran, Kerman, Mosul,

Mesopotamia, Seistan, and Oman. They hold persistency in the minor sins (Sughair) equivalent to polytheism (Shirk); whereas mortal sins are not damnable unless accompanied by persistency (Israr).

3. The Baghghasiyyeh, Banhasiyyeh, or Bayhasiyyeh, followers of Abu Baghghas, Banhas, or Bayhas. I have found no account of their 'doctrinal quiddities.'

4. The Safar, so called from their founder Ziyad ibn el Asfar, believe concealment of tenets ('Takiyyeh') permissible in word not in deed, and they extend infidelity (Kufr) even to such offences as neglecting prayer.

5. The Abazi or Bayazi, who form the mass of Arab population at Zanzibar, and who are also numerous in Oman. They are Karmati and anti-Moslem in the matter of Freewill, a vital distinction from the Sunnis; like the Ismailiyyeh and sundry mystic schools, they believe the Imamship to be a supreme pontificate, but not the succession, by grace, of the prophethood and the caliphate. They are opposed to the Mutazali by respecting the Shaykhayn (Abubekr and Omar), their exoteric reason being that El Islam then throve under a single head. Therefore they deem it lawful and right to abuse TJsman and Ali (damn-

ing the Shiahs for venerating the latter), Muawiyah and Yczid, Talhah, Zubayr,[1] and others, who brought calamities upon the Faithful, and who caused the spilling of Moslem blood. Tnthis age of decaying zeal they do not 'Sabb ' or blaspheme any one publicly by name, and by order of the late Sayyid they bless, during the Friday sermon (Ivhutbah), the two first Caliphs, and then generally the Sahabah (Companions of the Prophet), the Muhajirin (Meccans who accompanied the Flight), and the Ansar (Medinites who received Mohammed). As are all Moslems they may not use the word 'La'anat,' or curse, except to Satan—so Christians are forbidden to call others fools, and with equal success. Moravian-like they pride themselves upon preserving pure and undefiled the tenets and the ritual handed down to them from the Prophet's day, and, with the rest of the Moslem Ulema, who in this point are the most conservative and antiprogressive of men, they would model all modern civilization upon that of barbarous Arabia in the 7th century. One of their favourite sayings is,

[1] These two Asliab or 'Companions of the Apostle ' are popularly supposed to have been buried under a now ruined dome in a garden lying East of the Dahdah cemetery, Damascus. It is, however, a mistake; they were interred near Basreli where they fell in battle.

c ' All innovation (Bida'ah, i.e. a practice unknown to Mohammed's day) is error, and all error is in hell-fire.' Possibly, however, this may be the effect of Wahhabi neighbourhood.

The faith of the Bayazi is narrow and exclusive, a monopoly of righteousness, a moral study of the infinitely little. Amongst Christians I can compare him only with the [15] hard-grit ' style of Baptists, who aspire alone to people a Heaven in which the letter H is of no account. All who do not profess his tenets are Kafirs, and, as it is a standing belief that whoso calls a Moslem Kafir becomes a Kafir himself, they are replied to in kind. Each of the 73 schools naturally considers itself the 'Najiyah,' or Saving Paith; hut it is not justified in consigning to Jehannum those that do not agree with it. The Baydzi condemn all the Sunnis, and especially the Shafeis, who expect actually to see the Eeity (el Ru'uyah) during the next life. Quoting the debated passage of the Koran 'Sight shall not see Him '
the Kharijis agree that if .the Lord he visible, He must he material and personal, consequently created and unessential. In these matters they go beyond their depth; hut who, it may he asked, attempts the subject and does not ? The idea of the Godhead varies with every race, of which it is

the highest mental and moral expression; the higher the conception the higher will he the intellectual status, and vice versa; even the same race constantly modifies its hold for better or for worse. I do not believe that the sages of Greece and Home were polytheists or idolaters, although they may have sacrificed cocks to Esculapius. Under almost all mythologies, even the Hindu, there is an underlying faith in monotheism. But the God of the Jews, of the Christians, and of the Moslems, differs in kind as well as in degree, even as the God of Calvin would not he the God of Channing. A late writer has published several pages of very good writing and very had reasoning, upon the contrast of the Deity, as worshipped hy Christianity and by El Islam. His error has been to assume "Wahhabiism for the typical form of the latter. I might as well work out the theory that the Anabaptist Protestant is the Christian *par excellence.* Like the article on the Talmud which lately created so much attention, it is an able hit of special pleading and no more.

Amongst Moslems, Paradise is supposed to embrace the extent of the earth and firmament, and the late Sayyid used quaintly to remark, that his scanty orthodox subjects would people it hut poorly. The Bayazi, unlike others of the Saving

Faith, which we may better translate 'le Salut,' hold hell-fire to he the eternal portion of even their own sinners; thus literally interpreting the text, 'ever, to all eternity (dwelling) in it (hell),'— lid They have no prayer-station round the Ka'abah, and they relieve their chagrin hy proving these oratories to he 'novelties,' unknown to the Prophet's day.

The ritual differences between the Bayazi and other schools are small; in prayer the arms and hands are extended down the thighs, instead of being folded over the waist. Contrary to the practice of Sunnis and Shiahs, they may wear gold or silver rings of indefinite weight, and silks and satins, provided that the latter he removed during prayer. These sectarians cannot marry women with whom they have cohabited; divorce is imperative from wives whom they have visited at a forbidden season, and they allow legitimacy to children born within two years after the father's death. Amongst the Shafei the period extends to four years : physiological ignorance of ovarian dropsy fixed the time; and mistaken charity has refused to shorten it. In general the Baydzi, like the Druze, appears unwilling to explain his tenets, a remarkable contrast with the self-assertion and the controversial readiness of other Moslems.

When betrayed into argument they quarrel about their belief—a sign of weakness ; the calmly and thoroughly convinced, for instance an honest Scotch country minister, only smiles with pity upon the man who dares to differ from him. The studied simplicity and literalness of the sect and its fierce intolerance, combined with its crass semi-barbarism and isolation from the great family of nations, have favoured the progress of Wahhabi puritanism, and accordingly many Bayazi have ranged themselves under the uncompromising banner of puritanical ' Unitarianism '—literalism and Koranolatry.

Of old the Kharijis were the flowers of the Islamitic garden; and history will ever dwell upon the literary glories of Seville and Cordova. It was this heresy that produced the Allamat (doctissimus) El Ghazali, and the celebrated Persian grammarian and poet, the Imam Abri'l Kasim Mohammed bin Omar, El Zamakhshari. His wife attacked his vile belief in man's Eree-will with an argumentum ad hominem more demonstrative than purely logical. It caused him, however, to recant the error and to express his penitence in that glorious ode beginning—

\ij V>

'O TJiou who seest the midge extend her wing
Athwart the gathered glooms of gloomiest night,'

and to end life in the firm conviction of fate and predestination. His commentary (the KashsMf 'an Hik&ilc el Tanzil) displayed a logical reasoning, a profundity of learning, and purity of style which made it popular throughout El Islam, and it cleared the way for a long procession of similar productions.

In modern degenerate days the Baydzis of Zanzibar have little education and no learning: they must even borrow from the Sunnis commentaries (Tafsir) and other religious works, whence they can extract food for their own cravings of belief. Of these the most popular are El Bokhari, the Jelalayn, and El Baghawi; the abstruse Bayzdwi is seldom troubled. Logic is neglected: history, philosophy, and the exact sciences are unknown. Being Arabs, they do not require El Sarf (accidence or the changes of the verb), and the Alfiyyeh of Ibn Malik is the only popular treatise upon the subject of El Nahw (syntax, and the changes of non-verbal parts of speech). The Eazis of the Bayazi and the Sunni schools lecture in their own houses upon the religious sciences, and the elementary establishments may number on the Island 15 or 16. Here "boys learn to read the Koran, and to write the crabbed angular hand which distinguishes these Moslems. N akhodas master a little arithmetic and navigation at Bombay and Calcutta. Some few have been sent to England and Erance, where they showed no want of attention or capacity: on their return to semi-barbarism, however, almost all went to the bad; they robbed and plotted, an,d most of them died of drunkenness and debauchery.

The best education to be had at Zanzibar can only exercise the memory; it does little to cultivate the understanding or to improve the mind. Yet the people, averse to literary labour and despising learning in the presence of business, pleasure, or idleness, are shrewd and plodding 'thinkers,' and probably for the reason that their wits are not blunted by books and lectures, they are a match for Europeans in the everyday business of life. It is evident that where the profoundest ignorance of our elementary knowledge co-exists with practical wisdom, there is a large field for the labours of civilization, and that the western school, if kept strictly secular and pure of proselytizing, would be a blessing to the children of both sexes at Zanzibar.

CHAPTER XI.

COMPARATIVE ANTHROPOLOGY (ETHNOLOGY) OP ZANZIBAR—THE WASAWAHILI AND THE SLAVE RACES.

'Venti anni sono, il c.ommereio di Zanzibar era nullo ; ora il commercio li supera 50 milioni di franchi. Per aleuni arfcicoli, per esempio, pel garofano, per la gomma copale, e per l'avorio, il mercato di Zanzibar e divenuto il principale del Hondo.'—P. 17, La grandezza Italiana, by tbe learned geographer Cavagliere Cristoforo Negri. Torino, 1864.

THE Wasawahili, hounded north hy the Somal and the Gallas, south hy the so-called Kafir tribes, extend along the Indian Ocean from Makdisbu to Mozambique, a coastal distance of some 1050 miles; they also occupy the Zangian Archipelago, and the islets that fringe the shore. They call themselves Wazumba, ignoring the term Jabarti or Ghiberti (Gibberti), still applied to them hy the northern Moslems. It is given by El Makrizi to Zayla in Somaliland, and by other writers to the Abyssinian 'Moors; ' Yocatur quoque Jabarta, i. e. Eegio Ardens. This insititious race might be called Hamito-Semitic if anywhere we could discern that the mythical Ham, or his progeny, ever became negroes. They are, as they confess themselves to be, mulattos, descended from Asiatic settlers and colonists, Arabs, and Persians of the Days of Ignorance, who intermarried with the Wakafiri or infidels. The author of the Natural History of Man is correct in asserting their African origin, but he under-estimates the amount of Asiatic innervation. The traveller still witnesses the process of breeding half-castes: Maskatis and Baloch still trade to the coast harbours, and settle as agriculturists in the maritime regions, whilst the African element is maintained in the Island by a steady importation of slave girls. The Wasawahili differ in one essential point from their congeners of mixed blood, Egyptian, Nubian, Abyssinian, G-alla, Dankali, Somal, and the northern negroids; these have not, those like the Comoro men distinctly have, the negro effluvium, they are the 'foumarts, not the civets,' of the human race.

I am compelled by its high racial significance to offer a few words upon this unpleasant topic. The odour of the Wasawahili, like that of the negro, is a rank foetor, *sui generis,* which faintly reminded me of the ammoniacal smell exhaled by low-caste Hindus, popularly called Pariahs. These, however, owe it to external applications, aided by the want of cleanliness. All agree that it is most offensive in the yellow-skinned, and the darkest negroids are therefore preferred for domestic slaves and concubines. It does not depend upon diet. In the Anglo-American States, where blacks live like whites, no diminution of it has been remarked; nor upon want of washing,—those who bathe are not less nauseous than those who do not. After hard bodily exercise, or during mental emotion, the epiderm exudes a foetid perspiration, oily as that of orange peel: a negro's feet will stain a mat, an oar must be scraped after he has handled it, and a woman has left upon a polished oaken gun-case a hemispherical mark that no scrubbing could remove. This 'Catinga,' as the Brazilians call it, taints the room, infects every part of the body with which it comes in contact, and exerts a curious effect on the white races. A missionary's wife in Zanzibar owned to me that it caused her almost to faint. I have seen an Englishman turn pale when he felt that a crowded slave-craft was passing nnder Ms windows, and the late Sayyid could not eat or drink for hours after he had been exposed to the infliction.

The Wasawahili may he roughly estimated at half a million of souls. In 1850 Dr Krapf (Yoeabulary of six East African Languages) proposed 350,000 to 400,000. In Zanzibar Island they are divided into two great families, a distinction hitherto disregarded by travellers. The Shirazi, or nobles, derive themselves from the Shangaya settlement, also called Shiraz, on the coast north of Lamu in about S. lat. 2°; thence they extended to Tungi, four days' sail south of the Rufuma river. Asserting themselves to be Alawi Sayyids (descended from tbe Khalifah Ali) they take the title of Muigni, 'lord,' equivalent to the Arab 'Sherif,' whereas the other chiefs are addressed as B'ana—master. The last Msawahili Sultan in the days of the Arab conqueror, Ahmed bin Said, was Ahmed bin Sultan bin Hasan el Alawi. The actual head of the family is entitled Muigni Mku by his people; by the Europeans, 'King of the SawaMli.' His name is mentioned in the Khutbah or Eriday Sermon; he collects the poll-tax, and receives a percentage, some say one half, others only $2000, when paying it into the Sayyid's treasury. He was never, however, admitted to any equality hy the Arab ruler. The Shirazi clan does not now contain more than a hundred families.

The Wasawahili race appears, from the 'Kilwa Chronicle ' (Huma Chronica dos Keys de Quiloa) mentioned by He Barros (1st Decade of Asia, viii. 1, 5), to have been derived from the 'Emozaydis ' (Amm Zayd) or followers of their Imam, Zayd bin Ali Zayn el Abidin bin Husayn, the grandson of the Prophet. He was proclaimed Khalifah at Kufa in A. H. 122 (A.D. 739), under the Khalifat of El Hesham bin Abd el Melek, the Ommiade, by whom he was conquered and slain. The pretender's son, Yahya, fled to Khorasan, where the Abbasides were already making head against the Ommiades, and the tenets of his followers, the Zaydis, spread throughout Yemen, where they formed, and they still form, a numerous and influential class. Other 'Shiah ' partisans took refuge from persecution in East Africa, fortified themselves upon the littoral about Shangaya, and, extending southwards, became lords of the land. Some generations afterwards an emigration of Sunni Arabs from El Hasa, in three ships, commanded by seven brothers flying from the tyranny of their chief, visited the coast, founded Makdishu and Brava, and extended to Sofala. The 'Emozaydis,' unwilling to accept orthodox rule, retired into the interior, intermingled with the Kafir race, and became the Bedawin of the country. The second Persian emigration took place early in our eleventh century. A certain Ali, son of a 'Moorish' Sultan Hasan, who governed Shiraz, by an Abyssinian slave, finding himself despised by his six brethren, fled with wife and family in two ships from Hormuz to East Africa. At Makdishu and Brava, finding Arabs of another faith (Sunnis), he went to Kilwa Island, bought land with cloth, took the title of Sultan, and fortified himself against the Kafirs and against the Moslems of Songo-Songo and Changa, whose dominion extended to Mompana (Mafiyeh). The latter, together with other islets, was conquered by his son, Sultan 'Ali Bumalc,' and the dynasty lasted a grand total of 541 lunar years before the arrival of Cabral at Kilwa in July, A. D. 1500. These Shirazis originated the noble family of the Wasawahili, who do not claim descent from the older 'Emozaydis.'[1]

The Mahadimu, or serviles, a word derived from the Arabic Makhadim, the 'Mohaydin' of

---

[1] Further details will he given in Part II. chap xi.

Europeans, compose the mass of the Wasawahili race. They are popularly derived from the slaves left upon the Island hy the Portuguese. It must, however, he observed that most of the great families in Eastern and Southern Africa have congener clients, or rather outcastes, who are probably, like the Spartan Helots, remnants of subjugated rivals. Thus, to quote but a few, there are the Midgans amongst the Somal, the Walanghlo or Ariangulo and Dahalo amongst the Southern Gallas,[1] and the Wandurobo amongst the Wakwafi. The Wasumbara have then Washenzi; the Hottentots their Bushmen, and the Kafirs their Eingos. In a former volume I have shown that even the Arabs of Oman and Yemen are mixed with Khadims, a system of race within race, as contrary to the spirit of El Islam as of Christianity. These servile castes are distinguished by swarthier skins, weaker frames, and other signs

[1] A highly interesting account is given of this almost unknown race by the Bev. Thomas Wakefield in his 'Footprints in Eastern Africa, or Notes of a Visit to the Southern &alias ' (London, Beed. 1866, pp. 76—79). We are told that 'the Glalas never stab a Mlangulo, but removing the blades of their spears, they thrash him to death with the shafts or handles: ' moreover, that 'the Walangulo approach a Gala on their knees, crying, "tiririsho! tiririsho! tiririsho!" until their greeting is acknowledged by a grunt from their lord or by tbe latter spitting out a little saliva! '

of inferior development. The Mahadimu of Zanzibar are evidently the ancient lords of the Island, reduced to a manner of servitude hy northern conquerors. Though now free, and often slave-owners, these Helots are subject, at the Prince's order, to an occasional corvde, and to a poll-tax. The amount of the latter affords a rude census; the adult males range between 10,000 and 12,000, and the women, it is said, are proportionally more numerous.

The Wasawahili of the Island appear physically inferior to those of the seaboard: as in the days of Marco Polo, they are emphatically an ugly race. If the v girls in early youth show traces of prettiness, it is a grotesque order of the beauts du diable. Some of the men have fine, large, strong, and muscular fignres, without being able to use their strength, and as amongst uncivilized people generally, the reality falls short of the promise. The national peculiarity is the division of the face into two distinct types, and the contrast appears not a little singular. The upper, or intellectual part, though capped by woolly hair, is distinctly Semitic—with the suspicion of a caricature—as far as the nose-bridge, and the more ancient the family the more evident is the mixture. The lower, or animal half, especially the nostrils, lip, jaws, and chin is unmistakably African. There are a few Albinos with silk-cocoon-coloured hair, and tender-red eyes, their pinkish skins are cobwebbed by darker reticulations and rough from pellagrous disease. Leucosis, however, is rare; we saw only two cases, one on the Island, the other a youth near Tanga.

The Wasawahili are hy no means a jet-black people, as Pritchard, misled hy Dr Bird, has assumed ; nor, indeed, is this the distinction of the Zanzibarian races generally. The skin is a chocolate-brown, varying in shades, as amongst ourselves, but usually not darker than the complexion of Southern Arabia. About Lamu and Patta the colour is yellow-brown; at Mombasah and Zanzibar dark-brown; and south of Kilwa, I am told, black-brown. Mostly the hair is jetty, unless sunburnt; crisp, and curling short; it splits after growing a few inches long, and often it is planted like the body pile, in distinct 'pepper-corns.' The barbule is a degeneracy from the Arab goatee, and the mustachios are short and scanty. The oval skull, too dolichocephaious to he purely Caucasian, is much flattened at the walls, and sometimes the upper brow (the reflective region of Gall) is too highly developed for the lower. The eyes, with dark-brown pupils and cornea stained dirty bilious-yellow, are straight and well-opened, but the nose is flat and patulous, the mouth is coarse and ill-cut; the lips, often everted, project unduly; the teeth are obliquely set, and the jaw is prognathous. The figure is loose and pulpy, and even in early manhood the waist is seldom finely formed; in many men I have seen the nipples placed unusually low down, whilst the women have the flaccid pendulous breasts of negresses. Both sexes fail in point of hips, which are lank and angular, whereas those of the inner savages are finely rounded. The shanks are bowed forwards, the calf is high raised and bunchy, the heel is long, and the extremities are coarse and large. There is another proof of African blood which can hardly be quoted here : many overland travellers have remarked it amongst the boatmen of Egypt.[1]

Veritable half-castes, the Wasawahili have inherited the characters of both parents. Erom the Arab they derive shrewd thinking and practice in concealing thought: they will welcome a man with the determination to murder him; they have unusual confidence, self-esteem, and complacency;

[1] The carious reader will find it in the Travels of Marco Polo (chap. xxxvii. note 1, p. 432, of "Bohn's Antiquarian Library).

fondness for praise, honours, and distinctions; keenness together with short-sightedness in matters of business, and a nameless horror of responsibility and regular occupation. Africa has gifted them with comparative freedom from bigotry — they are not admodum dediti religionibus. Usually the Moslem combines commerce with proselytizing, opposed to our system, which divides by a wide gulf the merchant's career from that of the Missionary, and which unites them only upon the subscription sheet. These people care little to make converts: their African languor upon doctrinal points prevents their becoming fanatics or proselytizers. African also is their eternal, restless suspicion, the wisdom of serf and slave compensating for their sluggish imagination and small powers of concentration. They excel in negro duplicity; they are infinitely great in the 'Small wares and petty points of cunning,' and they will boast of this vile eminence, saying, 'Are we not Wasawa<u>hili</u>?' men who obtain their ends by foxship ? Natum mendacio genus, truth is unknown to it; honesty and candour are ignored even by name. When they assert they probably lie, when they swear they certainly lie. The favourite oath is 'Mi mi wad (or M'ana) hardml—I am a bastard if,' &c.,

&c., and it is never respected. The language is very foul, and such expressions as Komanyoko are never out of the mouth. The Msawahili will not ask a thing openly: he waits, fidgeting withal, till the subject edge itself in, and then he will rather hint than speak out. At the same time he is an inveterate heggar, and the outstretching of hands seems to relieve his hrain. When his mind is set upon an acquisition, he becomes a monomaniac, like that child-man the savage. His nonchalance, carelessness, and improvidence pass all hounds. He will light his pipe under a dozen leaky kegs of gunpowder; 'he will set a house on fire, as it were, to roast his eggs; ' he will wreck his ship because anchoring her to the beach saves trouble in loading; he might make his coast a mine of wealth, hut he will not work till hunger compels him, and his pure insouciance has allowed his valuable commerce to he wrested from him hy Europeans, Hindus, and Arabs. His dislike of direct action exceeds that of the Bedawi, and yet he quotes a proverb touching procrastination, 'Leo kabli ya kesho,'—to-day is before tomorrow — better than our 'To-morrow never comes.'

In disposition the Msawahili is at once cowardly and destructive: his quarrelsome temper leads him into trouble, but be fights only by being brought to bay. Sensual and degraded, bis self-indulgence is that of the brutes. He drinks, and always drinks to excess. He would stake and lose his mother at play. Chastity is unknown in this land of hot temperaments—the man places paradise in the pleasures of the sixth sense, and the woman yields herself to the first advances. Upon the coast, when an adulterer is openly detected, he is fined according to the 'injured husband's ' rank; mostly, however, such peccadillos are little noticed. Unnatural crimes are held conducive to health. *   *   *

The manners of 'the -perverse race of Kush ' are rough and free, especially compared with those of India, yet dashed with a queer African ceremoniousness. Their conversation turns wholly upon the subjects of women and money. With these optimists all that is is good, or, at least, it is not worth the trouble of a change for the better. They 'make a stand upon the ancient way,' and they hold that old custom, because it is old, must be fit for all time. This savage conservatism, combined with their traditional and now instinctive dread of the white face, and perhaps with a not unreasonable fear of present and future loss, has made them close the interior to Europeans. They have no especial dislike to, at the same time no fondness for, foreigners, who in mind as well as hody are separated from them longo interyallo.

The characteristic good points of the coast race are careless merriment, an abundance of animal spirits; strong attachments and devoted family affection. There is amongst men an artificial fraternity which reminds us of the 'fostering' of Ireland and the 'Lambmas brother and sister ' of the local Kermess, St Olla's Eair : a similar brotherhood is found at Madagascar. Amongst the negro races generally each sucks or exchanges blood from an arm vein, and the two then swear relationship. The operation is called Ku chanjana and the oath Sare or Sogu,—the Arabs, hy whose law it is forbidden, name it Mushati-beh. Girls, even though their parents be living, adopt a Kungwf or stead-mother, who may or who may not be of the family the latter attends her 'Mwari ' (adopted child) when the first ablution for puberty is performed, and at the wedding sits upon the couch till decency forbids. The connection reminds us of the Persian proverb, 'The nurse is kinder than the mother.' Like Orientals and certain peoples of Southern Europe, they make little distinction between near and distant relationship: a man's son may come from the same city and his brother perhaps from the same province. So in West Africa 'brother' has an extensive signification.

The Wasawahili from Makdishu to Mozambique (Mussumbeg) are all Moslems and Shafei, as they were in the 14th century when Ibn Batuta reported them chaste and honest, peaceful and religious. Possibly under the orthodox denomination they may still preserve, the heretical Zaydi tenets of their ancestors; but of this point I was not familiar enough with them to judge. If Persians, they must date from the days before the universal prevalence of Tashayyu (Shiitism), or they have abandoned their ancient faith. Peuds with the late Sayyid Said spread the school along the coast, and his Bayazi subjects became Sunnis in spite, even as Irishmen and Romans sometimes turn Protestants. El Islam, however, only fringes the Continent. With their savage irreverence for holy things, the Wasawahili calling themselves Moslems know little beyond the Kalmah, or profession of faith, rarely pray, and fast only by compulsion. Like Hindostanis, Persians, and Egyptians, nations professing El Islam at a distance from the fountainhead, amongst whom local usage has been largely incorporated with the pure practice of the Eaith, they have retained a mass of superstitions and idolatries belonging to their pagan forefathers. They have a terror of the sorcerers, with whom Maskat is said to swarm, and they tell frightful stories of men transformed into hyaenas, dogs, sheep, camels, and other animals. They defend themselves and their huts against evil spirits (Jann) and had men hy Koranic versets, greegrees, and various talismans, mostly bought from the pagan Mganga or Medieine-man. They believe in alehemy and in Kimbwata, or love-philters, the latter, as usual in the East, containing various abominations. The slave girls from about Mangdo, a small port near Kilwa, are famous for concocting draughts which, after bringing on a possibly fatal sickness, subjugate for ever the affections of the patient. Similarly in India, Sind, Egypt, and Persia, no man will touch sherbet under the roof of his betrothed and prepared by her mother, unless his future father-in-law set him the example. Some of the Eimbwata or philters are peculiar: a few grains of Jowari are 'forced' in an exceptional way till they sprout; they are then pounded and mixed with the food. This harmless adhibition causes, say the people, either death by violent disease or intense affection. It is a superstition common to the Western East, and I have found it in India and Sind, in Peru and Egypt. Ghosts and larva; haunt the houses in which men have died, a Fetish belief which does not properly belong to El Islam or to Christianity: the British Consulate has a bad name on account of the terrible fate of its owner, the late Sayyid's nephew. Descended from 'devil-worshippers,' the Wasawahili rather fear the 'Shaytani ' than love Allah, and to the malignant powers of preternatural beings they attribute sickness and all the evils of human life. A Zanzibar negroid will not even fetch a leech from the marsh, for fear of offending him to whom the animal is 'Ju-ju,' or sacred.

Generally, the Msawahili Alim or literato, though capable of reading the Koran, cannot write a common Arabic letter. Some, however, attain high proficiency: I may quote as an instance the Itazi Muhiyy el Din. These negroids begin arithmetic early, a practice which, perhaps, they have learned from the Banyans. They excel in memory and in quickness of apprehension from early childhood to the age of puberty: the same has been remarked about the Arabs, and Anglo-Indians observe it in the natives of Hindostan. Whether at the virile epoch there is an arrest of development, or the brain suffers from exclusive, excessive obedience to the natural law, 'increase and multiply' and its consequent affections, is a question still to be settled. Boys are sent to school when aged seven, and finish their Khitmah (perfection of the Koran) in one to three years; after this they are usually removed to assist their fathers in the business of life.

Upon the Island the Msawahili child receives some corrupted Moslem name, as Taufiki (Tanfik) Muamadi (Mohammed), Tani (ITsman), Shibu (Nasib), Muhina (Muhinna), Usy (Ali), or Uadi. Upon the coast the appellations are mostly heathen: I may quote the following from the Benu Kendij tribe—Bori, Chumi, Kambi, Kangaya, Kirwasha, Mareka, Mkame, Mkhokho, Mombe, or Mwambe, Mwere, Nungu, Shangora, Shenkambi, Zingaji. The wilder Wasawahili communities adopt very characteristic compounds : such are Machuzi wa Shimba (fish-soup), Mrima-khonde (mountain plantation),[1] Mkata-Moyyo (cutter-out of heart), Khiro-kota (treasure trove), Mchupio wa Keti

---

[1] Mr Cooley (G-eog. 37) tells us that 'Conda, in Congoese and also in Sawahili, means hill.' It certainly does not in Zanzibar, where Konda is an adjective, lean or thin. Konde means the fist (in Arabic   and Khonde is applied to a Shamba or plantation.

(leaper upon a cliair), Mshindo-Mamba (conqueror of crocodile), Khombe la Simba (lion's claw), Mguru Mfupi (short-legs), Mui' Mvua (Mister rain), Mkia ya Nyani (monkey's tail), Masimbi (cowries), and Ugali (stirabout).

Girls take Arabic names, as Mamai Khamisi (Mother Thursday), Fatimah, and Arusi, or they borrow from the pagans Magonera, Zawadi and Apewai (a gift), Timeh, Sitx, Bahiiti, Tinisi, and Maehoydo (their eyes). The ceremonial address to men is Bwana (pronounced B'dnd) master, possibly a corruption of the Arabic 'Abunait is prefixed to proper names, especially Arabic, as B'aria Muamadi. The diminutive Kib'and is the Italian ᵉ Signorino.' The feminine form Mwana (M'and) has equal claims of descent from the Arabic TJmmand, our mother. It means, however, 'child' generieally in the proverb M'ana uwwd Mze, Mze hawwd M'ana—child slays parent, parent slays not child—the equivalent of the Italian Amor descende non ascende, and the Arab's 'My heart is on my son, my son's is on a stone.' Amongst certain interior tribes it is still prefixed to the names of chiefs; hence probably the 'Emperor' Monomotapa (M'ana Mtdpa) which J. de Barros writes Benomotapa: the latter may not be a misprint, but represent '13'and Mtapa.' Muigni, contracted to Mui', is applied to Sayyids, Sberifs, and temporal rulers, and Shebe is the equivalent of Shaykh. Mkambi belongs to the sultan or chief, and the Anglo-Arab 'Seedy ' (Sidi = my lord) is unknown.

The marriages (Maowano) of the Wasawahili are operose, as might be expected amongst a race whose family festivals are, as in the far north of Europe, their only public amusements. I may, perhaps, here remark that in matching, as well as in despatching, even civilization has not thrown off all traces of the old barbarism, and that the visit to M. le Maire and the wedding breakfast, to mention no other troubles and disagreeables, should make us uncommonly lenient to those less advanced than ourselves. The relatives of the bridegroom, as soon as he reaches the mature age of 15, having found for him a fit and proper mate, repair to the parents; propose a Mahr, or settlement, varying according to means from $15 to $25, and obtain the reply ancipital. The women then visit one another; the answer emerges into distinctness, and all fall to cooking. In due time Ccelebs receives, as a token of acceptance, a large Siniyyah, a tray of rice, meat, and confectionery, a 'treat ' for his friends, forwarded by the future *father-in-law*. Tbe feast concludes tbe betrothal j[1] either of the twain most concerned is still at liberty to jilt; but in such a case, as usual throughout the Moslem East, enmity between the families inevitably results.

The wedding festivities outlast the month: there are great 'affinities of gossips;' tympanum et tripudium; hard eating and harder wetting of the driest clay with the longest draughts of Tembo K'hali (sour toddy), of Pombe beer (the Kafir Chuala), and of the maddening Zerambo. Processions of free women and slave girls, preceded by chattels performing on various utensils of music, perambulate the streets, singing and dancing in every court. At length the Kazi, or any other man of letters, recites the Eatiheh, and the two become one, either at the *bridegroom's* or at the bride's house. The women are present when the happy man enters the nuptial chamber, and they always require to be ejected by main force. Unlike the Arabs, they retain the Jewish practice of inspection: if the process be satisfactory, the bridegroom presents $10 to $50 to his new connections, while the exemplary

[1] M. Guillain (Part II. 108) calls the preliminary ceremony 'Outoumba,' and I cannot help thinking that he was grossly 'sold' by some exceedingly impudent interpreter.

young person is blessed, congratulated, and petted with small gifts by papa and mamma. Sbe often owes, it is whispered, ber blushing honours to tbe simple process of cutting a pigeon's throat. In case of a disappointment, there is a violent scene of abuse and recrimination ; but when lungs and wrath are exhausted, the storm is lulled without blows or even divorce. The first 'Mfungato,' i. e. seven (days) after consummation, is devoted to tbe wildest revelry, tbe 'Walrmeh,' or wedding feast, concluding only with the materials for feasting.

The Msawahili is allowed to breaths his last upon a couch, and the corpse, after being washed by an Alim or by some kinsman, is hastily wrapped in a perfumed winding-sheet. Women of the highest rank sit at home in solitary grief. The middle-classes stain their faces, assume dark or dingy-coloured dresses, and repair to the seashore for the purpose of washing the dead man's clothes before dividing them amongst his relations or distributing them to the poor. The slave girls shave their heads like Hindus, bathe, and go about the streets singing Nenise, and mourning aloud. Meanwhile a collection, technically known as Sdnda (the winding-sheet), is made amongst the people, who are almost all connected by a near or distant tie. One of the blood-kinsmen acts Munddi, or crier. As each one appears with Ms quotum, he shonts £ lo! such a person (naming Mm) has bought such and such articles for Ms brother's funeral feast.' TMs publicity tends of course to make men liberal. The corpse is buried, as is customary amongst Moslems, on the day, generally the evening, of decease, and there is a popular belief, in which some Europeans join, that deaths take place mostly when the tide ebbs, at the full and change of the moon. The custom of abusing the corpse, accompanied with the greatest indecencies, is confined to the least civilized settlements. After the funeral all apply themselves to eating, drinMng, and what we should call merriment; whilst music and dancing are kept up as long as weak human nature permits. The object is not that of the Yorkshire Arvills, to refresh those who attended from afar—it is confessedly to 'take the sorrow out of the heart.' So the Yelorio of Yucatan is para divertise—to distract kin-grief. As in the matter of marriage, however, so in funerals, we can hardly deride barbarous races whilst we keep up our pomp and expense of ridiculous trappings, taxing even the poor for mutes and carriages, for 'gloves, scarves, and hatbands.'

The Wasawahili have all the African passion for the dance and song : they may be said to exist upon manioc and hetel, palm-wine and spirits, music and dancing. The Ngoma Khu, or huge drum, a hollowed cocoarstem hound with leather braces, and thumped with fists, palms, or large sticks, plays an important and complex part in the business of life : it sounds when a man falls sick, when he revives, or when he dies ; at births and at marriages; at funerals and at festivals; when a stranger arrives or departs ; when a fight begins or ends, and generally whenever there is nothing else to do. It is accompanied hy the 'Siwa,' a huge pipe of black wood or ebony, and by the ᶜ Zumari,' a more handy variety of the same instrument. On occasions which justify full orchestras, an 'Upatu,' or brass pan, is placed upon the ground in a wooden tray, and is tapped with two bits of palm-frond. Some wealthy men possess gongs, from which the cudgel draws lugubrious sounds. The other implements are 'Tabl,' or tomtoms of gourd, provided with goatskin; the Tambire, or Arab Barbut, a kind of lute; the Malagash ᶜ Zeze,' a Calabash-banjo, whose single string is scraped with a bow; and finally horns of the cow, of the Addax, and the Oryx antelopes. These people are excellent timeists, but their music, being all in tbe minor key, and tbe song being a mere recitative without change of words, both are monotonous to the last degree. The dancing resembles that of the Somal, and, as amongst the slaves, both sexes prance together. The Diwans, or chiefs, caper with drawn swords, whilst the women move in regular time, shaking skirts with the right hand. The 'figures'[5] are, unlike the music, complicated and difficult: they seem to vary in almost every village. The only constant characteristic appears to be that tremulous motion from the waist downwards, and that lively pantomime of love which was so fiercely satirized by the eminently moral Juvenal. It is, indeed, the groundwork of all 'Oriental ' dancing from Morocco to Japan,

The principal occupation of the Wasawahili is agriculture ; they form the farmer class of the Island, and everywhere in the interior we find their little settlements of cajan-thatched huts of wattle and dab, with flying roofs, acting chimney as well as ventilator—a right sensible contrivance, worthy of imitation. The furniture consists of a few mats ; of low stools, mostly cut out of a single block; of chairs, a skin being stretched on a wooden frame; and invariably of a Kitanda, or cartel of coir. and sticks; even the beggar will not sleep or sit upon the damp face of his mother earth. The dwelling is divided into several rooms, or rather closets, hy partition walls the height of a man; as usual in tropical lands, the interior is kept dark. Sometimes the hovel boasts the convenience of a Cho'oni or Shironi (latrina), hut in no case is there a window. Gossips meet under the shade of huge Calabashes and other trees.

Like the Somal, the Wasawahili are essentially a trading race, a crumenimulga natio, and they do business with the characteristic dishonesty of Africans. They defraud and even offer violence to Banyans, and acting as trade-men to European merchants, they never allow a purchase without deducting their percentage. At the same time their plausibility, like that of the travelling Dragoman, so impresses upon the [civilized dupe, whom they hedge round with an entourage of their own, and whom it is their life-business to cozen, that nothing can convince him of their rascality. Some of them make considerable fortunes: I heard of one who lately purchased an estate for $14,000. They are also commercial travellers of no mean order. Upon the Zanzibar coast they cut rafters and firewood; they dig for copal, and they act as middlemen; they wander far into the interior, fraying hides, slaves, and ivory, and they have thus become familiar with the Lake Regions, which are now attracting our attention. The poorest classes employ themselves in fishing, and many may he seen hy day plying ahont the harbour in little 'Monoxyles,' which they manage with admirable dexterity. Others have learned to make the rude hardwares with which the mainland is supplied: there are also rough masons, hoat-hnilders, and carpenters of peculiar awkwardness.

Respectable Wasawahili dress like Arabs in 'Kofiyya,' here meaning red caps, and the long Disdashah, or night-gown; the loins are girt with a 'Kamarband '-shawl, and sandals protect the feet. Others are contented with the Iiammam-toilette, waist-cloth (Shukkah or Tanga) and shoulder-sheets (Izdr), always adorned with the favourite fringe (Tambua or Taraza). This is at once the simplest and one of the most ancient of attires; the plate from Montfaucon's Cosmas Indicopleustes (1706, Topographia Christiana) reproduced hy Yincent (Periplus, Appendix, part I.) shows the kilt to have been the general dress of the ancient Ethiopians, as the spear was their weapon. Before superiors they hare the shaven poll, an un-Oriental custom probably learned from the Portuguese. As amongst the Arab Bedawin, the Syrian Rayahs, and the Persian Iliyat, the women mostly go abroad unveiled. The ʽ Murun gawanah,' or freeborn, however, is distinguished out-of-doors by her rude mantilla, and ᶠ ladies ' affect an TJkaya, or fillet of indigo-dyed cotton, or muslin, somewhat like that of the Somal and the Syrians. The feminine garb is a Kisitu, or length of stained cotton, blue and red being the pet colours. It resembles the Kitambi of the Malagash, and it is the nearest approach to the primitive African kilt of skin or tree bark. Wrapped tightly round the unsupported bosom, and extending from the armpits to the heels, this ungraceful garb depresses the breast, spoils the figure, and conceals nothing of its deficiencies. The hair, like the body, drips with unfragrant cocoa-nut oil; and though there is not much material to work upon, it is worked in various fanciful styles. Many shave clean; some wear a half-crop, like a skull-cap of Astracan wool; others a full-grown bush covering the whole head. These part it down the middle, with an asinine cross over the regions of veneration; those draw longitudinal lines above the ears, malting a threefold parting ; there are also garnishings and outworks of stunted pigtails, forming stiff and savage accroche-coeurs. Two peculiar coiffures at once attract the stranger's eye. One makes the head look as if split into a pair of peaks, the side hair being raised from sinciput to occiput in tall double unpadded rolls, parted by a deep central hollow: this style is nowhere so pronounced as near the Gaboon river, where the heads of the Mpongwe girls appear short-horned. The other consists of frizzly twists trained lengthwise from nape to brow, and the whitish etiolated scalp showing itself between the lines as though the razor had been used: the stripes suggest the sections of a musk-melon or the meridians of a map.

The favourite feminine necklace is a row of sharks' teeth; some use beads, others hits of copal, but the amber so highly valued in the Somali country is here not prized. I have alluded before to the artificial deformity of ear-lobes distended by means of the Mpogo, a mixture of raw Copal (Chakazi) and Cinnabar. The left nostril is usually honoured with some simple der;oration—■ a stud or rose-shaped button of wood or bone, of ivory or of precious metal, and at times its place is taken by a clove or a pin of Cassava. The tattoo is not so common on the Island as upon the Continent. These women are said to he prolific, hut apparently they have small families : the child is carried in a cloth called Mbereko, and, curious to say, they do not hind up its head immediately after birth. They are hard-worked; and, like the dames of Harar, they buy and sell with men in the bazar. Their food is manioc, holcus, rice, and sometimes fish; a fowl is the extent of luxury, flesh being mostly beyond their means. Tew smoke, but almost all chew tobacco as lustily as their husbands, and their mouths are horrid chasms full of 'Tambul '—quids of betel-nut and areca leaf peppered with coarse shell-lime! This astringent, like the Kola-nut of the Guinea Regions, acts preventive against the effect of damp heat, and it is a stomachic, consequently a tonic. The habit of 'chawing ' it becomes inveterate : Hindostanis visiting Portugal, and unable to procure the favourite 'Pan-Supdri,' have imitated it with cuttings of cypress-apples and ivy leaves. Ibn Batuta declares the betel to be highly aphrodisiac, and hence partly the high esteem in which this masticatory is held.

[1] The areca-nut is called in Arabic Fofal, and in Kisawahili Popo : the betel-nut, Tambul and Tambuli, and the lime ISfurah and Choka.

The Wasawahili are not an honoured race; even the savage Somal call them 'Abld, or serviles, and bitterly deride their peculiarities. The unerring instinct of mankind has pointed them out for slaves, and they have readily accepted the position. As Moslems they should he free, and the Faith forbids them to trade in Moslems. Yet hy local usage, as the children become the property not of the parents, hut of the mother's brother, the latter can sell any or all of his nephews and nieces; indeed, he would he subject to popular contempt if, when poor, he did not thus 'raise the wind.'

The most interesting point connected with these coast negroids is their language, the Kisawahili. It was anciently called Kingozi, from Ungozi or the region lying about the Dana, or rather Zana, the river known to its Galla accoloo as 'Maro,' and ᶜ Pokomoni ' from the heathen Pokomo who, living near its course, form the southern boundary of Galla-land proper. The dialect is still spoken with the greatest purity about Patta and the other ancient settlements between Lamu and Mombasah. Oral tongues are essentially fluctuating; having no standard, the roots of words soon wither and die, whilst terms, idioms, and expressions once popular speedily fall into oblivion, and are supplanted by neologisms.

Thus the origin of words must often he sought hy collation with the wilder kindred dialects of the coast tribes; for instance, the root of 'Mhua' (rain), which has died out of Kisawahili, still visits in Kinyika—ku hua, to rain. In Zanzibar Island Kisawahili is most corrupted; the vocabulary, varying with every generation, has become a mere conglomerate which combines South African, Arabic, Persian, Hindi, and even Portuguese, an epitome of local history. On the coast it greatly varies, being constantly modified by the migration and mixture of tribes. Like the Malay of the Indian Islands, it has become the Lingua Pranca, the Lingoa Gera! of commerce from Ka'as Hafun to the Mozambique and throughout Central Intertropical Africa. This Urdu Zaban, or Hindostani of East Africa, is indispensable to the explorer, who disdains mere 'geography;' almost every inland tribe has some vagrant man who can speak it. My principle being never to travel where the language is unknown to me, I was careful to study it at once on arriving at Zanzibar; and though sometimes in the interior question and answer had to pass through three and even four media, immense advantage has derived from the modicum of direct intercourse.

, The base of Kisawahili is distinctly African;

and, totally unlike its limitrophe the Galla, it grammatically ignores the Semitic element. It is now time for writers to unlearn that, 'all the languages over the face of the earth, however remotely different and however widely spread, appear to he all reducible to the one or the other of three radically distinct tongues ' (Dr Belce, p. 352, Appendix to Jacob's Flight. London, Longmans, 1865)} It is only, I believe, the monogenist pure and simple who in these days would assert 'there exist three linguistic types, as there are three physical types, the black, the yellow, and the white ' (M. de Quatrefages, p. 31, Anthropological Beview, *No.* xxviii.). To the old and obsolete triad of Turanian, Semitic, and Aryan, or Turanian, Semitic, and Iranian, we must now add at least another pair—without noticing the Asianesian—namely, the American or Sentence language, and the prefixitive South African family.

[1] This is repeated by my friend (p. 59, The Idol in Horeb : Evidence tbat tbe golden image at Mount Sinai was a cone, and not a calf. London : Tinsleys, 1871), who, however, informs us tbat in 1846 Major, now Sir Henry, Kawlinson agreed with him in saying that, 'the class of languages to which the designation Semitic or Semitish is properly applicable is that comprising the whole of the aboriginal languages of Asia, Polynesia, and America.' This latter continent, however, should not have been included without proofs, and hitherto we have failed to find them.

These two great tongues, one extending oyer half a world, the other through half a continent, are, I believe with Lichtenstein and Marsden, unborrowed, indigenous, and marked with all the peculiarities which distinguish their inventors. Both are idioms which seem to indicate nice linguistic perceptions and high intellectual development •, history, however, supplies many cases of civilization simplifying and curtailing the complicated tongues of barbarians, thus making language the means, not the end, of instruction.

The limits of the South African family may be roughly laid down as extending from the Equator to the Cape of Good Hope. The Equatorial Gaboon on the Western Coast[1] evidently belongs to it; and upon the Congo river I found that whole sentences of Kisawahili were easily made intelligible to the people.[2] Though the language is evidently one in point of construction throughout this immense area, isolation and hostilities between tribes have split it into a multitude of

[1] Grammar of the Bakele language, &c.,by the Missionaries of the A. B. 0. E. M. Gaboon Station, Western Africa. New York: Pratt, 1854. Also Grammar of the Mpongwe language, Ac., by the same. New York : Snowdon and Pratt, 1847.

[2] A Vocabulary of the Malemba and Embomma Languages. (Appendix I. Tuckey's Expedition to the Iiivcr Zaire. London : Murray, 1818.) Also Fr. B. M. de Cannecatim's Diceionario da Lingua Bunda. Lisboa, 1804.

dialects. Almost every people, at the distance of 30 to 50 miles, has its peculiar speech, and in. these regions it would not he difficult to collect 'Specimens of a hundred African Languages.' The older travellers' remarked that the Tower of Babel must have been near the Gulf of Guinea; they would have found the same throughout the interior and Eastern Coast.

My experience[1] of the tongues spoken to the west of the Zanzibar coast proper is that their amount of difference greatly varies : some average that of the English counties, others of the three great Neo-Latin languages, whilst in some the degree amounts to that between English, German, and Dutch. And generally, I may remark, the East-West extremities of the lingual area are more closely connected than the North-South; the language of Angola, for instance, is more like Kisawahili than the Sichuana. I am at pain to understand why Dr Krapf should have named this linguistic family, Orphno-(dark-brown) Hamitic, Orphno-Cushite, Nilo-ITamitic, and Nilotic,[2] when it is far more intimately connected

[1] When travelling in East Africa I took as a base the vocabulary of Catherine of Eussia, and filled it up with five dialects, viz., those of the Sawahil, Uzaramo, Khutu, Usagara, and Unyamwezi.

[2] In these days, however, we cannot say, with the Opener

with the Kafir regions, the Congo and the Zambeze rivers, than with Ethiopia or the Nile Valley proper. Mr Cooley's term 'Zangian ' or 'Zingian ' also unduly limits the area to that of a mere sub-family.

The crux grammaticorum of the great South African language is its highly artificial system of principiatives or preformatives.[1] In the three recognized lingual types of the old world the work of inflexion, the business of grammar, and the mechanism of speech disclose themselves at the ends of vocables. In this prefixitive tongue the changes of mood, tense, case, and number, are effected at the beginning of words by prepositive modifying particles, which are evidently contractions of significant terms, and whose apparatus supplies the total want of inflexion. This development, arrested in other languages—the Coptic, for instance—here obtains a significance which isolates it from all linguistic society. The practised student at once discovers that he is dealing with a completely new family by the unusual difficulty which unvaried terminations

of Inner Africa (p. 123), 'The Nilotic family of languages nowhere extends into the basin of the Nile.'

[1] I have sketched the distinguishing points of the Hamitic tongues in my Preface (p. xxii.) to ' Wit and Wisdom from West Africa' (London: Tinsleys, 1865).

and initial changes present to one accustomed only to the terminal.

The minor characteristics of the Kisawahili are the peculiarities of the negative system in substantives and adjectives, pronouns, adnouns, and verbs; for instance, Asie, he or she who is not, Isie, it which is not. Secondly, are the broad lines of distinction drawn between words denoting the rational and the irrational, and in a minor degree the rational-animate (as man), and the rational-inanimate (as ass). In most cases the rational-animate affixes Wa as a plural sign: the irrational-animate Ma. Umbu, a sister, properly makes Waumbu, sisters: the ignorant, however, and the Islanders often say Maumbu (sisters) like Map'hunda (asses). Thus personality supplies the place of gender, a phenomenon that already dawns in the Persian and in other Indo-European tongues. Next is the artful and intricated system of irregular plurals, and last, not least, the characteristic alliteration, an assonance apparently the debris of many ancient dialects based upon an euphonious concord not always appreciable by us, and therefore not yet subjected by our writers to rule. We understand, for instance, that an alliterative speaker should say Mtu mema (a good man), and Watu wema (good men); but why is the regularity altered to Mahali pango (my place), p'hunda sango (my donkey), and Mtu *wa* Raskidi (Rashid's man), instead of mango, pango, and ma? These distinctions appear far too empirical, arbitrary, and artificial for the wants of primitive speech.

The Kisawahili is an oral tongue — an illiterate language in the sense assigned to the term by Professor Lepsius. The people, like the Somal and the Gallas, never invented a syllabarium. This absence of alphabet is a curious proof of deficient constructiveness in a race that cultivates rude eloquence, and that speaks dialects which express even delicate shades of meaning: it contrasts wonderfully with the Arabs and Hindus, who adapt to each language ■ some form of Phoenician or Dewanagari. The coast races use the modern Arabic alphabet, which, admirable for its proper purpose, represents African sounds imperfectly, as those of Sindi and Turkish, and is condemned to emulate the anomalous orthography or cacography of our English. The character is large, square, and old-fashioned, resembling later Kufic even more than that of Harar, and he must be a first-rate scholar who can read at sight all the letter of a man to his friend. Literature is confined to a few sheets upon the subject of Bao or TJganga (Banal or geomancy), to proverbs and proverbial sayings, mostly quatrains; to riddles and rabbit tales, which here represent the hare legends of the Namaqnas and the spider stories of the Gold Coast; to Mashairi, or songs rhymeless, measureless, and unmusical, and to 'Utenzi,' religious poems, and eulogies of the brave.

In Zanzibar Island Arabic is ever making' inroads upon the African tongue, and the student who knows the former will soon master the latter. The first short vocabulary, by Mr Salt, was published in 1811, and was presently followed by others, especially the 'Soahili vocabulary ' of the late Mr Samuel K. Masury, of Zanzibar (Memoirs of the American Academy, Cambridge, May, 1845), and Mr J. Boss Browne's 'Specimen of the Sowhelian Language' (Etchings of a Whaling Cruise. New York, 1846).[1] Strange to say, the 'Mombas Mission ' translated the Gospels into the obscure local Tvinyika, when only three chapters of Genesis and a version of the English Prayer Book (Tubingen, 1850—54)

[1] Mr Eoas Browne lias lately been *engaged in* writing a voluminous report to the Government at Washington upon the mineral resources of the Western States of the Union.

were published £ in the one language, hy the instrumentality of which the missionary and the merchant can master in a short time all the dialects spoken from the Line down to the Cape of Good Hope.' Dr Krapf's 'Outline of the Elements of the Kisauaheli Language' (Tubingen, 1850) requires great alterations and additions, especially in the alliterative and other characteristic parts of the tongue. Messrs Eebmann and Erhardt, who both were capable of writing a scholar-like book, or of perfecting the 'Outline,' turned their attention to the languages of the Nyassa, TJsumbara, and the Wakwafi. In 1857 M. Guillain published, as an Appendix to his third volume, a short grammar and vocabulary of the 'langue Souahlffili: ' they are mere bald sketches, and they convey but the scantiest idea of what they attempt to illustrate. A good study of Kisawahili would facilitate the acquisition of the whole sub-family. Eor my oAvn use I commenced a grammar intended to illustrate the intricate and difficult combinations and the peculiar euphony which here seems to be the first object of speech: unfortunately my transfer to West Africa left it, like my vocabularies, in a state of MS. My friend Mr Triibner has lately advertised a volume called 'East African folk-lore, Swahili Tales, as told by tbe natives of Zanzibar,' with an English translation by Edward Steere, L.L.D., Hector of Little Steeping, Lincolnshire, and Chaplain to Bishop Tozer (London: Bell and Daldy, 1870);[1] and Dr Krapf has proposed to publish the Juo ya Herkal (Book of Heraclius), c an account of the wars of Mohammed with Askaf, Governor of Syria, to the Greek Emperor Heraclius, in rhyme; a MS. in ancient Ki-Suahili written in Arabic characters.' Also 'Juo ja TJtenzi, Poems and Mottoes in rhyme,' the dialect being that formerly spoken in the Islands of Patta and Lamu. Both the e linguistie treasures ' were presented to the Oriental Society of Halle. The last publications which I have seen are *I* Specimens of the Swahili Language ' (Zanzibar, 1866) ; 'Collections for a Handbook of the Swahili Language, as spoken at Zanzibar,' by Bishop Tozer and Rev. E. *Steere* (Zanzibar, 1865), and the Rev. E. Steere's 'Collections for a Handbook of the Shambala Language ' (Zanzi-

---

[1] Messrs Monteiro *and Gamitto (0* Muata Cazembel, Appendix, 470) doubt whether the Tete grammar can be reduced to an intelligible system of verbs. I see no difficulty. Capt. Boteler, It. N. (A*ppendix, vol. i. Voyage to Africa, Bentley, 1885) easily collected a *I* Delagoa Vocabulary ' from George, his interpreter.

bar, 1887), the [6] tongue spoken in the country called, in our maps Usumbara, which is a mountainous district on the mainland of Africa, lying opposite to the Island of Pemba, and visible in clear weather from the town of Zanzibar.'

Kisawahili is at once rich and poor. It may contain 20,000 words, of which, perhaps, 3000 are generally used, and 10,000 have been published. Copious to cumbrousness in concrete, collective, and ideal words, it abounds in names of sensuous objects; there is a term for every tree, shrub, plant, grass, and bulb, and I have shown that the several ages of the cocoa-nut are differently called. It wants compounds, abstract and metaphysical expressions: these must be borrowed from the Arabic, fitted with terminal and internal vowels, to suit the tongue, and modified according to the organs of the people, harsh and guttural consonants being exchanged for easy cognates. Even the numerals beyond twenty are mere Semitic corruptions. All new ideas, that of servant, for instance, must be expressed by a short description. In the more advanced South African dialects, as in the Mpongwe of the Gaboon, a compound or a derivative would be found to include all require-merits. The sound, would he soft and harmonious were it not for the double initial consonants, aspirated or not; for the perpetual reduplications (the Arabic Itadif)a savage and childish contrivance to intensify the word, and for the undue recurrence of the coarse letter K. Possibly the fondness of the people for tautology may have tended to develop their tautophony and euphony. Abounding in vowels and liquids, the language admits of vast volubility of utterance; in anger or excitement the words flow like a torrent, and each dovetails into its neighbour till the whole speech becomes one vocable. Withal, every vowel has its distinct and equal articulation. It wants the short and obscure sound of the English and other European languages (e. g. a liar, *her,* flrst, actor, and lurried) called by us the original vowel sound. Like the Chinese and Maori languages, and the other South African tongues, it confounds the so often convertible letters, the L and the PA The slaves, the Wasawahili, and the wild natives mostly prefer the former, e. g. Mabeluki for Mabruki, and the Arabs and civilized speaker's

[1] In Kisawahili reduplication sometimes seriously modifies the root meaning, e, g. Mbliali means 'far' or 'distantMbhali-Mbhali is different or 'several,' meaning 'distinct.'

[2] The Tupys of the Brazil, according to tbe Portuguese, ignored both sounds—I presume initiative.

the latter, although Mr Cooley ((-biography of N'yassi, p. 20) asserts the contrary. The metastasis, however, appears to me often arbitrary, occasioning trouble, e. g. when ku ria (to eat) becomes ku lia (to weep). Dr Livingstone, (chap. xxx. First Expedition) complains of Loangoa, Luenya, and Bazizulu being transformed into Arroangoa, Buanlia, and Morusurus, but he also similarly errs when he converts Karagwali into Kalagwe, and when (p, 266) he uses indifferently Maroro and Maloli. The It is often inserted pleonastically, to prevent hiatus, as Ku potera for Ku potea, to lose ; Ku pakira for Ku palda, to pack. Sometimes, again, it is omitted, as TT'ongo for Urongo, a lie. In pronouncing it the tongue tip must be more vibrated than in our language, which loves to slur over the sound. Aspirated consonants are found, as in Sanskrit, especially B'h, P'h, D'h, T'h, K'h, and G'h. Quiescent consonants are rare in the middle of words; thus the Arabic Mismar (a nail) is changed to Misumari, and treble are unknown. There are only five peculiar sounds [1] which are

[1] These are
1. B—an emphatic and explosive perfect-nnite, formed by .compressing the lips apparently to the observer's eye.
2. D—which is half T, formed somewhat like the Arabic Ta (-) by touching tbe lower part of tbe central upper incisors

generally mispronounced by the Arabs, and these are mostly of little importance. The dialect is easily learned: many foreigners who cannot speak understand, after a short residence, what is spoken to them. It may be said to have no accent, but a sinking or dropping of the voice at the .terminal syllable—possibly the case with Latin hexameters and pentameters— seems to place the ictus upon the penulti-

with the thickened tongue-tip. Strangers write indifferently Doruma and Toruma, Taita and Daida.

3. G—harder and more guttural than ours, the tongue root being applied thickened to the soft palate. An instance is ©ombe, a large cow (G-nomhe), which Arabs and Europeans pronounce Gombe, meaning a shell. Incrementation is also effected by simplifying the initial sound, as Gru, a large foot, from Mgu; Dege, a large bird, from Kdege.

4. J—a semi-liquid: the J is expressed by applying tbe fore part of the tongue to the palate, above the incisors closely followed by a half-articulated T. It is often confounded with D and Y, e. g. Unguja, Unguya, and Ungudya, for Ungujya (not Uguya, as Mr Cooley believes), and Yambeho or Jambeho for Jvambeho. The sound is not 'peculiarly African it exists in Sindi and other tongues, and a likeness to it occurs at the junction of English words, as 'pledge you.[1] Even the Arabs distinguish it from their common Jim, and it is well worth the conscientious studenCs attention.

5. K—half G-, a hardened sound whilst the mid tongue is still applied to the palate. It might be taken for a corruption of the Arabic Ivaf (jj).   ^

At Motnbasah we shall remark other sounds mostly peculiar to the coast Kisawahili. As a rule, however, the stranger will be understood even before his tongue has mastered these minutias.

mate, as Wasawahili for Wasawahili.[1] Hence when first writing proper norms I preferred Mtony and Pangany to Mto-ni and Panga-ni. Similarly the W when placed between a consonant and a vowel is often so slurred over as hardly to he detected. Por instance, Bwanfi, master, becomes B'and, and Unyamwezi might be both written TJnyam'ezi were it not liable to confuse the reader. There is also a Spanish h (Nina),- as in Nika, the hush, and Nendo, the P. N. of a district, which I express by Ny, e. g. Nyika and Nyendo. Pinally, being a lazy language, which well suits the depressing climate, it takes as little trouble to articulate as Italian: hence, even in the first generation, Arabs and Baloch exchange for it their own guttural and laborious tongues, and their offspring will learn nothing else. This is more curious than the children of the Scandinavians abandoning the father-tongue for Norman and Anglo-

[1] Nothing can be more erroneous than the following sentence: 'But the Mohammedan natives of the Eastern Coasts of Africa, who are comprehended under the name of Sawahili, do not pronounce the hard *h* of the Arabs; the vowels, therefore, between which it stands in their name, unite to form a diphthong-, like the *Italian ai or the* English i in wile ; and Sawahili is pronounced Sawlli ' (Inner Africa Laid Open, p. 88). The 'Wasawahil merely change the hard Arabic h (^-) into tbe softer guttural (a).

Scandinavian, vulgarly called Anglo-Saxon. In East Africa adult settlers forget their mother-tongue.

And now of the slave races proper.

The treaty of 1815, which modified Capt. Moresby's, of 1822, and Capt. Cogan's, of 1839, forbade exportation from the Zanzibarian ports north of Lamu and its dependencies (S. lat. 1° 57') and south of Kilwa (S. lat. 9° 2') : thus the upper markets were cut off, and the traffic was confined to the African dominions of the late Sayyid. The object of these provisions was, of course, to avoid interference with the status of domestic slavery, in the dominions of a foreign and friendly power. It actually, however, led to what it was intended to prevent. The vigilance and the summary measures of our Cape cruisers, especially when commanded by men like Admiral Christopher Wyvill, inflicted severe injuries upon, and in some places almost abolished, the contraband. I have said that the diminution of export has materially benefited the Island and its population. But at Zanzibar, as in the Guinea regions and the African interior, prasdial slavery appears still an evil necessity: upon it hinges not only the prosperity but the very existence of the present race. An abolition act passed in this

Island would soon restore it to tlie Iguana and the Turtle, its old inhabitants.

The slave, on the other hand, has lost by not being exported. It is the same in the Oil rivers of West Africa, where in 1838 Sir T. Powell Buxton proposed to substitute for illegal and injurious, harmless and profitable trade leading to 'Christianity, which would call forth the capabilities of the soul, and elevate the savage mind.' It was expected that at Benin, for instance, man would become too valuable as a labourer to be sold as a chattel. Unhappily the reverse took place ; man became so cheap, that, to work and to starve him to death paid better than to feed him. A fresh gang could be purchased for a few shillings, and the price of provisions was of far more importance than the value of life. The Buxtonian idea was founded upon simple ignorance of Africa, and upon the ill-judged assertion that slavery was caused hy foreigners. The internal wars, whose main object is capturing serviles, are the normal state of Blackland society; they continued and they will continue, whether slavers touch the coast or not. Briefly, the results to the captive are now not sale, but slaughter or sacrifice in the interior, and death by starvation upon the coast.

When I visited Zanzibar, in 1857, the English

public, periodically stimulated by tbe Liberal press, had split up, on the subject of the African slave trade, into two sets of opinions, both honestly believed in, both diametrically opposed to each other, and both somewhat in extremes. The one sanguinely represented it as crushed, and congratulated the nation upon having dealt its death-blow to a system which was rotting the roots of prosperity and progress. The others despondently declared that, although in some places the snake was scotched, yet that it was nowhere killed ; they proved that whilst slavery had increased in horrors, the result of our interference, yet the average quantity of the wretched merchandise had not been diminished ; they opined that nothing save the special interposition of Providence could end that which had so long baffled many best efforts; and being well acquainted with details, they maintained that the average opinion was a mere pandering to popularity at the expense of truth. And, when weary of the self-glorifying theme whose novelty had engrossed the attention of their fathers, the public readily attributed selfish motives to those who would enliven their,zeal.

Pact, as usual, lay between the two assertions, but the inner working of the slave-abolition measures was known only to few, and those few hardly cared to speak out. England, ripe for free labour, had resolved to throw off the African; she kicked away, to use a popular phrase, the ladder by which she had risen, and she made slavery, for which she had shed her best blood in the days of Queen Anne, the sum of all villanies in the reign of King George. This was natural. The steps by which nations attain to the summit of civilization appear, as they are beheld from above, gradations of mere barbarism : to revert to them would be as possible as to enjoy the nursery tales which enlivened our childhood.

Other European peoples were not in the condition of England to dispense with slave labour, but the termination of a long continental war was made the inducement to sign abolition treaties. All were so much waste-paper, not being based upon public opinion. As long as Cuba and the slave-importers of the Western world required (a.d. 1830—57) an annual supply of 100,000 men, their demands were supplied. Neither the word piracy, nor the prospect of hanging from the yard-arm—a remedy more virulent than the disease—could deter adventurers from engaging in a trade where a 'pretty girl ' was to be 'bought for a few rolls of tobacco, fathoms of flannel, and pieces of calico,' and whose profits were estimated at 200 per cent. As long as sugar, tobacco, and dollars increase, so long will the desire for more support the means by which the supply may be increased. Of old one cargo run home out of three paid: presently one in four was found sufficient. The losses, however, added greatly to the misery of the slave; ships were built with 18 inches between decks, one pint of water ahead was served out per diem, and five wretches were stowed away instead of two. With curious contradiction and 'wrong-headedness,' these evils, caused by an abolitionary squadron, were quoted against the slaver, as if the diabolical malignity of the latter could be gratified only by destroying his own property.

It was soon discovered that the slaves, being often condemned criminals,[1] could not be returned under pain of death to their homes. The natural result was to disembark them free upon English ground, and thus certain British colonies were amply supplied with the hands of which their

---

[1] I regret to read such statements as the following in the Journal of the Anthropological Society : 'It may be asserted, without fear of exaggeration, that it is to this demand for slaves that are to he attributed pie desultory and bloody wars which are waged in Central Africa.' (On the Negro Slaves in Turkey, No. 29, April, 1870.)

government was depriving foreign powers. This proceeding added jealousy to the ill-will with which our 'meddling and muddling ' philanthropy was regarded. But both those chiefly concerned—the slaver and anti-slaver—gained ; for the former the price of his wares was kept up, whilst the latter made not a little political capital out of his position. Slave exportation might at once have been crushed at head-quarters: Madrid could have ended it in Cuba; Lisbon, and Bio de Janeiro, in Africa and in the Brazil; it was, however, judged best to let it die quietly, and to make as much use as possible of its dying throes. Some five years ago, after defying for a generation the squadrons of civilized Europe and the United States, it perished of itself, and to-morrow it would revive if the old conditions of its existence could be restored.

The Zanzibar slave-depôt is so situated that its market was limited only by the extent of Western Asia. Erom Ba'as Hafun to the Kilima-ni river was gathered the supply for the Bed Sea, for the Persian Gulf, for the Peninsula of Hindostan, and for the extensive regions to the East. A spirited trade was carried on, and few obstacles were placed in its way. The Anglo-India Government did not in this matter rival the zeal of the

THE SLAVE SUPPLY.

Home Authorities. It lacked earnestness, judging slavery leniently, and finding the practice conducive to the well-being of its subjects. A squadron of at least four steamers was required : the work was left to a sloop and a corvette stationed in the Persian Gulf, with orders, amongst other things, to arrest slavers. The Cape squadron, whose beat extended to the Equator, rarely visited these seas, and the French ships of war were popularly said to do more harm than *good*. Even in after years, when a considerable impulse was given to our cruisers, they could capture only 6.6 per cent. : thus, from Zanzibar and Kilwa, in 1867-9 were taken 116 daus carrying 2645 slaves, leaving 37,000 to escape. There were neither special agents nor approvers; steam-launches and crews sufficiently numerous for arduous boat-service were wanting. An infinite deal of nothing in the shape of bescribbled foolscap was collected, by way of sop for the Court of Directors and for Exeter Hall; but the counsels of such authorities as Lieut.-Colonel Hamerton and Capt. Felix Jones, I. N., were passed over with the scant attention of a compliment. The fact is, in British India, as to a certain extent in France, no political capital could be made out of Abolition. Few men retain, after long residence in the East, that lively horror of the institution which distinguislies the home-hred Englishman, and which has arisen partly from his crass ignorance of negro nature and from the misrepresentations of very earnest hut also deluded anti-slavers. The Anglo-Indian has seen many a chattel happy and contented, enjoying an enviable lot compared with the poor at home free to starve or to die in the workhouse: possibly he has dined with some emancipated slave: certainly he has heard of Mamluk Beys and purchased Pashas; and, whilst he owns in the abstract that one man has no right to buy another, in practice he is lenient to the 'patriarchal system.'

The apathy of the Anglo-Indian Government gave the cue to its executive. When it was proposed that the Cutch 'Nakhodas' (skippers) should be compelled to keep crew-lists for inspection, some 'collector ' objected that such men cannot write—surely he must have known that every vessel carries its own ͨ Kirani,' or accountant. That imperium in imperio the Supreme Court, was enough to paralyze the energies of a fleet ; the captured slave-dau was carried to Bombay, whence, after a year's detention by the claws of the law, it was probably restored to its owner. The officers of the Indian Navy would not exercise increased vigilance, necessitating exposure of their men and neglect of other more important duties, when their labours were so likely to be made futile. And as very little prize money was followed by a very large amount of correspondence, slaver-hunting appeared as undesirable to them.as to the officers of the Erencli squadron on the West Coast of Africa.

At Zanzibar, where the Erench Consul, or in his absence the first 'Drogman ' (like all consuls here, their office is rather political than commercial), could fine and imprison an offender, and even ship off a merchant skipper to the nearest port, the English functionary was a magistrate absolutely without magisterial or criminal jurisdiction. He could not deport an Indian convicted of slave-dealing. Whilst the Arab Courts were not allowed jurisdiction over British subjects, the latter, unless merchant seamen ashore, were not liable to be arrested for felony. All this might easily have been remedied by extending eastward the British Order in Council for the exercise of power and jurisdiction By English functionaries (e.g. Consuls for the Levant), in the Ottoman Dominions (June 19, 1844), and by adding power ashore to Article 124 of Consular Instructions, making offences on the high seas cognizable by the Consul.

THE SLAVE SUPPLY.

Thus, despite Order upon. Ordinance, Asia was supplied hy the whole slave-coast of Eastern Africa, without hardly the decency of concealment. Boys and girls might he seen on hoard every native craft freshly trapped in the inner wilds, unahle to speak a word of any language hut the Zangian, and bearing upon their heads the trade-marks of the Hindu Banyan. The commerce was openly carried on by aliens sailing under British protection. Kidnapping was common and daring, as about Lagos and Badagry. Scarcely a vessel manned hy crews from Sur or Ba'as el Ivhaymah, the greatest ruffians of these pirate seas, left Zanzibar city or mainland without stealing a few negros or negrets. By the temptations of a bottle of rum or of some decoy girl, they were enticed into the house or on hoard, and they suddenly found themselves safe under hatches : even Arabs, men and women, have been carried off in mistake by these inveterate thieves. A child here worth from £1 5s. to £3 would fetch in Persia £14 to £20 ; hence the practice. And the anti-slave exportation treaties became exactly worth their weight in words, because the sword was known to be sheathed.

The slaves on 'Zanzibar Island are roundly

estimated at two-thirds of the population ; some travellers increase the number to three-fourths. The annual loss of males by death, export, and desertion, amounted, I was told, to 30 per cent., thus within every fourth year the whole gang[1] upon a plantation required to be renewed. The actual supply necessary for the Island is now estimated at a total varying from 1700 to 6000, and leaving 12,000 to 16,000 for the export slave-market. As usual in Moslem lands, they may be divided into two distinct classes : first, the Hawaii id or Mutawallid, the Mazaliya of the Wasawahili, the famulus or slave born in the family, or rather on the Island; secondly, the captive or imported chattel.

The Muwallid belongs solely to his mother's owner, who sells him or gives him away at pleasure. Under no circumstances can he claim manumission—one born a slave is a slave for ever, even in the next world, amongst those nations which, like the Dahomans, have a next world. If notoriously ill-treated, however, he may compel his proprietor to dispose of him. Tew Arabs behave cruelly to their 'sons;[5] they fear desertion, which here is always easy, and the master, besides being dependent for comfort upon his household, is also held responsible for the misdeeds of his pi'operty. He is also probably living in concubinage with the sisters of his slaves, and in this case the latter can take great liberties—they are the most unruly of their kind. I need hardly remark that the issue of a slave-girl by an Arab or by any other * Hurr ' (free-born man) has been legitimate in El Islam since the days of Ishmael, inheriting like the son of a lawful wife, and that neither mother nor child can be sold. It is to be regretted that in this matter the Christian did not take example of the Mohammedan.

The domestic slave-girl rarely has issue. This results partly from the malignant unchastity of the race, the women being so to speak in common ; and on the same principle we witness the decline and extinction of wild tribes that come in contact with civilized nations. The chief social cause is that the 'captive ' has no interest in becoming a mother; she will tell you so in the Brazil as in Zanzibar; her progeny by another slave may he sold away from her at any moment, and she obviates the pains and penalties of maternity by the easy process of procuring abortion.

The wild slaves are brought over in daus which carry from 10 to 500 head. Most of those intended for the Island market are comparatively young: the Portuguese settlements at Mozambique give higher prices for able-bodied adults. Since the last treaty the value has more than trebled; what then cost $10 has now risen to $30 to $35. A small boy fresh from the mainland commands from $7 to $15; a girl under 7 or 8 years old, from $10 to $18. The live cargo pays duty to the Zanzibar and Kilwa custom-houses, as at Zayla, Tajurrah, and the slave-exporting harbours of the Red Sea: the sick and the refuse, however, enter free. About 1835 the import duty varied from 10.50 to $1, according to the port whence the 'black ivory ' was shipped: some races had such an ill fame that only excessive cheapness found purchasers. Presently $2 and at last $1 were levied upon all, good or bad. Of late years (1857) tbe annual maximum collected was $23,000: this enables us to rate the import at an average of 14,000 to 15,000 per annum, the extreme being 9000 or 18,000. In 1860-61 it rose to 19,000, in 1861-62 it fell to 14,000, and in 1862-63 there was a further declension.[1]

The impudence and audacity of the wild slaves almost passes belief. Such is their habit

---

[1] Concerning Kilwa further details will be found in Vol. II.

of walking into any open dwelling and carrying off whatever is handy, that no questions are asked about a negro shot or cut down in the act of simple trespass. At night they employ themselves in robbing or smuggling, and at times in firing a house, when they join the crowd and spread the flames for the purpose of plunder. They are armed burglars, and not a few murders are laid at their door. In the plantation they gratify their savage, quarrelsome, and ungovernable tempers, by waging desultory servile wars with, neighbouring gangs; hundreds will turn out with knobsticks, stones, and a few muskets, and blaze wildly in the direction of one another : at the first casualty all will run. gome proprietors have had as many as 2000 blacks—∎ not half the number often owned in the Southern United States, and in the Brazil—hut at those times the negro was worth only from S3 to $10. They were allowed two days out of the week to fish for themselves, and to work at their own patches of ground.

Of late years the Zanzibar serviles have attempted to compete with the honest and hard-working porters of Hazramaut; hut they cannot keep their hands from picking and stealing, and thus they have ruined several of their 'Akidahs,' or headmen, who rendered themselves responsible to the merchant. Being capable of considerable although desultory exertion, they get a living by day-work on hoard European ships, and they prefer this employment because they receive rations of rice and treacle, with occasionally a bit of beef or pork. When there is no work upon the plantation its slaves are jobbed at the rate of 8 to 10 pice per diem, and of this sum they receive 2, about the wage of an Indian 'biggareef Of course they do their best to defraud their masters of the hire.

The following are the distant races of whom a few serviles find their way to Zanzibar.

Circassians and white slave girls being exceedingly rare, are confined to the harems of the rulers. They are brought from Persia, and are as extravagant in tastes as they are expensive in prime cost. A ᶜ Jariyeh bayza ' soon renders the house of a moderately rich man unendurable.

Abyssinians, or rather Africans from Guragué, Amhara, and the continent north of the parallel of Cape Guardafui, are mostly imported from El Hejaz. Boys and lads range from $60 to $100: girls, from $60 to $150. The former are circumcised, and having a good reputation for honesty, intelligence, and amiability, they are educated as stewards, superintendents, and super-cargos. The latter, though exceedingly addicted to intrigue, are favourites with men, and, it is said, with Arah women.

Galla captives of many tribes, especially of the Arisha and a few of the southern Somal, are shipped from Hafun, Brava, and Planir or Maltdishu. They fetch low prices, and are little prized, being considered roguish and treacherous. In appearance they are savage likenesses of the Abyssinians.

The coast of Zanzibar, which before the days of the Periplus supplied the eastern world with slaves, has of late years been exhausted by overdriving. It may be divided into two sections : the northern country, which exports from Mombasah and the little adjacent harbours as far south as the Pangani river; and the southern regions between Pangani and Kilwa. Details concerning all these servile races will be given when we visit their respective ports.

CHAPTER XII.

PREPARATIONS EOR DEPARTURE.

'The port of Zanzibar has little or no trade; that to Bombay consists of a little gum and ivory, brought from the mainland, with a few cloves, the only produce of the island; and the import trade is chiefly dates, and cloth from Muscat, to make turbans. These things are sent in small country vessels, which make only one voyage a year. The trade is consequently very trifling.'—CAPT. HABT, **Commanding If. M. 8. Imogene,** *1834.*

THE dry season—and uncommonly dry it had been—was judged hy all old hands unfit for travel, and I was strongly advised to defer exploration of the interior till after learning something of the coast. The Rev. Mr Erhardt's Memoir on the Chart of Eastern and Central Africa, which threw into a huge uninterrupted Caspian half-a-dozen central lakes, and called it in the south Niandslia (Nyassa), in the north Ukerewe, and on the coast Hiasa and Bahari ya Uniamesi, had proposed a choice of three several routes. The first was through Dshaga (Chaga), and the lands of the Wamasai. It numbered 59 days, over level land, though studded with many isolated hills and mountains, and it traded to the Wanyamwezi, of the race of Wazambiro,[5] probably the Wafioma of the Usambi'ro *district,* near Karagwah, The middle caravan was reported to start 'from Bagamoyo and Mboamaji to Uniamesi.' The general features of the country, the distances, and even the position of Ujiji, were remarkably well laid down. The 'Stadt Ujiji,[5] inhabited partly hy Arabians, partly by Wahas (Wakkas), of course, did not exist: the saline stream of the Wapogo,[1] and the people, whose teeth became yellow by drinking of another water, were evidently the creations of some lively negro[5]s fancy. The 'third or southern caravan line,' set out from Kilwa, and after 200 miles struck the £ Niasa or Niandsha[5] Lake.

[1] Tbis salt stream might have been some confusion with the salt Lake Naivasha or Balibali, in about S. lat. 1° 40', first laid down by the Bev. Thomas Wakefield, 'Boutes of Native Caravans from the Coast to the Interior of Eastern Africa, chiefly from information given by Sadi bin Ahedi, a native of a district near Gazi (Gasi ?), in ITdigo, a little north of Zanzibar ' (pp. 303—339, Journal of the Boyal Geographical Society, vol. xl. 1870). Of this very valuable paper I shall have more to say in Vol. II.

In this section the distances were miscalculated, and except the Wafipa and the Wabembe, the tribes were incorrectly named and placed.

In his plan for exploring the Great Lake, and laid before the Royal Geographical Society in 1854, M. Erhardt proposed to land at Kilwa, where he had touched with Dr Krapf; to collect a party of Wasawahili, and with an outfit of $300 to march into the continent. This might have been feasible in 1854; it was impossible in 1856. Tbe sum mentioned was inadequate; tbe missionaries bad spent as much upon a fortnight's march from Pangani to Puga. Slaves are the only porters of the land, and the death of Sayyid Said had then made the coast Arabs and the Mrima people about Kilwa almost independent of Zanzibar. My directions from borne were to follow, if possible, this lino; Lient. Christopher, I. N., however, who visited the coast in 1843, *more* wisely advised explorers to avoid the neighbourhood of Kilwa. Lieut.-Colonel Ilamerton, moreover, strongly objected to ony landing anywhere but under the guns of Zanzibar, as it were. He informed me that the Wangindo, a tribe settled behind Kilwa, had lately murdered a native trader, at the instigation of those settled on tbe coast; and that nothing* less than a ship of war stationed at the port would open the road to a ' Muzungu ' (white man).

The Consul had also warned me that my inquiries into the country trade, and the practice of writing down answers—without which, however, no report could have been compiled—were exciting ill will. The short-sighted traders dreaded, like Orientals, that competition might result from our discoveries, and their brains were too dull to perceive that the development of the resources of the interior would benefit all those connected with the coast. Houses that had amassed in a few years large fortunes hy the Zanzibar trade, were exceedingly anxious to 'let sleeping dogs lie.' As far as dinners and similar hospitality, the white merchants resident on the Island received us with the usual African profuseness. There were, of course, honourable exceptions : I have especially mentioned Captain Mansfield, Mr Masury, and M. Bdrard; hut not a few—exempla sunt odiosa — spread reports amongst the natives, Banyans, Arabs, and Wasawahili, which were very likely to secure for us the disastrous fate of M. Maizan. Captain Speke, who subsequently ignored this fact, threatened to throw one of the 'first houses ' out of the window; and Lieut.-Colonel Hamerton declared that unless more discretion in spreading[1] evil reports were shown he would withdraw British protection from another well-known firm. The son of a Hamburg merchant had written to his father for leave to supply us with sums to he recovered from the Loyal Geographical Society. When informed of this peculiar kindness I inquired the object, and the answer was that, intending himself to visit India, he wished to prepare his father for the expense of travel in the East. Certainly knowing all these intrigues, I see no reason why they should not be published.

The Arabs were as much alarmed at the prospect of opening up the African interior as 'were the foreign merchants; they knew that Europeans had long coveted a settlement upon the sea-board, and they had no wish to lose the monopoly of the copal coast and the ivory-lands. Nothing indeed would be easier, I repeat, for a European power than to establish itself upon the mainland; and if it followed the wise example of the-»early Portuguese, who limited their possessions to the principal ports and to the great centres of trade, it would soon monopolize an enriching traffic. With respect to copal, and to the articles most in demand, our commercial relations with Zanzibar might he altered for the benefit of both contracting parties. It is at present an unnatural, exclusive system, a monopoly claiming advantages of which it will not, or cannot, avail itself. But all steps in these matters must be taken by the Home Governments; the petty jealousies of rival powers here render all local interference unadvisable.

At length the Kazi Muhiyy el Bin, the 'celestial doctor' of the Wasawahili, was detailed by the curious to investigate the subject, and to represent the terrors of the public. He retired, satisfied that our plans were not of conquest. The Arab chiefs pressed Lieut.-Colonel Hamerton to swear upon the 'Kalmat Ullah' that the expedition was to be conducted only by English officers, upon[1] whose good-will they could rely ; that it was not a proselytizing movement of the Wanajuoni (sons of the book, missionaries), and that it would not be accompanied by 'Dutchmen,' as certain gentleman from Germany were called by the Zanzibaris.[1] Had the Consul liesi-

[1] I leave these words as they "were written in 1857, a time when German nationality did not exist, and when the name of German had perhaps reached its lowest appreciation. Throughout the history of the nineteenth century there is nothing more striking than the change which the last decade has worked in Europe, than the rise of the mighty power, which in a month crushed the armies of France, and which tore from

tated to satisfy them, the course of events is clear to all who know the Eastern man. The surface of Arab civility would have run unruffled, but the undertow would have carried us off our legs.

Persuaded at last by the earnestness of our *energetic* supporter, the Sayyid Sulayman bin Hamid bin Said—a noble Omani never neglects the name of his grandsire—came forward in our favour. This aged chief, a cousin of the late Sayyid, rejoiced in the nickname of Bahari Maziwa (Sea of Milk), the Ethiopic equivalent for 'soft-sawder.' He had governed Zanzibar during the minority of Sayyid Khalid, who died in 1854, and his influence was strong upon the sea-board. He gave us his good word in sundry circulars, to which the Prince Majid added others, addressed to Kimwere, Sultan of Usumbara; to the Hiwans or Wasawahili head-men,

her side the provinces of Alsace and Lorraine. By an Englishman. who loves his country, nothing can be more enthusiastically welcomed than this accession to power of a kindred people, connected with us hy language, hy religion, and by all the ties which hind nation to nation. It proves that tbe ISTorth is still the fecund mother of heroes, and it justifies us in hoping that our Anglo-Teutonic blood, with its Scandinavian 'baptism,' will gain new strength hy the example, and will apply itself to rival our Continental cousins in the course of progress, and in the mighty struggle for national life and prosperity.

and to the Baloch Jemadars, commanding the several garrisons. On the other hand, Ladha jDamha of Mandavie, the Banyan Collector of Customs, provided me with orders upon the Hindu coast-merchants, to raise the requisite moneys, without which our reception would have been of the coolest. Tlie horizon now began to clear, and even to look bright, as it generally will when the explorer has time and patience to await the change of weather.

If we travellers in transit had reason to be proud of our countryman's influence at Zanzibar, the resident foreigners should have been truly thankful for it. When Lieut-Colonel Hamerton first made this Island his head-quarters (1811), he found that for nine years it had not been visited by a British cruiser, and that interested reports had been spread, representing us to be no longer masters of the Indian Seas. Slavery was everywhere rampant. Bozals, green or wild slaves, here called Baghams *({*>)*, were thrown overboard when sick, to avoid paying duty; and the sea-beach of the city, which acts Marine Parade, as well as the plantations, presented horrible spectacles of dogs and birds of prey devouring swollen and spotted human carcases—the remnants of 'slaves that never prayed.'[1] The Consul's representations were listened to hy Sayyid Said, who, through virtue of certain dry floggings and confiscations of property, a la Mohammed Ali, instilled into the slave-owners some semblance of humanity.

Negro insolence was dealt with as summarily. The Arabs had persuaded the Wasawahili, and even the Creoles, that a white man is a being below contempt, and the ' poor African ' eagerly carried out the theory. Only 17 years have elapsed (1857) since a certain trading-consul, Mr W—, in consular hat and sword, was horsed upon a servile back, and was solemnly 'bakur'd,' in his own consular house, under his own consular flag. This occurrence was afterwards denied by the best of all authorities, the gentleman who told the tale: I have, however, every reason to believe it. A Msawahili would at any time enter the merchant's office, dispose his sandaled or bare feet npon the table or tbe bureau, call for cognac, and, if refused, draw his dagger. Impudent fishermen would anchor their craft below the windows of the British Consulate,

---

[1] **Dr Euschenberger remarked the skeletons on the beach to the North and to the East of the Island.**

and, clinging to the mast-top, enjoy with derision the spectacle of feeding Kafirs. The Arabs jostled strangers in the streets, drove them from the centre, and compelled them to pass hy the wall. At night no one dared to carry a lantern, which would inevitably have been knocked out of his hand; and a promenade in the dark usually caused insults, sometimes a bastinado. To such a pitch rose contempt for the 'Earanj,' that even the 'mild Hindus,'—our 'fellow-subjects ' from Cutch and other parts of Western India,—could not preserve with a European the semblance of civility.

Time was required to uproot an evil made inveterate, as in Japan, by mercantile tameness, and by the precept quocunque modo rem. Patience, the Sayyid's increasing good-will, and at times a rough measure which brought the negro man to a 'sense of his duty,' were at last successful, and the result now is that the Englishman is better received here than at any of our Presidencies. The change is wholly the work of Lieut.-Colonel Hamerton, who, in the strenuous and unremitting discharge of his duties, has lost youth, strength, and health. The iron constitution of this valuable public servant—I have quoted merely one specimen of his worth—has been undermined by tbe terrible fever, and at fifty bis head bears the £ blossoms of tbe grave,' as though it had seen its seventieth summer.

Before we could set out a guide, a Mahmandar, a Cafilah-bdshi or Kirangozi, was requisite, and this necessary was soon provided by the 'Sea of Milk.' Said bin Salim el Lamld, the companion of our way for many a weary league, must not depart this life unsketched. He is a half-caste Arab, as is shown by the wiry, woolly hair, which he generally, however, removes with care ; by his dead yellow skin; by scanty mustachios, and by a beard which no pulling will lengthen. Short, thin, and delicate; a kind of man for the pocket; with weak and prominent eyes, the long protruding heak of a young bird, loose lips, and regular teeth dyed by betel to the crimson of chess-men, he owns to 40, and he shows 45. Of noble family on the father's side, the Benu Lamk of the Hinawi, he was born when bis progenitor governed Kilwa, bence bis African blood; and lie has himself commanded at tbe little port Sa'adani. Yet has not dignity invested him with the outer show of authority. He says 'Karrib,'—draw near!—to all, simple and gentle. He cannot heat his naughty bondsmen, though he perpetually quotes Ali the Khalifeh—

'Buy not the slave but with staff and sword;
Or the lord will slave, and the slave will lord.'

I have heard him address, with 'rotund mouth,' his small boy Earaj, a demon of impudence; yet he is mostly ashamed to scold. This results from his extreme timidity and nervousness. He never appears abroad without the longest of daggers and a two-handed blade fit for Kichard of England. lie will sleep in an oven rather than open the door when a leopard has been talked of: on hoard ship he groans like a colicky patient at every 'lop,' and a shipped sea brings from his lips the involuntary squeak of mortal agony. In the hour of perfect safety he has a certain quietness of manner and mildly valorous talk which are exceedingly likely to impose. He cannot bear hunger or thirst, fatigue or want of sleep, and until Eate threw him in our way he probably never walked a single consecutive mile. Though owner of a wife, and of three quasi wives, he had been refused hy Allah the gift of issue and increase. Possibly the glad tidings that a slave girl was likely to make him a father—he swore that, if a boy, Abdullah should be his name—suddenly communicated to him on his return from our first cruise, caused him to judge my companionship canny, and once more to link his destiny with ours.

Safd hin Salim is a Bayazi of the Khariji schism. He prays regularly; fasts uncompromisingly; he chews but will not smoke tobacco; he never casts away a date-stone; and he £ sips water ' but 'swills milk ' as the Moslem saying directs. His mother tongue is the Kisawahili: he speaks, however, the grotesque Arabic of Oman, and sometimes, to display his mastery of the humanities, he mixes hashed Koran and terminating vowels with Maskat 'baragouinage,' Paradise Lost and Thieves' Latin. He has read syntax; he writes a pretty hand; he is great at epistles, and he loves to garnish discourse with saw and song. When in the 'doldrums ' he will exclaim—

>'The grave's the gate all flesh must pass—
>Ah! would I knew what lies behind.'

I have heard him crooning for long hours—

>'The knowledge of this nether world,
>Say, friend, what is it ?—false or true ?
>The false, what mortal cares to know ?—
>The true, what mortal ever knew ?'

Sometimes he will break out into rather a 'fast ' strain, e. g.—

>[1] At Meccah I saw a lass selling perfume,
>She put forth a hand, and I cried, " 0 sweet! "
>(Three sniffs, crescendo.)

> She leant over me, casting a glance of love,
>   But from Meccab I sped, saying, " [Farewell, sweet! " '
> (Three Kafir clicks, diminuendo, signifying 'No go.')

The reader will ask what induced me to take a guide apparently so little fit for rough and ready work ? In the first place, the presence of Said bin Salim el Lamki, el Hinawi, was a pledge of oar utter ᶜ respectability,' and as a court spy, he could report that we were not malignants. Moreover, he was well known upon the coast, and he had a knowledge-box filled with local details, which he imparted without churlishness. During the first trip I found him full of excellent gifts, courteous, thoroughly good-tempered, and apparently truthful, honest, and honourable—a bright exception to the rule of his unconscientious race. When I offered him the task he replied, ' Yerily, whoso benefiteth the beneficent becometh his lord; but the vile, when well treated, will turn and rend thee.' I almost hoped that he would not disappoint me in the end; but the delays, the dangers, and the hardships of the second journey proved too much for Said bin Salim. The thin outer varnish disappeared from the man, and the material below was not inviting. The Maskat Arab, especially the half-caste, easily becomes the Bedawi, the Ishmael, the Orson. These people have rarely any ' stay ' in them; they are charming only as long as things run smooth, and after once shoAving true colours, they care not to conceal them. Arabs, however, are not the only handsome shoes that badly pinch. Ho.\v often would fellow-travellers have avoided one another like fire, had they been able to see a trifle below the surface ! Said bin Salim, offended by certain remarks in my Lake Legions of Central Africa (passim), and wishing to ᶜ prove his character for honour and honesty,' persuaded Capt. Speke to give him another chance, and began by telling a gross falsehood, which Capt. Speke at once believed. He accompanied the second East African expedition: he played his usual slavish tricks, and he had to be 'dropped,' utterly useless, at Kazeli, with the Arabs.

I had engaged at Bombay two Portuguese boys, Yalentino Itodrigues and Caetano Andrade, who resolved that Avhat Sahib Log could endure, that same could they. Having described them once there is no object in saying further of them, except that they Avere, despite all deficiencies, a great comfort to us; and that they proved themselves, in the long run, better men than the Arab. Taking no interest in 'African exploration,' and desirous of seeing only the end of the expedition, they mnst, poor fellows, have yearned sadly for home, even Goa; and I am rejoiced to think that they hoth reached it alive.

The outfit and expenses of an African journey are always interesting to travellers. Tor the personnel, we expended in two months a total of $172 ($50 to Said, and $20 per mens, to the two Goanese), including $82 for ship hire, and the inevitable £ Bakhshish ' which accompanies it. As presents to the native chiefs who might entertain us, we took 20 Jamdanis, or sprigged muslin for turbans ($15); a score of embroidered Surat caps (Alfiyyah=$17.50); a broad-cloth coat and a Maskat Sabai, or loin-cloth of silk, cotton, and goldthread ($20.50) for the Sultan Kimwere; two gaudy cotton shawls, yellow and scarlet ($2.50), and 35 lbs. of smallwhite-and-pink Venetian beads ($14). This item amounted to $69.50. I made the mistake of ignorance by not laying in an ample store of American domestics (Merkani), the silver of the country, and a greater quantity of beads, which are the small change. About $250 represented the expenses of living and travelling ($94 in January., and in February $84): this included the expenditure of the whole party. The provisions were, rice (three bags), maize flour (one barrel), dates (one bag), sugar and coffee (each 20 lbs.), salt, pepper, onions, and curry stuff, oil and clarified butter, snuff and tobacco. Of course soap and candles were not forgotten, and we had a small but necessary supply of cords for baggage—these, however, soon followed the way of our knives. The several items form a grand total of $480, equal to about £50 per mensem. I must observe, however, that we travelled in humble guise, hired poor vessels, walked the whole way, and otherwise practised a somewhat rigid economy.

Ladha Darnha, who had provided us with these necessaries, also hired for the coasting cruise an old Arab Beden, or 'Awaysiyeh ' (foyst) called the Bidmi. She was a fine specimen of her class; old and rotten, the boards and timbers of the deck were breaking up; the tanks were represented by a few Glirbahs, or empty skins; the sails were in rags; the ropes and cables broke every half-hour, and the awning leaked like a cheap waterproof, despite bits of cotton rudely caulked in. Ants effected lodgment in our instrument cases, cockroaches dropped upon us all day, and the rats made marriage, as Said said, during the live-long night. The crew was picked up out of the bazar : one was a tailor, a second stuttered unintelligibly, a third, was maimed and purblind, a fourth was sick, and a fifth, the Chelebi (fop) of the party, was a malingerer, who could do nothing hut shave, pluck his eyebrows, and contemplate a flat face in the glass. The only man on hoard was old R&shid, a scion of that Suri race, the self-styled descendants of the Syrians, well-known for beggary and niggardness, for kidnapping and safe piracy. They are the most uncourteous of the Arabs; and while ever demanding Hishmah (respect) for themselves, they forget their own proverb,[c] Politeness has two heads,' and they will on no occasion accord it *to* others. Hfishid, however, proved a hero and a treasure, by the side of our Nakhoda Hamid, a Saudawi or melancholist of the most approved type—never was brain of goose or heart of hen-partridge hidden by brow so broad and intellectual; never did liver of milk wear so Herculean a beard! He squats upon the deck screaming and abusing his men; now silent and surly, then answering every question with El 'ilm 'ind Allah (God knows!), and in danger he weeps bitterly. With such fellows the only system is to be as distant as possible: the least familiarity ends badly; they will hate you more for one cross word than love you for a thousand favours. The civility of a pipe or a glass of sherbet infallibly spoils them: they respect only tbe man who tells them once a day that they are unworthy to eat with a Walad Amir (gentleman). They will call you proud; but that matters little, and if you pay them well they will speak of you accordingly.

On the evening of Sunday, Jan. 4, 1857, we bade a temporary farewell to our kind friend and host, Lieut.-Colonel Hamerton, and transferred ourselves on board the Biami, expecting to set out. Simple souls that we were! There was neither wood nor water on board, and our *gallant* captain lost no time in eclipsing himself. The north-east wind coursing through the clear sky was dead against us, but he pretended that the sailors had remained in the bazar. He came on board next morning, when we made sail and ran down to Mto-ni, there filling our skins with bad saltish water. Hamid again went ashore, promising to return in half an hour, and leaving us to spend the day in vain expectation. Said bin Salim solaced himself by wishing that the Shay tan might appear to Hamid on his death-bed and say, 'O friend of my soul, welcome home!' But when the truant came off, he was welcomed by the half-caste Arab with a cup of coffee and a proverb importing that out of woe cometh weal; this considerably diminished the effect of my flea in the ear and threat of the 'bakur.' Finally, after the loss of two nights and a day, we fished np onr ground-tackle and began onr journey. I afterwards learned that in this part of East Africa the traveller must ever be prepared for three distinct departures—the little start, the big start, and *the* start.

Amongst our belongings was a lif e-boat which we determined to tow, and the trouble which it gave was endless. In consequence of a lecture delivered at the United' Service Institution (May 2, 1856), by Major, now Sir Yincent, Eyre, of the Bengal Artillery, I wrote through him to Mr Joseph Erancis, of New York, whose application of iron had taken the place of the old copper article in which Lieut. Lynch, of the United States navy, descended the Jordan rapids. The total length, 20 feet, was divided into seven sections, each weighing under 40 lbs. The pieces were so numbered that experienced men could put the thing together in one hour, and it was provided with rivets, bolts, nuts, and japanned waterproof awning. A flat keel and a cork fender were proposed by Major Eyre to the manufacturers, Messrs Marshall, Lefferts, and Co., and were rejected: the former would have offered greater hindrance to the joints, and the latter would have been only additional weight.

This life-boat, after being set up with some difficulty at Zanzibar, accompanied us on our trip northwards. The galvanized and corrugated iron, in longitudial furrows, like the roofing of railway stations, hut only sixpence-thick, proved far superior to the softer copper formerly used. The Arabs, who could not sufficiently admire her graceful form, the facility with which she was handled, and above all things, her speed, called her the Sharradeh, or runaway (mare). The 'Louisa' was indeed sadly given to breaking her halter and to bolting. We lost her during a storm near Mombasah, but an article so remarkable and so useless to any but ourselves was of course easily recovered. Compelled by want of carriage on the coast to reduce my material, I left her most unwillingly at Zanzibar. Buoyant as graceful, fireproof, wormproof, and waterproof, incapable of becoming nail-sick or water-logged, she would indeed have been a Godsend upon the Tanganyika lake, sparing us long delay, great expense, and a host of difficulties and hardships.

APPENDIX.

THE UKAEA OE UKEEEWE LAKE.

<small>A DEDUCTION EROM THE REV. MR 'SVAKBFIELD'S 'ROUTES.'</small>

Thk following paper was read out oil December 11,1871, before a meeting of the Eoyal Geographical Society, Major-General Sir Henry Eawlinson, President of the Society, being in the chair.

Much light had been lately thrown upon the dark points of Eastern Africa, especially those which gather round the much-vexed Ethiopic Olympus, Kilima-njaro, by the labours of the Eev. Thomas Wakefield.. This gentleman, we are informed (Preface by Mr Samuel S. Barton, General Mission Secretary, to 'Footprints in Eastern Africa.' London: Eeed, 1866), was one of four missionaries sent out to Mombasah in 1861 by the United Methodist Free Churches under charge of Dr Krapf, who first established the now -world-renowned 'Mombas Mission.' After a residence of five years he published the interesting series of 'Notes on a Yisit to the Southern Galas ' above alluded to ; and in 1866-7, accompanied by the Eev. C. New, he marched from Mombasah to TJpokomo, on the Dana river. He is therefore an African traveller of some experience ; and as he has evidently mastered the Kisawahili tongue, he is unusually well qualified to supervise and to correct the 'Routes of Native Caravans from the Coast to the Interior of Eastern Africa, chiefly from information, given by Sadi bin Ahedi, a native of a district near Gazi (Gasi Bandar ?) in Udogo, a little north of Zanzibar.' Especially advocated by my old and tried friend Mr Alexander Eindlay, F.R.G.S., this valuable paper was published in the Journal of the Royal Geographical Society (pp. 303— 339, No. xi. Yol. xl. of 1870), and I felt somewhat surprised that the extent of its importance has not attracted more attention in England.

I will consider this addition to our scanty knowledge of one of the most interesting regions in tropical Africa under two heads—the philological and the geographical.

Firstly, Mr Wakefield, like Doctors Livingstone and Kirk, all being practical linguists, invariably uses the system of Zangian orthography, adopted by the ' Mombas Mission,' and by myself since 1859. He speaks, for instance, of Kilima-njaro and Unyamwezi, not the Monomoezi of Mr Cooley or 'the authentic word Mueni Muezi,' translated landlord, or petty chief country (p. 11, The Memoir on the Lake Regions of Bast Africa reviewed, &o. &c., by W. D. Cooley. London: Stanford, 1864). We find in Mr Wakefield's Notes (p. 316) [1] *Lima,* a term denoting extraordinary size—Mlima being the general term for mountain,' whilst (p. 321) Ki-Mrima is justly applied to the dialect spoken on the Mrima or mainland facing Zanzibar Island. We read also (323) 'Mtanganyiko,[1] Kisawahili, meaning the place of *mingling* or *mixture* (rendezvous).' This is precisely the meaning attached by me

---

[1] Possibly a clerical error for Mtanganyika: similarly in the Notes (p. 313) we find Risimani, evidently a misprint for Kisima-ni. I shal write to Mr Wakefield upon the subject.

to the Lake's name, yet I was assured, in the Memoir above alluded to (p. 7) that nothing can be ¹ more ridiculous ' than my explanation of Tanganyika. Even in philological details of the Kisawahili dialect Mr Wakefield agrees with me. He writes, for instance, TJdogo (Notes, p. 313), Ugala (Footprints, p. 67, 68), and TTlangulo (Ibid. p. 63).

I was assured in the Memoir (p. 9) that IT is prefixed to the names of countries only by Dr Krapf and Captain Burton—this, too, after I had for years been talking of Europe as Uzungu, literally, Land of white men. Mr Wakefield speaks of Wasamba, of Wasawahili (or Wa-Sawahili), and of Wanyamwezi, thus sanctioning the use of Wamrima, continental men, and Wakilima, hill-men. He adopts Kisawahili, Kikwavi, Kimasai, and so forth, prefixing an adjectival particle 'Ki' to the root, and denoting chiefly dialect, yet I was assured *by Mr Cooley* (Memoir, p. 9) that 'Ki ' has never an adjectival form. I may now invite the author of Inner Africa Laid Open to revise the verdict (Memoir, p. 7) which pronounces me 'totally ignorant ' of the language of which I affect to be master.

It may be deemed trivial to dwell upon these philological minutiae, but, firstly, nothing is unimportant when it affects the accuracy of a traveller, especially of an explorer, in the smallest matters of detail. Secondly, without an exact nomenclature all topographical literature must be imperfect and of scant value. And, finally, as Mr Cooley and I have been differing upon these points for the last ten years, it is well that the portion of the public which takes an interest in the subject should see who is right and who is not. I have no personal *feeling in the* matter; and if the 'Geographer of N'yassi ' will bring, as I have done, independent testimony to bear upon the points in question, and not evolve his learning out of the depths of his self-consciousness, I am at all times ready and willing to own myself wrong.

Far more important and generally interesting, however, is the geographical knowledge brought home or rather confirmed to us by Mr Wakefield's ' Routes.' We now know that the block whose apices are Mounts Kilima-njaro and Kenia (alias Doenyo Ebor, Mont Blanc) to be a great upland, bounded on the South by the Panga-ni river in S. lat. 5°, and on the hi. West by a lacustrine region in S. lat. 6°; whilst it may possibly anastomose to the North, as was suggested by my friend Dr Beke, with the Highlands of Harar and of Moslem Abyssinia, lying upon the same meridian. The breadth between N. West and S. East will be included between East long. (Gr.) 37° and 39°. Assuming, therefore, roughly the bounding lines to measure 240 by *120* direct geographical miles—we obtain a superficies of 28,800 square geographical miles, more than a fourth of the area assigned to the British Islands. We can now '••a.felv believe, with Dr Krapf and Mr Rebmann, the explorers, that the block is a high volcanic country, separating the watershed of the Nilotic Basin from that of the Indian Ocean ; sending off, like the Highlands of Abyssinia, its own tributary or tributaries to the White river, and corresponding with the Oamarones or Theon Ochcma in West Africa (N. lat. 4°) ; that it is a land of high plains and thickly forested hills, rising to summits capped, not with delornite and quartz, but with glaciers and eternal snows; and that it abounds in the lakes and swamps, sweet and salt, necessary to feed the inland 'smoke mountains ' or volcanoes,[1] whose

---

[1] Mr Keith Johnston, jun., who appended some very sensible and

existence before appeared so problematical. And now the two mighty summits, Kilima-njaro, explored by the late lamented Baron von der Decked and Doenyo Ebor, reported to Dr Krapf under the alias Kenia or Kirenia, and unexpectedly confirmed by fresh evidence, have obtained local habitations as well as names.

But the interest of Mr Wakefield's Routes culminates in the fact that they show even to a certainty the existence of a lake before unknown, and they lead to the conclusion that the area of 29,900 square geographical miles, assigned to the so-called Victoria Kyanza, contains at least four and probably a greater number of separate waters; that it is, in fact, not a Lake, but a Lake Region.

Mr Keith Johnston observes (p. 333), 'It is remarkable that not one single name of a district, people, or place (with the exception of that of the Wamasai, a general name for the people of the white region west of the Lake)[1] given in these new routes has any such remote resemblance to names reported by »Speke and Burton as to warrant any identification with any one of them.' The reason will presently appear in the fact that we are speaking of

well-considered remarks to the 'Routes,' observes (p. 337) that [1] the Njemsi volcano in this region has a special interest, since, if the report be true, it is the only one which is known to present any signs of activity in the African Continent.' I cannot at present place my hand upon a private note addressed to me by Mr Trank Wilson of Fernando Po, and describing how the Camarones Peak was seen to be in eruption shortly after my departure from the West African coast (1864). I had found it in one place still smoking.

[1] The routes as well as the information given by me in tbe Lake Regions of Central Africa, and in my forthcoming work upon Zanzibar, City, Island, and Coast, prove the Wamasai to be a special tribe. M. Richard Brenner (Mittheilungen, 1868, p. 175, &c., and map facing p. 384) shows that this fierce pastoral people has approached the coast and seized the right or southern bank of the Sabiiki or Melinde river.

different waters. The annotator further observes (p. 333) that 'the arguments which Captain Burton used in recommending a division of the Nyanza had not a sufficient basis of proof to give them moment, as is shown by the acceptance of the Lake as one sheet hy the whole geographical world.'

The mapper will readily understand that it is much more sightly and convenient to have a basin neatly outlined, and margined sky-blue, like the Damascus swamps, than to split it into fragments as I did. A volume published by the late Mr Macqueen and myself (The Nile Basin. London: Tinsleys, 1864), offered a sketch of what was actually seen by the second expedition, and the aspect of disjecta membra was not inviting. Afterwards, however (p. 334), Mr Johnston remarks, 'Captain Burton's recommendation would seem to receive some slight support from the new information obtained by Mr Wakefield.' To this I would add that his language might have been less hesitating, as these 'Routes,' so important to the geography of Eastern Africa, at once establish the existence of two lakes wholly independent of the so-called Victoria Nyanza.

The first is that which we named from hearsay Bahari ya Ngo, contracted to Bahari Ngo, sea or water of Ngo(-land). In the atlas of Mercator (Gerhard Kauffmann) we find it written Barcena for Barenca or Barenga. Mr Wakefield prefers (324) Baringo, meaning a 'canoe,' and 'possibly so called from its form.' I shall follow his example, at the same time observing that African negroes rarely adopt such general and comprehensive views of larger features or venture upon such comparisons unless they ran command a birds-eye glance at the prospect. Route No.

5, from ' Lake Nyanza' to Lake Baringo, conclusively proves that the latter is not[1] a sort of backwater ' connected with the former 'by a strait, at the same distance from the East of Ripon Falls as the Katenga river is to the West/ Nor is it a 'vast salt marsh' without effluent: the saline water has evidently been confused with the lately reported Lake Na'irvasha or Balibali lying S. West of Doenyo Ebor. Native description supplies the Baringo with the Northern Nyarus—the southern effluent of the same name being clearly an influent. Nyarus thus corresponds with the old Thumbiri, Tubirih, and Meri, afterwards called Achua, TJsua, and Asua, words probably corrupted from Nyarus.

The map of 1864, printed by Mr now Sir Samuel Baker in the Proceedings of the Royal Geographical Society, affirms the Asua to have been a dry channel 150 yards wide when he crossed it, in Jan. 9, 1864, but rolling 15 feet deep in the wet season. He can hardly be speaking of the drain from the Baringo Lake, which must be large and perennial, and which therefore must besought farther north, unless it anastomoses with some other stream. M. d'Arnand, the French engineer sent in 1840-1841 by Mohammed Ali Pasha to explore the Tipper Nile, reported (Journal Royal Geographical Society, vol. xviii. p. 73) that about 30 leagues south of where the expedition was stopped hy shallow water in N. lat. 4° 42' 42", and therefore in N. lat. 3° 12', the several branches unite, the chief one flowing from the east.

The Baringo Palus must act reservoir to the whole N. Western declivities of Doenyo Ebor, whose snows have given it a name. Ptolemy (iv. 8) distinctly mentions the x/oms, or (melted) snows which feed the Nile; and though he places them in S. lat. 12? 30', he is correct as to the exist-

N.° 1   BURTON & SPEKE. May 1858

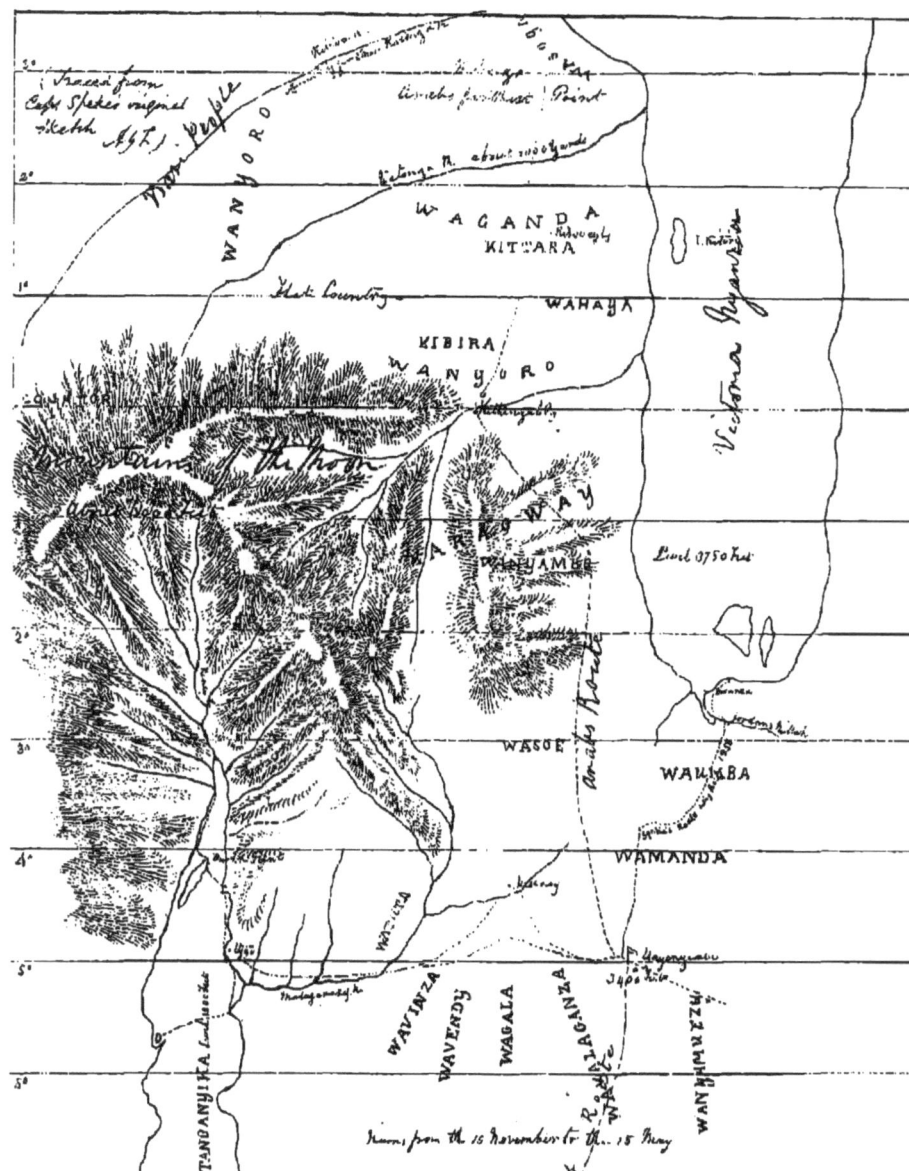

No 3.   SPEKE & GRANT. *1853*

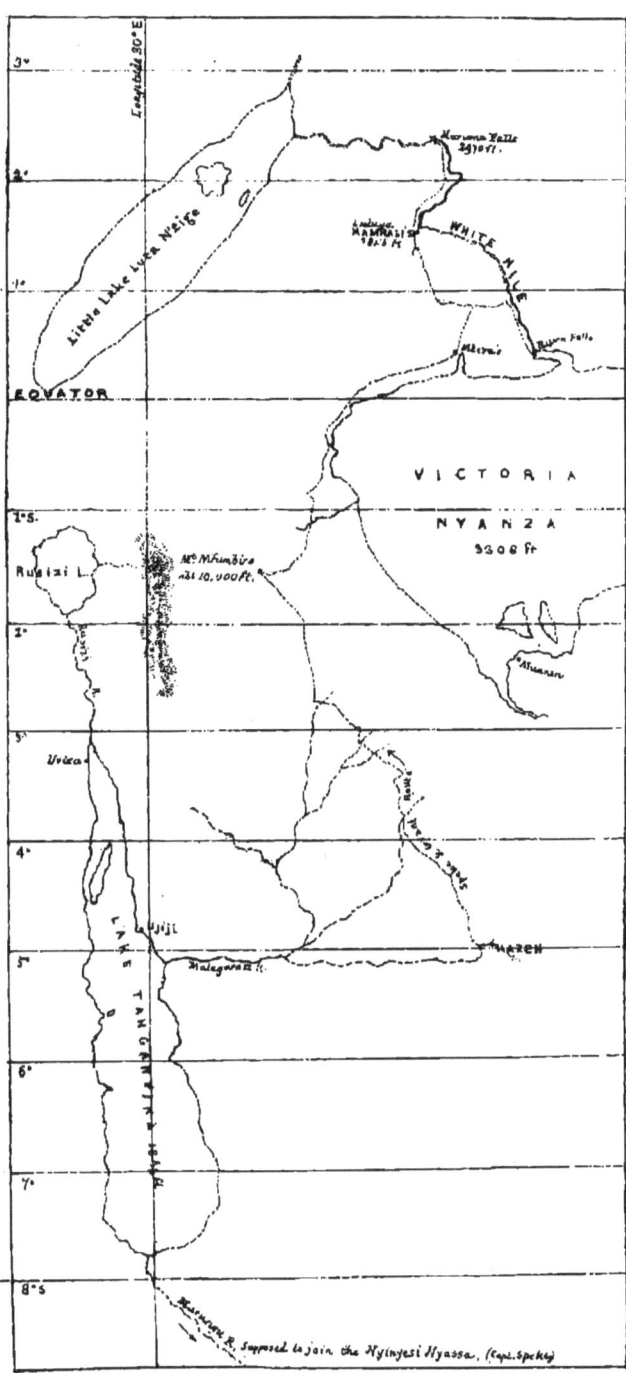

No 4   SIR S. W. BAKER. 1864

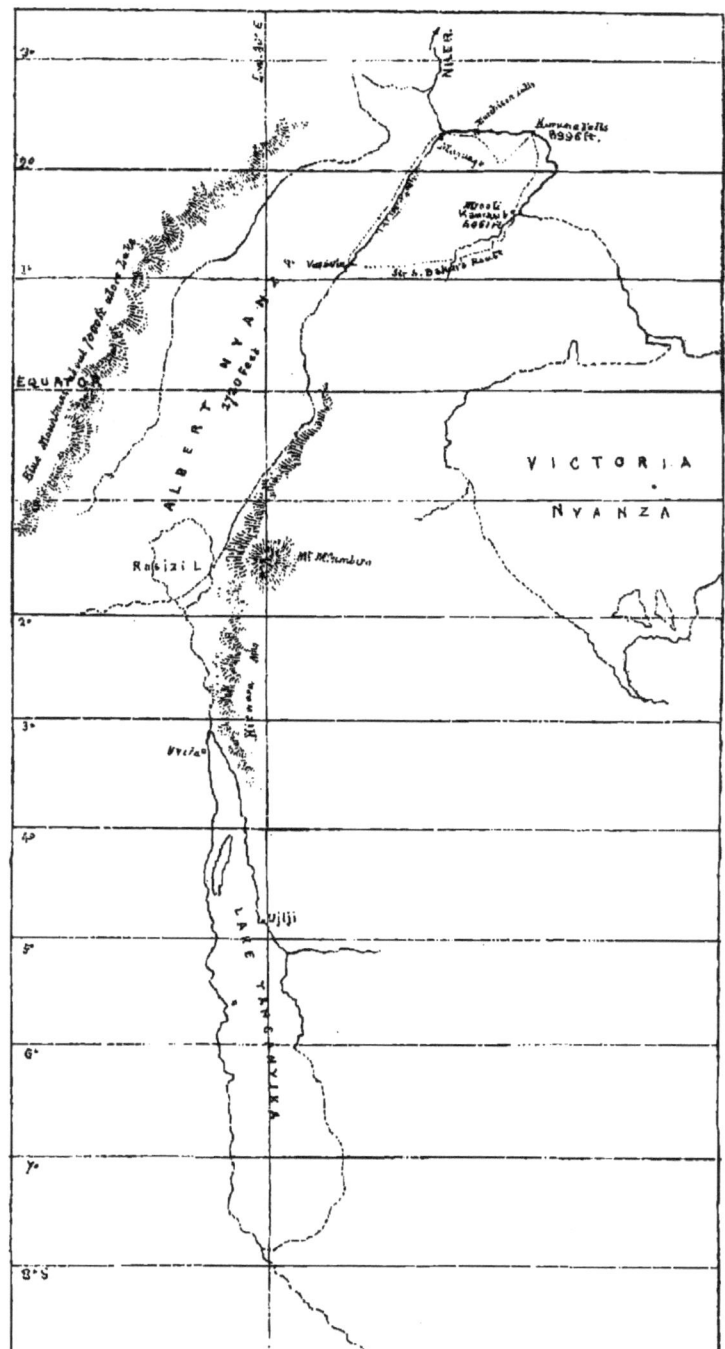

ence of snowy feeders. Some years ago a Swiss traveller drew my attention to the fact that glacier-water would explain. the term White river aa opposed to Bine river. The quantity of melted snow' or glacier-water which finds its way to the true Nile may be comparatively inconsiderable, but that little may perhaps modify the colourless complexion of rain-water when its suspended matter has been deposited, and distinguish it from the pure azure of a stream issuing from a Lake Geneva. In 1857 Captain. Speke, an experienced Himalayan, easily detected, when drinking from the Pangar-ni or Rufu river, the rough flavour of snow water.

More important, however, than Burin go is the new Lake announced to us by Mr Wakefield's African Pandit, Sadi bin Ahedi. The latter ignoring Nyanza, calls it Nyanja, possibly a dialectic variety, and therefore a difference neither to be dwelt upon too much nor wholly to be neglected. Of greater value is the name Bahari ya Pili., or Second Sea, not called so, v^{r}e are expressly informed, because inland of the First Sea—Indian Ocean—hut evidently because leading to a neighbouring w'ater on the west. Most suggestive of all, and therefore adopted by me, is the term 'Bahari ya Ukara/ or Sea of Ukara, the latter being the region on the Eastern shore. Here we detect the true origin of the ancient Garava, and of Captain Speke's Ukewere, which he applied to a peninsula projecting from the Eastern shore, and which the Wanyamwezi, translating 'island water,' gave to the Oriental portion of the so-called Victoria JSfyanza.

Respecting the length of the TJkara Lake, Sadi was informed that it could be crossed by canoes in 6 full days, paddling from sunrise to sunset; but if the men went on night and day, the voyage is to be accomplished in three days. Now the native craft used upon, these dangerous plateau-waters never dare to cross them: the voyager may rush over the narrow parts of the Tanganyika Lake, but of course he would not attempt the physical impossibility of navigating without chart or compass beyond sight of land. It is impossible to believe in a canoe-cruise of 6 days across the lake : it is evident that a coasting-cruise is meant. The total of hours, allowing- the day to be 12, and without halts, would be 72. Upon the Tanganyika I estimated the rate at a little more than 2 knots an hour. Thus, in round numbers, we have 145 miles, which probably require reduction : an estimate of the mean amount of error distributed on the whole of Mr Wakefield's 'Routes ' gives, according to the annotator, an exaggeration of 1.24 : 1.0; and of course, when estimating the length of these distant and dangerous navigations, exaggeration would be excessive. We may, therefore, fairly assume the semi-circumference of the Ukara Lake at 120 miles, and the total circumference at 240. Sadi, we are told (p. 309), made Bahari-ni on the Eastern shore the terminus of his long journey from Tanga Bandar to the 'Lake Nyanza' (Nyamia?). Let us protract the full 145 miles as the exceptional rate of 3 knots an hour upon Captain Speke's last map, without allowing anything for the sinuosities of the coast, and the end would strike the entrance of 'Jordan Nullah' off the 'Bengal Archipelago,' about half the width of the so-called 'Victoria Nyanza.'

As regards the breadth of the Ukara Lake, we read (p. -310), 'Standing on the Eastern shore, Sadi said he-could descry nothing of land in a western direction, except the very faint outline of a mountain summit, far, far away on the horizon.' This passage is again suggestive. The sandy and level Eastern shore of the Nyanja (i. e. water) or Ukara Lake about Bahari-ni, whence Sidi sighted, it is probably in E. long. (G.) 35° 15'. The easternmost, that is, the nearest, point of the Karagwah, or, as Captain Speke writes it, the Karague Highlands, is in E. long. (Gr.) 32° 30'. Thus the minimum width is 165 miles, whilst man's vision under such circumstances would hardly cover a dozen. Here, again, we have room for a First as well as for a Second Sea. Mr Johnston suggests that the mountain-summit in question might he an island rising high in the midst of the Lake ; but, he adds, such a feature could not well have been missed entirely by Captain Speke. Here I join issue with him for- reasons which can he deduced from these pages— my companion and second in command never saw or heard of the Uliara Lake. But it is highly improbable that those who could tell Sadi the number of days required to cross or to coast along the Lake would not have known whether the summit was that of a mountain on terra firma or of a lacustrine islet. The latter feature is not unfamiliar to Mr Wakefield's informant: he does not fail to mention (p. 324) the small conical hill in the southern waters of the Baringo Lake.

When Sadi declared that 'he travelled 60 days (marches ?) along the shore without perceiving any signs of its termination,' he evidently spoke wildly, as Africans will. His assertion that the natives with whom he conversed were unable to give him any information about its northern or southern limit, simply means that in this part of the African interior neither caravans nor individuals trust themselves in strange lands, especially with the prospect of meeting such dangerous plunderers as the Wasuku. Similarly a 'two months' journey' and 'going to Egypt,' asserted by 'all authorities without exception, African and Arab,' signify nothing but the total ignorance of the informant concerning the country a few leagues beyond his home. A lake 120 miles in length, that is to say, even a little smaller than the Baringo is supposed to be, will amply satisfy all requirements in this matter.

Finally, we have Sadi's report that 8 or 9 years ago (before 1867 p) tbe Ukara Lake was navigated by Europeans. Certain very white men, we are told, who bought only short ivories (Scrivellos), refusing long tusks, and who purchased large quantities of eggs—Africans have learnt by some curious *process* to connect Eurojieans with oqahagy—came up in a large vessel, carrying three masts and another in front (bowsprit?), with many white cloths (sails). Tbe event took place only a month and a half before he reached the Lake, and it is described with an exactness of detail which seems to vouch for its *truth*. If *this be* a fact, it is clear that the Nyanja cannot be Captain Speke's Nyanza, and that the visitors could not have made it via his ¹ White Nile,' with its immense and manifold obstructions. But it may be that of which he heard (Journal, p. 333) from the 'Kidi officers,' who reported a high mountain to rise behind the Asua (Nyarus ?) river, and a lake navigated by the Gallas in very large vessels. We now understand why the 'King ' Mtesa (Ibid. p. 294) offered to send the traveller home (to Zanzibar) in one month by a frequented route, doubtless through the Wamasai and other tribes living between the Nyanja and the Nyanza. Thus Irungu of Uganda (Ibid. p. 187) expressed his surprise that Captain Speke had come all the way round to that country, when lie could have taken the short and safe direct route up the mid-length of his own lake—viaUrnasai and Usoga, by which an Arab caravan had travelled.

The Ukara Lake will be found laid down (A.D. 1712) in the Africa of John Senex, F.U.S. (quoted by the late Mr John Hogg, F.R.S., 'On some old maps of Africa, in which the central equatorial lakes are laid down nearly in their true positions'). It is evidently the Grarava of Mercator (A.D. 1623), whose atlas supplies it with a northern effluent draining to the Kile. The 'Couir ' of H'Anville's folio atlas (A.D. 1749), and placed where the Lake Ho and the Bakr el Ghazal actually exist, may be a confusion with the equatorial Lake Kura Kawar, given by Ja'afar Mohammed bin Musa el Khwarazmi (A.D. 833) in the Rasrn el Arzi, published in Lelawel's Geographic du Moyen Age (Brussels, 1850), and, like Garava, both may be derived from Ukara.

The third water is evidently the Uyanza of which I first heard at Kazah of Unyamwezi. whence Captain Speke was despatched on a reconnoitre between July 29 and August 25, 1858. After returning, he reported that this lake being nearly flush with the surface of the level country to the south, bears signs of overflowing for some 13 miles during the rains. The second expedition found no traces of flood on the marshy lands to the Horth and the H. West of the so-called 'Victoria Nyanza.' This fact, combined with a difference of level amounting to 400 feet in the surface of the two water,?, speaks for itself. We are justified in suspecting a fourth lake, or broadening of a river along whose banks Captain Speke and Grant travelled northward to Uganda, and there must be more than one, if all his effluents be correctly laid down.

Briefly to resume: Mr Wakefield's very valuable 'Routes' teach us these novelties:

1. That the Baringo is a Lake distinct from the so-called Victoria Nyanza; that it has a northern effluent, the Nyarus, and consequently that its waters are sweet.

2. That the Nyanja, Ukara, TJkerewe, Gfarava or Bahari va Pili, is a long narrow formation like the Baringo, perhaps 20 miles broad, with 240 of circumference, and possibly drained to the White River or true Nile by a navigable channel.

And I have long ago come to the following conclusions:

1. That the 30,000 square miles representing upon our maps the area of the so-called Victoria Nyanza represent not a lake, but a Lake Region.

2. That the Victoria Nyanza Proper is a water—possibly a swamp—distinct from the two mentioned above, flooding tbe lands to the south, showing no sign of depth and swelling during the hot season of the Nile, and vice versa.

3. That the Northern and N. Western portions of the so-called 'Victoria Nyanza' must be divided into sundry independent broads or lakes, one of them marshy, reed-margined, and probably shallow, in order to account for three large effluents within a little more than 60 miles.

I cannot finish these lines without expressing my gratitude to Mr Wakefield for the interesting information with which he supplied us. He has returned to his labours at Mombasah, amongst the Wasawahili and the Wanyika, and as he has, I am assured by my friend Captain George,

APPENDIX.

R. N., qualified himself to take astronomical observations, we may rest assured that with his aid the 'Mombas Mission' will lose nothing of its well-won fame for linguistic study and African exploration.

www.ingramcontent.com/pod-product-compliance
Lightning Source LLC
Chambersburg PA
CBHW051157300426
44116CB00006B/338